In Memory of My Father

VISUAL BASIC

A Programmer's Guide to Managing Component Based Development

Eran Marom

To join a Prentice Hall PTR mailing list, point to:
http://www.prenhall.com/register

Prentice Hall PTR, Upper Saddle River, NJ 07458
http://www.prenhall.com

Library of Congress Cataloging-in-Publication Data

Marom, Eran.
    Visual Basic : a programmer's guide to managing component based development / Eran Marom.
        p.   cm.
    Includes index.
    ISBN 0-13-591504-X
    1. Microsoft Visual BASIC.   2. Computer software--Development.
    I. Title.
    QA76.73.B3M3744   1996
    005.265--dc20   96-36077
                                                                                 CIP

Acquisitions editor: *Paul Becker*
Editorial/production supervision and interior design: *bookworks*
Marketing manager: *Dan Rush*
Manufacturing manager: *Alexis Heydt*
Cover design: *Design Source*
Cover illustration: *David Chen/Stock Illustration Source, Inc.*
Cover design director: *Jerry Votta*

© 1997 by M&D Advanced Systems, Inc.
Published by Prentice Hall PTR
Prentice-Hall, Inc.
A Simon & Schuster Company
Upper Saddle River, New Jersey 07458

The publisher offers discounts on this book when ordered in bulk quantities.
For more information, contact:
    Corporate Sales Department, PTR Prentice Hall
    One Lake St.
    Upper Saddle River, NJ 07458
    Phone: 800-382-3419   FAX: 201-236-7141   E-mail: corpsales@prenhall.com

For information:
    Eran Marom, M&D Advanced Systems, Inc.
    161 Hilburn Road, Scarsdale, NY 10583
    (914) 722-4241
    EMarom@AOL.COM

Visual Basic, MS Word, MS Excel, MS PowerPoint, MS Project, Windows 95, Windows NT, SQL Server, and SourceSafe are registered trademarks of Microsoft Corporation. Erwin ERX is a registered trademark of Logic Works Corporation. Delphi is a registered trademark of Borland, Inc. PowerBuilder is a registered trademark of Powersoft Corp. PVCS is a registered trademark of Intersolve Corporation.

Printed in the United States of America

10   9   8   7   6   5   4   3   2   1

ISBN 0-13-591504-X

Prentice-Hall International (UK) Limited, *London*
Prentice-Hall of Australia Pty. Limited, *Sydney*
Prentice-Hall Canada, Inc., *Toronto*
Prentice-Hall Hispanoamericana, S.A., *Mexico*
Prentice-Hall of India Private Limited, *New Dehli*
Prentice-Hall of Japan, Inc., *Tokyo*
Simon & Schuster Asia Pte. Ltd., *Singapore*
Editora Prentice-Hall do Brasil, Ltda., *Rio de Janeiro*

Contents

4

Those Pesky End Users 38

5

**Why Is It Impossible to Justify a DP Project Financially
and What Should Be Done Instead? 41**

6

**Why Correct Scheduling Is Crucial and How to Schedule a
Visual Basic Project 50**

7

**How to Budget for a Project Including How to Deal
with Accountants 65**

22

How Is Report Generation
Accomplished in Visual Basic?   *204*

23

Every Application a Component
(Object Linking and Embedding)   *211*

24

How to Optimize Visual Basic Code   *219*

25

Application Security   *224*

Preface

This book is a practical guide on how to fully exploit the features of Visual Basic in order to achieve drastic improvements in the project life cycle. Such efficiency is possible with Visual Basic since it is a component-based language. Thus, developing in VB better resembles an assembly project than the more traditional craft-work of third generation languages. But in order for this paradigm shift to materialize into real cost and time improvements, the method by which one goes about managing a software development project must change. Following the real-life, pragmatic recommendations in this book will provide the reader with the tools to carry through such a transformation.

The first few chapters of the book introduce the Visual Basic language and development environment, and contrast them with those of some of the more traditional languages. Special attention is paid to the difference between the component-based technology displayed by VB and the object-oriented approach of languages such as C++. This discussion is combined with everyday analogies to other industries and situations where assembly techniques had proven very successful.

Next, the book turns to some more elementary aspects of project management, such as scheduling, budgeting, and staffing. For each item, the discussion first demonstrates how Visual Basic affects the function and then suggests ways that best take advantage of the language to reap the most benefits. Specifically, this section answers questions such as "How to justify a VB project?," "How to decide which project to pursue?," "How to schedule a VB project?," "How much to budget for?," "How many people to hire?," and "How to best organize the team?"

Moving slightly away from the nuts and bolts issues and toward the more touchy–feely aspect of management, the book next deals with management style, motivational techniques, and productivity measurements. As with the previous items, these aspects of project development are also affected by the rapid pace at which Visual Basic projects are carried out and, thus, must be modified accordingly. This part of the book is concluded by summing up the development approach through the definition of a new development model.

For the remainder of the book, the discussion moves back and forth between the logical steps of the development life cycle—specifications, design, development, testing, and implementation—and the building blocks that are pertinent to each step. The latter is covered on a technical level, but with a strong emphasis on managerial implications. Among such technical issues is a chapter dedicated to the selection and usage of client–server databases as a component in the Visual Basic environment. Another chapter covers the process by which reports are generated with VB. Optimizing applications is the subject of yet another technical discussion. Finally, client–server application security is looked at extensively.

No book on component-based technology would be complete without defining Open Database Connectivity (ODBC), Object Linking and Embedding (OLE), and Dynamic Link Libraries (DLL). Sure enough, these three subjects each have their own chapter that specifically points out their usage in the VB project.

Two standards guidebooks are included: One instructs on the Visual Basic coding conventions, the other is a sample of a graphical user interface manual.

The material in this book represents precisely the type of information I wish I had access to when I first encountered Visual Basic and, later on, as I learned to fully exploit its advantages. It is sure to help you jump start the learning curve if you are a Visual Basic novice, or climb it more easily if you are a veteran.

CHAPTER 1

Happy Days Are Here Again

Whether you are a chief information officer, an MIS director, a project manager, or a system consultant, you probably question, quite frequently, whether your job is as rewarding as it should be. If your experience is like many of us in the field, the answer is a resounding "No." Your life is most likely full of frustration and despair trying to perform the impossible for a bunch of incompetents using the talents of a few incorrigibles.

- The company's top management believes you are spending too much money and demands that you cut costs.
- The users want their system finished and tested by yesterday morning, never mind that they will finish writing the specifications in about a week or so, give or take a year.
- The boss wants to know how come your project is so far behind schedule when the 30 person-days you were allocated for rewriting the company's entire accounting system was, in his opinion, *sand bagging* it.
- Each and every one of your programmers had threatened to quit by tomorrow, 10:00 A.M., unless they are given a raise.
- You are stuck with a 20-year-old mainframe because you are not allowed to move the CPU-specific applications to a faster machine.

And, as if all of this was not enough, you were just informed that your vendor is discontinuing support of its communication module, beginning today. "What do you mean you never got the memo?"

Let's face it: Managing large systems development in today's *give-it-to-me-by-yesterday-but-don't-ask-me-to-pay* environment is just no fun anymore.

Alas, help is here! Thanks to the ingenuity of the Microsoft development team and the foresight of its founder, Bill Gates, a specific component-based language known as Visual Basic can and will, if used correctly, return the fun to your job. So promising is this product that on every package of Visual Basic the following familiar inscription should be prominently displayed:

Give me your poor, your tired, your huddled masses. . . .

Or maybe it should read:

Give me your cost-conscious companies, your frustrated MIS directors, your army of programmers. . . .

Indeed, it has long been kept a secret that Visual Basic increases programmers' productivity by an order of magnitude never before experienced in data processing. This is because Visual Basic virtually eliminates the need for substantial chunks of specifications, coding, documentation, and testing. So powerful is this new development environment that a project developed using Visual Basic and one that deploys the language's full capabilities can cut a project's costs by as much as a half compared with conventional development (see financial analysis at the end of this chapter).

But to gain these enormous benefits data processing managers must change the way their groups develop applications. After all, one cannot develop tomorrow's systems using yesterday's methodologies. Take, for instance, the hardware selection process. Visual Basic is a language developed for the personal computer and PC networks. Therefore, in order to take advantage of Visual Basic you must migrate a substantial portion of the design, development, and installation from the mainframe world to the personal computer network world and from UNIX to Windows.

It is not my intention to devote much space to argue that PCs and Windows are more suited than mainframes and UNIX for meeting the current and future needs of the business community. Doing so would be beyond the scope of this book. I will, however, point out that while the old guard is struggling to develop ever more complicated systems on hardware and operating systems that are ill fitted to meet users' needs, their competitors are using Visual Basic (VB) to develop PC systems in a fraction of the cost and time. At current trends, those who refuse to change and join the PC world may end up arguing the merits of a mainframe system or a UNIX operating system from outside the data processing field.

Don't believe me? Listen to this one statistic: "CFOs surveyed by Deloitte & Touche and Hyperion Software Corp. said that 82% of the new accounting systems that they are installing will be on 'client-server platforms'. . . . James Perakis, president of Hyperion, based in Stamford, Connecticut, said that the annual spending for client-server networks will grow from today's $1.5 billion to $5 billion in 1999. 'Client-server accounting networks are much more flexible and easy to change and maintain than mainframes,' he added."[1] This is an amazing statistic considering that we can hardly get 82% of any population to agree on what day it is, let alone on what technology to use!

And if you think PCs do not provide the same level of performance as your mainframe, or that Windows is not as robust as UNIX, think again. Even the smallest of today's PCs are faster and better than the mainframe on which many older business systems were originally developed.

But if you are one of those who is still not convinced—and surely I could not sway you from your faith in just two paragraphs—note that I am not at all advocating disposing of the mainframe. I am merely suggesting that your trusted machine may better serve you as, say, a data warehouse than it would as the full-blown information system it was originally designed to be. So you are hereby invited to take your user interface, electronic mail system, spreadsheets, data processors, accounting systems, and payroll systems off of that old contraption and move on down to the PC. Welcome to the late twentieth century.

Rule #1: Don't let yesterday's technology stand in the way of today's decision-making process or you will be unable to benefit from component-based languages.

The second change that you must make requires you to forget everything you know about programming and the management of systems development. This coerced amnesia is necessary since, if you attempt to manage a VB project the way traditional software projects have been developed, you risk losing all of the productivity improvements that could otherwise be gained. Instead you must learn a new methodology that better fits the rapid application development (RAD) paradigm.

Rule #2: To capture the benefits of a component-based system development, you must change your management methodology.

The rest of this book details this new management methodology starting with justification for using VB on through the development cycle and right up to system deployment.

WHO IS THIS BOOK FOR?

By now, some of you are probably reaching for a firearm and dialing frantically to inquire my whereabouts. After all, my contention that (a) Visual Basic is the greatest thing in computers since, well, computers, and that (b) mainframes are, at best, peripheral technology, is hardly popular among computer professionals. Yet, before you attempt to inflict any bodily harm on

---

[1] *The Wall Street Journal*, Dow Jones, Inc., March 21, 1996, p. B6.

yours truly, please understand that this book is limited in scope and by no means attempts to address the entire data processing world. Some of you, for example, will find both Visual Basic and the material in this book so helpful that you will not know how you got along without such wonders. Others might as well return this book to the counter and ask for their money back. Still others may fall somewhere in between the two groups, receiving some benefit from the methodology this book advocates yet finding no practical use for Visual Basic, or vice versa.

To save you the aggravation of reading the first 200 pages to discover which group you may belong to, I have prepared a chart of how different users may benefit from the material of this book:

If you are . . .	You will . . .	Because . . .
A corporate data processing manager or an aspiring manager who is building database-intensive systems to support such business functions as accounting, inventory, sales, finance, payroll, personnel, and so on,	love Visual Basic and benefit from using the component-based methodology of this book	you could save buko bucks, deliver your systems in no time flat, and become a folk hero among your peers.
A consultant or systems house manger who specialize in data-intensive systems,	love Visual Basic, benefit from the methodology, but become very frustrated when your clients insist on using other technology	Visual Basic could allow you to earn the same amount of money you make now but spend much more time on the beach or golf course.
	Also you may find a lucrative niche market in providing custom software that does not fit within the component-based paradigm	there is always somebody who wants a very specific design and is willing to pay any price to get it. Remember, Rolls Royce is thriving by building cars the way they were built 50 years ago.
Component builders (the ones producing the objects used by VB),	agree with everything said in this book, but probably find the material useless. Booch's analysis and design methodology, and such languages as C++ may fit your needs better than VB	your work is more of a craft than an assembly. Although your products are being used in the assembly process you may have to resort to older technology to manufacture such parts.

If you are . . .	You will . . .	Because . . .
A data processing professional developing exotic systems such as artificial intelligent applications, space exploration modules, and so on,	find this book not very interesting	you are currently working on the cutting edge of software development. The components this book talks about will not be developed for your application for a year or two, by which time you will most likely be working on something even more advanced.
The average third-generation language programmer,	hate VB, hate this book, hate me, and hate Microsoft	VB and the component-based paradigm threaten to take away your craftsperson status and turn you into an assembly worker.
	nonetheless, you must continue to read,	you do not want to become unemployed.
The average "reformed" (read-VB) programmer,	benefit from the methodology and the management training	you probably already know about VB.

WHY DO WE NEED COMPONENT-BASED DEVELOPMENT TOOLS?

For as long as I have been involved in data processing, I have been hearing and reading about the ultimate data processing vision. I even started to believe that development managers dream only one dream: that someday, they would be able to build big systems by gluing together program objects, each answering a different functional need. In this dream, the programmer's job is transformed from that of a creative artist who crafts software systems to that of an assembly worker, slapping together interchangeable building blocks that are easily reused.

The desire to achieve this dream is easily understood: Software development is a labor-intensive, expensive, and time-consuming effort. Whether you are building an investment management system for your company's treasurer, an inventory system for the factory, or a payroll system for the accounting department, you must first spend thousands of person-hours specifying the needs of the system in view of the available hardware. You then have to hire some very highly paid prima donnas—read, software engineers—to program the system, expending a fortune on pay and benefits in the process. As a consequence, over the next few years, your job transforms into that of a wrestling match referee who must keep the users who "absolutely, positively must have a certain feature if you want us to use your damn system" from your programmers who "absolutely, positively, would not implement this feature if they are to be considered the data processing gods that they so obviously are."

If you are lucky, in a year or two your team will have built a system that has to be tested *ad nauseum* just to prove that it could do what used to be done before with pen and paper. From then on, you must maintain the system, nursing and babying it to perform as you originally intended. Yet, if yours is like any other software shop, by the time the system goes into production your programmers have long moved on to other projects leaving you with new hiring and training costs and, probably, a suicide wish.

Slowly though, problems are solved, beepers are passed out, documentation is written, and you begin to think that maybe it was all worthwhile. Just then you discover that the hardware is no longer capable of supporting the burden the new system has placed upon it. Oh, and by the way, new government regulations require some changes to the system that cannot be physically implemented by any living, breathing human being. The only solution: a new system. You must begin the cycle from scratch.

If only you could develop software the way Henry Ford built cars your life could be so much easier. Then, instead of specifying and programming systems from scratch, you could walk on down to the data interface shop on the corner of Main and Elm Streets and pick up a data interface object. You could mail order for a data entry screen. You could send your secretary for an error handler. And when, within a week or two, all the parts arrive and sit on the receiving floor, you can dispatch Joe, the low-paid technician, to assemble them and try the whole thing out. If one part in the system does not work, you could send the defective culprit back to the factory and replace it with another, better part. After all, *"parts is parts."*

Of course, the best aspect of this scenario is that in the ample free time you will gain as a result of this component-based development, you could write and send rejection letters to all those prima donnas who would now be begging you for a job. No doubt, your promotion to CEO would be virtually assured.

Still, for all these years, the promised land had eluded data processing managers. Now, think about that for a second. Since computers first gained commercial prominence, we landed on the moon, fought and won a cold war—not to mention a few hot ones—gained, lost, and regained the world manufacturing leadership, and proved beyond all reasonable doubt that a gearhead, Harvard dropout from the state of Washington can beat any IBM hot-shot marketer any day of the week. Yet, not until recently had we been able to develop a commercially available system that even remotely resembles the object-oriented programming described earlier.

Why is that, you ask? Well, for one thing, we were never very successful in narrowing the scope of software objects. Although we always perfectly understood that when we purchased a new car, we were essentially buying the same car whether it was blue, green, or gold, we had refused, in the past, to limit our software development tools to those needed by 95% of the user population. Instead we designed and built tools to satisfy not only each and every one of the contemporary potential users but also anyone who might come along and think about a feature we missed. As a result, the tools we built had a tendency to be cumbersome, complicated, and not very interchangeable.

In addition, not until recently were we able to package the software tools we did manage to develop so they could be easily used by a wide variety of users. Unlike an engine piston in Henry Ford's interchangeable parts engine, a software building block could not, until now, be given a part number and stacked on the shelf to be readily retrieved and used. The functions of a certain piece of software, basically a bunch of written lines of code, could not be freely determined by just looking at the text nor could it be easily installed without referring to extensive documentation. As a result, cataloging, storing, searching, and retrieving functions in our software warehouse became insurmountable obstacles when we applied them to traditional software objects.

Consequently, attempts to create software building blocks in the past had generated huge libraries that no one had the ability or the inclination to use. When attempts were made to employ these tools, large amounts of resources were required to manage, administer, and enforce reusability. Naturally, such non-revenue-generating librarian functions became instant targets for cost-conscious management when economic conditions deteriorated.

Some people blame management for failing to commit enough resources to do the *right thing*. But in reality, any effort that costs so much in terms of dollars and other corporate resources and produces so few benefits in return could not and should not be allowed to survive. The funds might, instead, be better spent in attempting to find a better solution.

There are, of course, other reasons for the failure to develop object-oriented tools. Edward Yourdon blames, among other factors, the NIH (not invented here) syndrome, and the failure of management to reward reusability.[2] NIH is a contributing factor, no doubt, as many software engineers pride themselves on their ingenuity, creativity, and originality. Suggest a better, preexisting solution to a programmer and you put your life at peril. Yet, even Mr. Yourdon agrees that no self-respecting programmer builds a whole project from scratch. "Software engineers eventually grow tired of reinventing solutions to problems they themselves have already solved. . . . The journeyman software engineer gradually builds his own personal library of previously solved problems through which he rummages whenever faced with a new problem that has familiar overtones."[3] Consequently, I believe that in the final analysis most programmers would have welcomed a reasonable reusability scheme.

---

[2] Edward Yourdon, *The Decline and Fall of the American Programmer*, Yourdon Press Computing Series (Englewood Cliffs, NJ: Prentice Hall, 1993), p. 217.

[3] Ibid., pp. 217-218.

Likewise, management's failure to reward reusability must be viewed in light of the previously mentioned difficulty and enormous expense of maintaining a software library. After all, why reward something that may bankrupt your company and/or get you fired?

But just as we were about to give up on the concept of software building blocks and settle for a life full of misery and pain, along came several different solutions. These include Microsoft Visual Basic®, Powersoft's PowerBuilder®, and Boreland's Delphi®. At long last, the Gordian knot of software reusability had been cut, opening the way to the long sought after nirvana.

This book concentrates on one such solution, namely, component-based development, and, in particular, on Microsoft's Visual Basic, a language that uses the component methodology to its ultimate ability.

WHAT IS A COMPONENT AND WHAT IS COMPONENT-ORIENTED PROGRAMMING?

Before we go any further, we must define some basic concepts:

The word *component* as it is used in the context of this book is sometimes referred to as an *object*. The Microsoft Press Computer Dictionary defines such an object as follows:

> A shorthand term for object code (machine readable code); in object-oriented programming, a variable comprising both routines and data that is treated as a discrete entity.[4]

The dictionary defines object-oriented programming (or, here, component-based programming) as:

> A programming paradigm in which a program is viewed as a collection of discrete objects that are self-contained collections of data structures and routines that interact with other objects. A class defines the data structures and routines of an object; an object is an instance of a class that can be used as a variable in a program. In some object oriented languages, objects respond to messages which are the principal means of communication. Other object oriented languages retain the traditional procedure-call mechanism.[5]

In nontechnical terms, component-oriented—or component-based—programming is a method of using self-contained software building blocks that encapsulate within them all the necessary code, variables, and data to be used by other software. An example of a component might be a text box for the user to type in text in any given data entry screen (see Figure 1.1). This object includes software to accept the text and store it until it is needed by the

---

[4] *Microsoft Press Computer Dictionary,* 2nd ed. (Redmond, WA: Microsoft Press, 1993), p. 276.

[5] Ibid., p. 277.

Password: [   ]

Figure 1.1 *An example of a text box object along with a caption object to its left*

calling program. A component of this nature also includes a bit map picture of a text box which we could place anywhere on the screen. The component may also have variables that the calling program can set to change the text font, size, and properties. Finally, this component may include event-handling procedures so that, for example, when the user first enters the text box a certain algorithm is run. In its most sophisticated form, event handling is accomplished by initiating a procedure in the calling program (see Figure 1.2).

In Visual Basic, a component can be a **control,** which is an externally supplied extension of the language (usually known as a VBX, OCX, or DLL), or it can be another application connected through OLE automation. But more about that later.

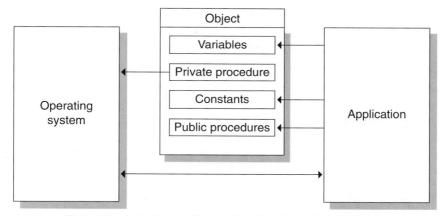

Figure 1.2 *A simple view of how an object interfaces with the application*

Purists insist that true objects must display three characteristics:

Encapsulation	Be a stand-alone program entity that can be moved, stored, and used as a single unit.
Polymorphism	Ability to change easily in order to perform slightly different tasks and functions.
Inheritance	Ability to create new objects from existing ones whereby the new objects inherit all the attributes (constants, variables, procedures, data structures, etc.) of the parent object which can then be modified as needed.

I have no problem with the first two requirements but, clearly, inheritance cannot apply to the definition of a component. In fact, a component that displays inheritance miserably fails the needs of the business application development environment by making objects too easy to modify. An object, after all, is supposed to be a building block of a well-defined system and not some abstract concept to be molded into shape depending on the problem at hand.

In fact, any attempt to make objects modifiable defeats the whole concept of object-oriented programming. The bottom line, as you may recall, is to transform the software development task from an art form to an assembly task. Inheritance throws this concept right out the window.

Consider, for example, our car engine analogy: One would not expect inheritance properties in mechanical objects used to construct the engine. That is, we do not normally go to a hardware store and ask for an object of a bolt class that we will be able to modify so it will fit any of the holes we drilled into the engine block. Instead we ask for, say, a 1-inch long, 3/8-inch diameter, schedule L threaded, hexagonal head bolt that is specifically and uniquely designed to fit only one type of hole. Yet no one would argue that a bolt of this type is not an object or even that one cannot build an efficient engine using such readily available bolts.

This is an important point since, as you will see later, the success of any component-oriented language—and any project using such language—does not depend on the inheritance of its objects, as may be commonly believed. Rather attainment of efficient programming relies on the ability to package objects in such a way that they can easily be used by a multitude of different applications. Just as the bolt described earlier can be used in constructing an engine, in building a shelf rack, or in the manufacturing of an aircraft carrier, software objects must be equally adaptable. To be so they must conform to expected standards, be self-contained in a single, easily stored and retrieved package, and behave in the same manner regardless of application.

Thus, unless you are in the business of building the components themselves, inheritance is hardly necessary.

Finally, note that I make a big distinction between flexibility and inheritance. Not making an object modifiable (inheritance) does not necessarily make it rigid. In fact, some objects on the market today have hundreds of properties (accessible variables), and many event-driven procedures. They are, in my opinion, an overkill in flexibility. Yet no one is allowed to modify them into something else outside of their natural user features. They thus retain their encapsulation and meet our criteria of being a true component.

HOW DOES COMPONENT-ORIENTED PROGRAMMING COMPARE TO OTHER SOFTWARE DEVELOPMENT?

Throughout my career in data processing, I programmed in just about every language there is, on just about any type of hardware in existence. Usually I found that third-generation languages were easily compared to each other and that experts could readily point out the distinctive features of each. Yet a component-based language such as Visual Basic is not simply weighed against other languages. Such comparison is difficult because the benefits VB provides are mostly economical rather than purely technical.

Take, for example, two third-generation languages such as C and COBOL. In comparing the two, one may point out that in the realm of memory optimization C is better than COBOL for database applications since it allows for dynamic structures. COBOL, on the other hand, may be better than C for reporting purposes since program output is position specific. (Then again, a C zealot would hardly agree on anything that a COBOL fanatic says and vice versa, but I gather you get the drift.)

However, when you compare Visual Basic to COBOL or C, many technical issues become trivial in view of the huge economic benefits the language provides. Sure, VB has many of the features of C, Pascal, COBOL, and so on. And even if at the moment it does not support a certain feature, I am sure Microsoft will include whatever is missing in the next version. But if you consider that you can develop a full-blown application using VB in about three months, a process that could take you two years with C, you quickly and willingly forget such trivialities as VB does not have a C-like pointer mechanism. After all, who, other than your fanatic C programmers, cares?

Furthermore, the ability to import into a Visual Basic application other commercial applications as components of your system means that many of the advanced features of other languages are, actually, no longer needed. For example, being able to use dynamic structures in C and C++ is an essential feature when developing a database application from scratch. That is, the payroll application must be able to add and delete employees to the database, and these records must be added and removed from memory with minimum waste. But if you can use an off-the-shelf database engine as a component, you quickly discover that you no longer need to program addition and deletion algorithms and so the need for dynamic structures disappears. The component does all the work for you.

So in order to do justice to Visual Basic in particular and component-based applications as a whole, the following chart compares different language types not only on technical merits but also on economic factor.[6]

Rule #3: Don't be tempted to compare Visual Basic to other languages on technical ability alone. Consider economic benefits and the use of readily available components to achieve technical prowess.

---

[6] The format of this grid as well as items marked with an asterisk (*) were taken from A (Visual) Basic Programming Decision, N. Jones and M. West, *Application Development and Management Strategies*, Gartner Group.

Factor	Visual Basic	Third-Generation Languages (C, Pascal, COBOL, etc.)	3GLs with Objects Displaying Inheritance (C++)
Programming metaphor	Component-based, extensive visual tools for GUI development, event-driven, whole development environment.	Procedural, textual source code.	Object-oriented, textual source code, some visual tools for developing GUI components.*
Commercial risk	➤ Low. Microsoft is a large and stable vendor.* Availability of hundreds of third-party components.	Medium. With object-oriented programs coming along, development with these languages is too slow.	➤ Low. Several vendors provide C++ compilers and development environments. There is some danger of lock-in to vendor-specific class libraries.*
Technical risk	➤ Low. Commercially available component can be approved once and be used repeatedly.	Medium. There is a large knowledge base for these languages but they are ill fitted to develop GUI applications.	Medium to high. Requires experienced staff and specialist debugging tools and skills.*
Productivity	➤ Very high. Low-cost programmers combined with very fast development.	Low. Code has to be written from scratch.	Low. Code development may be faster than 3GL languages but programmers are very expensive and hard to come by.
Performance	Medium to high. Speed is hurt a bit by component technology but business applications perform very well.	Not applicable (A 3GL Windows program uses mostly Windows APIs, which make performance measurement pointless.)	➤ Superior run-time performance.* . . . but compile cycle slows development.
Flexibility	Extremely flexible.	Flexible.	Extremely flexible.*
Portability	Limited to MS Windows and DOS.	➤ Good. Compiler and cross compilers have been built for just about every platform.	➤ Good. C++ systems are available on a range of platforms. Third-party tools and class libraries can support cross-platform GUI development.*

Factor	Visual Basic	Third-Generation Languages (C, Pascal, COBOL, etc.)	3GLs with Objects Displaying Inheritance (C++)
Staff skills	➤ Very easy to learn. Can be used by less skilled staff. Training may take one to three months.*	Somewhat hard to learn but is well taught in universities and even high schools.	Requires skilled staff. Very hard to learn and harder to master. Training may take around a year.*
Supporting infrastructure requirements and availability	Extensive third-party tools available commercially. And tool set is ever growing. Entire development environment is included. Suitable for large project development.	➤ Standards, methodology, change management, and other infrastructure are well established.	Needs standards, additional tools (e.g., for storage, change management, analysis and design, testing), and review procedures. With these, can be used for substantial projects.* Many third-party tools available to assist with C++ development.*
Reuse issues	➤ High reuse of components. Code reuse done through third-party tools such as VB Assist or Microsoft SourceSafe.	Limited reuse through code copying.	Full object-oriented reuse through inheritance. Third-party class libraries available. Third-party components available.*
Project size	➤ Suitable for all sizes of projects.	Suitable for all sizes of projects.	Suitable for all sizes of projects, although strong infrastructure and tools will be required for large applications.*
Ease of database connectivity	Native tools as well as third-party tools make database access almost trivial.	Difficult. Need to use database API calls and handle errors separately.	Difficult. Need to use database API calls and handle errors separately.
Ease of OLE integration	Very easy. Allows for bringing in whole applications as objects. Easy to create OLE servers.	Easy only if the product is capable of becoming an OLE client.	Very easy. Allows for bringing in whole applications as objects. More difficult to build an OLE server.

Factor	Visual Basic	Third-Generation Languages (C, Pascal, COBOL, etc.)	3GLs with Objects Displaying Inheritance (C++)
Ease of maintenance	➤ Extremely easy. Very readable code combined with untouchable components that make up most of the code makes for easy maintenance.	Depends on the language. Code needs to be documented well to be easily maintained.	Very hard. Code is not easily readable and class libraries disperse portions of the code around the project.
Ease of testing	Fast testing. Most of the code has been tested by the components vendors or, often, by a corporate approval team that signed off on the components.	Testing is a nightmare. Every aspect has to be tested from scratch every time changes have been made.	Somewhat easier than 3GLS only if a class library is well maintained. Still, not nearly as easy as VB.

TEN MYTHS ABOUT VISUAL BASIC

> There is nothing more difficult to take in hand, more perilous to conduct, or more uncertain in its success, than to take the lead in the introduction of a new order of things.
>
> Niccolo Machiavelli (1459–1527 from *The Prince*)

Surely, by now, you have probably read enough to be itching to get back to your office and proclaim the dawn of a new era. No sense fooling around with other technologies when there is such a wonderful tool out there that can solve all your problems and make you rich and famous in the process.

Well, not so fast. Before you go and attempt to convince your programmers and managers that the future has arrived and is knocking on the door, let me warn you about what you might encounter. Judging from my own experience, and from a mountain of anecdotal evidence, if you attempt to introduce Visual Basic to your unsuspecting organization you will, most likely, win no popularity contests.

Basically, component-based programming is the biggest threat to come around the information processing world since the paper and pencil were replaced by the computer. A whole generation of programmers had become accustomed to being treated as gods who regularly walk on water and clear tall buildings in a single leap. Such honor was bestowed upon them by people who think that what a programmer does on a daily basis is hardly distinguishable from pure magic. In fact, programmers have become the true craftsman and craftswomen of the late twentieth century, comparable to the artisans who built all those magnificent European cathedrals during the Renaissance. One hardly surrenders such status voluntarily.

Be forewarned, therefore, that your current organization's establishment of conventional programmers and managers who know nothing else but third-generation languages will fight a fierce rear-guard action to defeat any effort to introduce Visual Basic. To help you deflect such attacks, I compiled a list of the ten most popular arguments used by the establishment against Visual Basic. This list also points out why these arguments resemble the stuff farmers spread on their fields in the spring.

Myth #1: **VB is too slow to update the display, or, you-can-watch-the-screens-being-drawn syndrome.** The many holders of this opinion claim that when they attempted to program a quick VB application that, for example, obtained data from a database and then displayed them on the screen, the screens were being drawn with excruciating slowness. So hindered was this process that it seemed as though the display was slowly sifting into the screen. In comparison, C is said to be screamin' fast where displays are updated faster than the eye can see.

This is perhaps the most typical of arguments against VB and is the one that represents the basic problem with VB acceptance. Namely, people who argue against VB try to program it like their favorite third-generation language. Thus, it is my favorite criticism to dispute.

The reason display updates appear to be slow to the resisting conventional technologist is because the typical 3GL programmer writes a procedural algorithm like this:

Display Screen → Get Data → Put Data in Screen

Alas, VB is an event-driven programming language that uses the Windows messaging infrastructure to accomplish its tasks. Therefore, the foregoing algorithm programmed procedurally really translates to:

Send Message to Display Screen <u>Whenever</u> → Get Data <u>Now</u> → Put Data in Screen

Subsequently, what is happening behind the scenes is the screen is drawn at leisure by the operating system while the CPU is busy obtaining the data. Thus, display updates appear to be slow as molasses.

To solve this problem, a good VB programmer will construct the following algorithm:

Send Message to Display Screen → Wait to Finish Displaying the Screen → Get Data → Put Data in Screen

Better yet, a superb VB programmer will conceive the following:

Load the Screen into Memory → Get Data → Put Data in the Screen → Send Message to Display Screen

If this is done correctly, VB is as fast as any other language.

Reality: VB is not at all slow if you program it right.

Myth #2: **VB is good only for prototyping and is useless for large projects.** This view is typically articulated in the following passage: "When choosing between Visual Basic and C++, the biggest risk is that Visual Basic will be used for large projects or complex applications under the assumption that its productivity will automatically scale up. . . . We recommend Visual Basic for tactical and relatively simple applications developed by individuals or small teams. C++ is more applicable."[7]

Hogwash!

I myself developed and was part of several teams that built VB projects rivaling in size any existing business application. Never had I encountered a problem limiting the size of VB programs. VB is scaleable and with clever design and implementation is a much better choice for large projects than any other language.

Then, again, I suppose that if you attempt to develop large VB projects like you would a C++ application, you will surely conclude that VB is a bad choice for large applications.

Reality: There is no technical reason whatsoever that limits the size of a VB system.

Myth #3: **Visual Basic is not readable.** This is, perhaps, the most preposterous of all arguments against VB. So ridiculous is this criticism that I will not even bother verbalizing a response. Instead let me ask you to determine for yourself what is more readable from the following two examples of code: Each of these examples determines whether the name being inserted into the database is already present; if so, the new definition will supersede the old one. Otherwise, a new entry is created.

C or C++[8]:

```
struct nlist *lookup(char *)
char * strdup(char *)

/* install: put (name, defn) in hashtab */
struct nlist *install(char *name, char *defn)
{
    struct nlist *np;
    unsigned hashval;

    if ((np=lookup(name)) == NULL) { /* not found */
        np = (struct nlist *) malloc(sizeof(*np));
        if (np == NULL || (np->name = strdup(name)) == NULL)
```

---

[7] N. Jones and M. West, A (Visual) Basic Programming Decision, *Application Development and Management Strategies*, Gartner Group.

[8] Brian W. Kernigham and Dennis M. Ritchie, *The C Programming Language*, 2nd ed. (Englewood Cliffs, NJ: Prentice Hall Software Series, 1988), p. 145.

```
            return NULL;
        hashaval = hash(name);
        np->next = hastab[hasval];
        hastab[hasval] = np;
    } else         /* already there */
            free((void *) np->defn); /*free previous defn */
        if ((np->defn = strdup(defn)) == NULL)
            return NULL;
        return np;
}
```

Visual Basic 3.0:

```
Function Install(Name as String, Definition as String) as Integer
    Dim CurrentNames as Dynaset
    On Error Goto ErrorHandler
    Set HashTable = Database("Hashtabs")
    Set CurrentNames = HashTable.Seek(Name)
    If CurrentNames.EOF Then            ' Not found
        HashTable.Add
        HashTable("Name") = Name
        HashTable("Definition") = Definition
    Else                                ' Already there
        CurrentNames.Edit
        CurrentNames("Definition") = Definition
    End If
    Install = TRUE

    Exit Function

ErrorHandler:
        msgbox "Sorry, there was an error"
        Install = FALSE
End Function
```

By the way, the boldface and italics signify text in other colors in the Visual Basic development environment.

Reality: VB is much *more* readable than other languages.

Myth #4: **VB is not a serious language.** This argument flows from the fact that, at one time, BASIC was a beginners' language. It was developed in the 1960s as a teaching tool by Dartmouth professors John Kemeny and Thomas Kurt. In fact BASIC stands for Beginner's All-purpose Symbolic Instruction Code.

But, excuse me! Wake up! Haven't things changed since the 1960s, thank God? We no longer wear ugly clothes, we often cheer rather than jeer our troops going into battle, and we don't think drugs are cool (well, most of us don't). BASIC has also changed. "Over time, it has grown to be much more: a highly developed language with all the features needed for professional use. Some of BASIC's newfound strength comes from conceptual enhancements such as syntax extensions and support for structured programming. But much comes from pure added horsepower: robust integrated development environments . . ."[9] and so on.

Add to that the fact that Visual Basic is a visual development environment and that it uses events to initiate actions and you have your normal, run of the mill, fourth-, fifth-, and sixth-generation language.

Reality: Visual BASIC is not your father's programming language.

Myth #5: **The Visual Basic Wall.** This is a term that means different things to different people. It is supposed to signify the point at which a programmer cannot continue developing in VB since the application had either stopped running, is too slow, or is too complicated. At this point, it is said, most organizations and/or developers give up and start developing anew in, say, C++.

I have never seen this wall. Could someone, please, show me where it is? Or maybe it has gone the way of the Berlin Wall?

In all seriousness, though, many of the people who have *hit the wall,* so to speak, have done so with Visual Basic version 1.0 which, admittedly, was not a completed product. They then gave up on the product even though later versions of VB brought down this alleged wall.

Those who proclaim a wall with later versions of VB are, well, let's get it out in the open, bad programmers. I once had a guy complain that he could not declare any more global variables because VB has a 64Kbyte limit for such declarations. What in the name of all saints this guy was doing declaring 64Kbytes of global variables is well beyond my comprehension. I often don't declare any more than a handful of such variables. But I suppose that no tool, no matter how sophisticated, could stop a bad programmer from cutting his toes off.

Reality: The VB wall is a nonissue.

Myth #6: **Many companies tried Visual Basic but returned to developing C shortly afterward.** Oh, really? Can you name some of these companies? Chances are you cannot. In fact, I am not aware of any organization that has ever tried VB on a large scale and has since returned to its former development environment. Although, I suppose that would be quite conceivable given that some people kept on riding in horse and buggies long after the automobile was invented.

What I have seen is something like this: Imagine, if you will, an MIS director who is pacing in his office. He has been reading about Visual Basic in this book and other publications and decides it is time to try it out. He calls in Jim, his crack C project leader.

"Jim," he says, "I am hearing a lot of good things about Visual Basic. Why don't we try it out for size?"

[9]S. Canter et al., "Not So Basic Anymore," *PC Magazine,* September 28, 1993, 12, no. 16, p. 233.

Jim is shocked: "Do we have to? What's wrong with C?"

"Well, Jim, they say VB is more economical. Why don't you develop the new payroll system you just started in VB rather than in C? Give it a shot, will you? And let me know what you think."

A few months later, the MIS director takes a phone call from Jim who is telling him about his VB experience:

"So what have you found out about VB, Jim?" asks the MIS director. "Really? That bad? . . . And no pointers? . . . Couldn't have a lot of globals? . . . The VB wall? Yeah, I've heard of it. . . . Well, I guess we will have to scrap it. It may be good only for prototyping. . . . OK, go ahead and finish the job in C. I'll put out a memo this afternoon." Click.

You see, moving over to VB cannot be a half-hearted effort since the establishment is too entrenched to allow such an attempt to succeed. In this example, the MIS director was correct in trying VB slowly but then chose the wrong team to test it. He basically gave the people who have the most to lose from Visual Basic the responsibility of approving it. No wonder the company *went back to C.*

Reality: Companies who evaluate Visual Basic by employing nonbias techniques never return to C except for some select performance-enhancing routines.

Myth #7: **VB is not maintainable or reusable.** According to this, VB requires programmers to write each part of the application over again each time a new project is started or a problem is discovered, generating mountains of code in the process.

First, I find it hard to believe that most of the people who claim such difficulties are C++ programmers. These are the same people who often have to program a single feature in several different parts each in a different module. Surely they do not think C++ is more maintainable?

Second, in a typical VB program, over 90% of the code resides in encapsulated components. Even if whatever is left is hard to maintain—and it is not—are we not better off by an order of magnitude compared to whichever mythical language VB is being compared to?

In reality, however, VB is no harder to maintain than any other language. Moreover, there are several tools on the market that help with code management so the task becomes even easier.

Reality: VB is easy to maintain.

Myth #8: **VB does not have dynamic data structures.** This is a favorite argument of those who are used to programming databases and, thus, are accustomed to creating and destroying data elements or linked lists. Such people get lost in the Visual Basic environment that may not have the exact similar capabilities.

In fact, though, VB does have some dynamic structures. Controls and forms (extension components such as text boxes, radio boxes, etc.) can be created and destroyed on the fly, as needed. Actually any VB object, whether native or user defined, is kept in dynamic collections.

Also, arrays do not have to be statically declared and can grow and shrink as required. This, combined with the ability to define structures, approaches PASCAL's and C's dynamic structured capabilities.

But, of course, to some purists, these are not enough since they seek the more traditional C++ dynamic pointers. Rather than spend unnecessary time and space arguing this hair-splitting technical issue, allow me to revert to my standard argument: Using Visual Basic, you can import a whole database application as a component that will, in turn, manage all your dynamic needs. Why anyone would need a dynamic structure when such a powerful tool is at his of her disposal is beyond me.

Reality: VB does have dynamic structures but most dynamic capabilities are redundant.

Myth #9: **VB wastes memory.** VB requires that the entire code set of a component module be loaded into RAM with the program whether it is used or not.

So what?

At $40 per megabyte of RAM, memory is cheap. Include this extra cost in your financial analysis comparing VB with any other language and it will be lost in incidental expenses. That is, even four additional megabytes per work station hardly covers the cost of about one hour's pay of a hot-shot C++ programmer.

Additionally, newly manufactured personal computers are being delivered with increasing amounts of memory so they can support the ever expanding appetite of commercial software such as word processors and spreadsheets. Rarely will a business application's memory requirements even come close to the memory needs of these other systems.

Reality: Extra costs incurred due to memory requirements of a Visual Basic application are quickly drowned by the cost savings of the language itself.

Myth #10: **VB cannot handle large files.** This contention is usually uttered by 3GL programmers who are used to handling large text files with caching algorithms. Thus, they miss the pointer mechanisms of C and C++ to handle these files.

Actually, VB has a better way of handling caching with such commands as SEEK and LOC but, again, who needs to write his or her own cache any more?

Should you want to bring in a large text file for the user to view or edit, connect any OLE server word processor to your program (as a component) and you have a ready-made file manger with built-in caching.

Reality: Smart VB programmers can handle any size file.

So you see, the criticisms against VB hardly hold water.

Rule #4: Don't let the turkeys get you down. VB is as flexible and robust a development environment as any on the market today.

In Figure 1.3 you will find a sample of a typical project's cost justification comparing Visual Basic to other languages. This justification is based on some rudimentary assumptions that may not fit your particular need. It serves to show, however, how much cheaper VB can be in comparison to the alternatives.

Visual Basic Cost Justification on a System-wide Basis

Comparison of developing a 25-screen, database application for use on 25 workstations.

Platform	PC		PC		PC		Mainframe	
Language		VB		C		C++		C
Technical Labor Costs								
Programmer salary per day	$	600	$	750	$	1,000	$	600
Person-days to develop a 25-screens database application		75		450		300		675
Total Programming Costs		45,000		337,500		300,000		405,000
Tester salary per day		400		400		400		400
Number of person-days to test system		20		68		45		101
Total Testing Costs		8,000		27,000		18,000		40,500
Document preparers salary		300		300		300		300
Number of person-days to document		25		25		25		25
Total Documentation Costs		7,500		7,500		7,500		7,500
Trainer's salary (assuming programmer will train)		600		750		1,000		600
Days to train users		5		5		5		15
Total Training Costs		3,000		3,750		5,000		9,000
Total Technical Salaries	$	63,500	$	375,750	$	330,500	$	462,000
Workstation Related Costs								
Personal computer (90MHz Pentium, 32MB, 1MB Disk)	$	5,000	$	5,000	$	5,000		
Components		300						
OLE applications (database, word processor, etc.)		300						
Smart terminal								500
Misc. hardware (cables, printers, etc.)		1,000		1,000		1,000		1,000
Total Workstation Cost		6,600		6,000		6,000		1,500
Technician salary per day		300		300		300		300
Number of days to install per workstation		1.0		1.0		1.0		1.5
Total Installation Costs per Workstation		300		300		300		450
Total cost per workstation		6,900		6,300		6,300		1,950
Number of workstations		25		25		25		25
Total Workstation Cost	$	172,500	$	157,500	$	157,500	$	48,750
Total Project Cost (Hardware and Software)	**$**	**236,000**	**$**	**533,250**	**$**	**488,000**	**$**	**510,750**
Cost of developing a VB system as % of others				44%		48%		46%

Note that this is only an incremental analysis. It disregards sunk costs such as the cost of the mainframe and existing database or the cost of a network. It also ignores supervision costs and other overhead as those would be incurred no matter what development environment is used. (Technically, some accountants would argue that the time value of overhead costs should be included. i.e., since a VB project could be completed so much faster, managers could be assigned to other tasks sooner. Nonetheless, we chose to ignore this time-value principle so as not to muddy up the issue.)

Figure 1.3 *Visual Basic cost justification*

CHAPTER 2

What Is a Business Application?

Some people will concede that Visual Basic is an excellent development tool but only for business or database-intensive applications. Naturally, I disagree with this disclaimer but I also think that it is irrelevant. In this chapter we will examine the full range of business applications to see if there are any types of applications that are not database driven and with which we need to concern ourselves. In the process, we will also define the scope and type of applications to which the material of this book applies.

The vast majority of business applications can be divided into four types:

1. Data depository, entry, and retrieval
2. Transaction processing
3. Decision support
4. Analytic

We shall soon see that all but the last are database-intensive applications and that the case can be made that even the analytic application is database driven. That is, the first three applications accept, store, manipulate, and retrieve data. An analytic application does not necessarily provide such data functions but most do.

A data depository application is one that prompts the user for information and then stores the information in a database. Upon demand, this application reports the information back to the user on the screen or on paper. An example of a data entry application can be a directory of clients used by sales-people to log customer information. Such an application is very common and is really nothing more than a sophisticated rolodex. Nonetheless, these applications are irreplaceable in today's office. Aside from providing every user information at his or her fingertips, data depository applications also serve as data validation tools, improve data accuracy, and vastly improve data entry time.

Incidentally, data depository applications do not always follow the rolodex paradigm. Word processors such as Microsoft Word™, presentation applications such as Microsoft PowerPoint™, office bulletin boards such as Lotus Notes™, and mail programs such as Microsoft Mail™ are also nothing more than merely data depository, entry, and retrieval programs.

The next level up from the data depository application is the transaction processing application. This type of application also has data entry screens and provides reports but the data are used to affect business operations rather than simply as a library of information. Examples of transaction processing applications include inventory systems, order entry systems, stock trading systems, accounting systems, and others.

In a typical transaction application, the user enters information, say, a customer order, through a data entry screen. The information is recorded in the database just as it is with the data depository application. But, in addition, a secondary process goes into play producing a shipping order to the warehouse. When the order is shipped, the ordered item is automatically subtracted from inventory. At each step, a corresponding entry is made into the company's general ledger. Thus, transactions are recorded not only when the user enters information but also as a result of background computer processing. Generally, transaction applications must also conform to accounting principles and, thus, most also provide such services as audit trails and ability to adjust accounts.

Decision support systems are slightly more complex than the previous two types of applications. A typical decision support system applies the data that are in the database—entered either by the user or as a result of a transaction—toward a user-defined scenario. The scenario's parameters are, therefore, provided by both the database and the user. An example of a common decision support tool is Microsoft Excel™. The typical Excel user defines complex models in this spreadsheet application and then tweaks the parameters to determine the business outcome. In a more modern spreadsheet, much of the data are obtained from the database server or market data feeds using Visual Basic for Application, leaving the user to alter the parameters that are truly variable in real life. A stock trader can, thus, determine what effects his portfolio experiences as a result of movements in the bond market. The underlying data defining such movements may be entered manually or obtained automatically from an electronic feed. The portfolio holding definition can be directly loaded from the company's central database.

Clearly, with the advent of application linking and the use of Visual Basic for Applications, decision support applications are fast becoming indistinguishable from the other two database application types described previously. In fact, many programmers will tell you that the set of program components that must be assembled to make a decision support software is very much the same as that needed for a transaction processing application.

Finally, we are left with the analytic application. This type includes any business application whose sole purpose is to calculate outcome based on input parameters. An example of an analytic application is a program to calculate the yield curves of a certain interest rate portfolio. The algorithms for such calculation are usually based on complex mathematics and proprietary technology that once derived rarely change over time.

Without the aid of a dedicated computer application, it could take a very long time to calculate the yield. Yet the information is needed on a timely basis. Take, for instance, the bond trader who relies on the bond analysis to make timely trades. If he is to make correct trades, he needs the results of the calculation almost instantaneously. Subsequently, decision support applications are developed as stand-alone calculators using C and sometimes Assembly languages.

The problem, of course, is that the understanding of the code and the algorithm often resided in the head of the mathematician who developed it. And with C and Assembly being so difficult to understand, when the developer leaves, the knowledge base also disappears.

Today one would have a hard time explaining why these calculations cannot be done using spreadsheets such as Microsoft Excel with the help of a Visual Basic for Applications utilizing the horsepower of a 200-MHz Pentium Pro processor chip and distributed computing client-server technology. Such a setup can outperform any application developed only a few years ago in any language. Furthermore, the ease of readability and maintenance relieves the worry of losing the knowledge base with personnel turnover.

But for those of you who would still maintain that analytic applications are better done in traditional languages, I will be happy to concede. These applications represent such an insignificant portion of business applications that in the final analysis they matter little to the overall choice of development language.

Either way, database applications represent the majority, if not the entirety, of business software development. If you are one of those people who believes that Visual Basic is great but only for database applications, then, by definition, you should use it in developing your business applications.

_____ CHAPTER 3 _____

What Is Visual Basic?

This chapter is designed to provide a brief overview of the Visual Basic language and development environment for those readers who know little about this application. If you are an experienced Visual Basic programmer, you may wish to skip this chapter and move on to more interesting items.

Visual Basic is a rapid application development tool set for creating Microsoft Windows applications soon to expand to other platforms. It is a complete development environment including a WYSIWYG text editor (What-You-See-Is-What-You-Get), a syntax checker, a rich set of debug tools, a graphical screen-design interface, a database interface, and an interpreter by which execution is accomplished. These elements are integrated together seamlessly so they appear to the user to be a single application.

But the integration does not stop within the development environment. Visual Basic is also completely integrated within the Microsoft Windows environment. The user can, thus, cut and paste text and images to and from any other Windows application into the Visual Basic workbench. Consequently, whatever tool native Visual Basic is missing, such as a bit map editor, for example, is easily made up with the availability of such a tool in Windows.

Most important, Visual Basic is a component-oriented development environment that is fully extensible. The user can add or remove components to and from the system during development and then instantly be able to use these components while developing the applications. Once added, these components become indistinguishable from the native development environment. For example, the user can bring up a property dialog box for a third-party supplied control, say, a fancy List Box, much the same way she invokes a property dialog box for the built-in Text Box control.

Finally, Visual Basic is an event-driven program. It processes code not in a simple serial fashion as do traditional programs but also as triggering events occur. For example, while serially executing a piece of code to load and display some record set of data, the program uses the Windows messaging interface to determine that an event had occurred, say, a mouse click. Depending on the program's design, the program can immediately suspend normal execution and launch the code that is currently associated with a mouse click. Following this *interruption*, normal execution can resume.

A somewhat more limited version of Visual Basic is the Visual Basic for Applications (VBA) that Microsoft now uses as the macro language for many of its applications. VBA shares in appearance the editor, debugger, and even some of the objects of VB but is, currently, not a stand-alone workbench. Luckily, one can develop an application in VB and then import it into a VBA application.

CONTROLS

Before we proceed any further, we must define some terms used in the Visual Basic environment. (See Figure 3.1.) The most prevalent of the terms is a *control* also know as a VBX—Visual Basic Extension—or OCX—OLE Control Extension. A control is an application component that can be included as part of the development environment. To be a bit more technical, a control is part of or a complete DLL or OLE program loaded into memory at the time of development and during execution. The VB application interacts with the

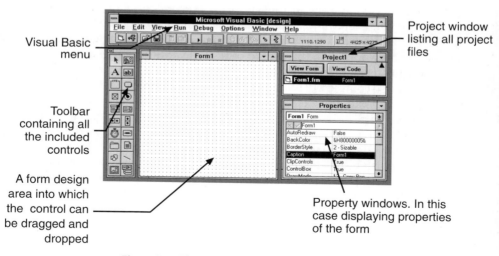

Visual Basic menu

Toolbar containing all the included controls

A form design area into which the control can be dragged and dropped

Project window listing all project files

Property windows. In this case displaying properties of the form

Figure 3.1 *The Visual Basic development work bench*

control either via the Windows messaging system or a shared stack. (Relax. If you did not understand the last few sentences, you need not panic. We will be talking about DLLs and OLE later on in the book.)

A CONTROL IS A PROGRAM COMPONENT. An example of a control is a text box. This is the typical rectangular white box into which a user can enter new or edit existing text. This control can be placed on the application window wherever needed during development. Physically, this entails dragging the control from the control pallet (with a mouse, of course) and dropping it onto the appropriate design element. The properties of this control such as background color, text color, and text alignment can be modified during development as well as during real-time execution. Most important, the application can write to or read from the control the contents of the text box.

The Visual Basic development environment provides a basic pallet of controls that can be extended or shrunk based on the application's need. The basic set includes such controls as labels, push buttons, text boxes, list boxes (three kinds), picture boxes, panels (for three-dimensional effect), check boxes, radio option buttons, basic grids and many others. Third-party controls can also be added as needed. These include complex grids, tabs, voice and multimedia interfaces, and many others.

At last glance, there were over 200 control vendors around the world and over 500 different third-party controls on the market.

PROPERTIES

As mentioned earlier, each control has a set of *properties*. (See Figure 3.2.) These properties are predefined by the control's maker and can be set either during development by the developer or during execution by the application. The Text Box control, for instance, has such properties as TextSize, BackColor, Text Alignment, and so on. The developer can use the property dialog box to set these properties during design time. Alternately, the application can be programmed to set the properties during execution. The following line of code changes the TextSize property of a Text Box called txtBox1:

```
txtBox1.TextSize = 12
```

METHODS

In addition to properties, each control also has *methods*. Methods are executable procedures that exist inside the control—remember, it is really a program component—and that are not accessible for modifications. The application can run these methods during execution. An example of a method is the Clear or AddItem method of the ListBox control. During run time, the program may issue the following lines of code to populate a ListBox called lstCountries:

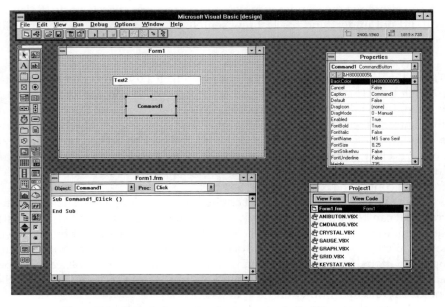

Figure 3.2 *Control placement and programming in the VB environment*

```
lstCountries.Clear                    ' Empties the list box
lstCountries.AddItem "USA"            ' Add countries
lstCountries.AddItem "England"
lstCountries.AddItem "Canada"
lstCountries.AddItem "France"
```

Note that the programmer of the application need not write the Clear procedure or the AddItem procedure. These are integral parts of the ListBox control residing deep within its mechanism. Rather, the user needed only to include the ListBox control in his development environment and the preceding logic in his program.

EVENTS

Many controls also make use of *Events*. An event is quite literally an action that triggers the Visual Basic interpreter to initiate a specific segment of code as directed during design. For example, the Push Button control has a click event. Whenever the user clicks on the push-button with the mouse during normal execution, a click event is generated by Windows causing the associated VB code to be executed immediately. Other push button events include GetFocus, DoubleClick, LoseFocus, and many others.

Events are similar to methods in that they are hidden pieces of executable code residing in the corresponding control. The difference is that in events the procedure is not completely predefined by the encapsulated component and must be completed by the developer. If, for instance, he wants the program to display a message whenever the user clicks on a button called btnDisplayMessage, he adds code to the btnDisplayMessage_Click procedure that was automatically generated when he created the button. The procedure looks like this:

```
Sub btnDisplayMessage_Click     ' automatically generated
      MsgBox "Hello"            ' we added
End Sub                          ' automatically generated
```

PROJECTS, FORMS, MODULES, AND CLASSES

During development, the Visual Basic application is defined as a *Project*. A project contains the following elements:

1. Zero or more *Forms*. A form is an MS Windows window (a screen or dialog box, if you will) that holds menus, controls, text, pictures, and others. A form commonly has minimize and maximize buttons on the upper right-hand side, a control box on the upper left-hand side, and a banner and a caption on top. Sometimes it has a menu underneath the banner.

     Forms contain not only controls and display elements but also the event procedure for the controls. They can also hold code relating to the form but good programming standards advise against such implementation.

2. Zero or more *Modules*. A module is where the main elements of code are placed. In essence, this is very similar to the traditional modules built in more traditional languages.

     Note that an application needs to have only one module and no forms. Similarly, it can have only one form and no modules if all code is resident within the form. However, a project must have either at least one module or at least one form. Practically speaking, most projects have both forms and modules. This is because for performance reasons, it is a good idea to lighten the size of a form. As a result, code that could be placed in forms ends up being put in modules.

3. Zero or more *Classes*. A class is the definition of a Visual Basic program component. It does not actually take shape and execute until a new instance of the class is created within a module. Classes contain all the code, properties, events, and methods necessary to form an encapsulated component.

     Classes differ from controls in that they reside inside the Visual Basic program and are created by the developer as opposed to being taken "off the shelf," so to speak.

4. Related project definitions such as executable name, location of files, DLLs used, and so on.

To put an application together, the developer first opens a new project. She then designs numerous forms by dragging and dropping controls, using the mouse, from the tool bar to the form and sizing everything appropriately. She also sets the suitable properties of each control. This visual design phase is actually no more complex than drawing screens using conventional *etch-a-sketch* applications such as Corel Draw® or even MS Paint®.

When the visual design phase is complete, the developer can demonstrate the look and feel of the application and the flow of the screens by writing some very rudimentary event procedures (rarely more than one line each). Such a prototype can be put together very quickly and modified in the presence of the end user. But do not let the word *prototype* mislead you. This *prototype* is already a completed application, one for which an executable can be generated and handed to the user for review. It may not do much more than simply take the user through the screen flow, but a stand-alone application it is.

Once the prototype is approved, the developer can then *fill between the lines*, so to speak, by placing elements of the logic in the currently empty, or mostly empty, modules and event procedures. She may also add, as needed, several classes and modules that are independent of the forms. This phase resembles the more traditional development cycle with one important exception: By the time the developer starts *coding*, over 80% of the application is already done. The screens, screen elements, and screen flow are fully functional and well integrated.

Incidentally, Microsoft has done an excellent job designing the editor that is used to generate the *filler* code. Some of the features of this editor include:

1. Comments are automatically displayed in green. Key words are automatically displayed in blue. Other such assignments can be added and the existing color scheme can be modified.
2. Syntax errors are caught as soon as a line of code is typed. Then again, experienced programmers like to turn this feature off so they can jump around the code more freely.
3. A set of developer directives instructs VB on whether or not variables must be declared, and on such matters as the first index of an element in an array (zero or one).
4. Multiple modules can be opened at any one time, making code comparison easy.
5. Moving around the code and finding and replacing strings are easily accomplished with a set of robust tools and short-cut keys.

DEBUGGING

Next to the visual design process described previously, the biggest time saving VB provides is generated by the debugging environment. Since VB is an interpretive rather than a compiled language, stepping through the code is done in real time on the actual code.[1] The developer can actually see what statement is being executed, move the cursor to another location and continue executing there, reset or assign new values to variables, query variable values, and even execute new statements in real time through what is known as the *Immediate Window*.

The most impressive feature, however, is the ability to change the code while it is being executed. To do so, the developer pauses the program, writes in new code or corrects the syntax of an existing line, and then continues execution. When the program is done, the developer can save her changes to the disk since the modifications were recorded in the actual program as if written there before execution began.

No other major development environment on the market today has this great time-saving feature.

CONTEXT-SENSITIVE HELP

Visual Basic, just like any other Microsoft application for Windows, supports context-sensitive help. Subsequently, developers need not remember by heart the documentation for each and every aspect of the language. Instead, programmers can point to a control or syntax they want to know more about and press the F1 function key. The Windows help utility pops up with the relevant topic.

Here, too, development is speeded up considerably since the programmer can concentrate on the design and implementation instead of having to page through endless manuals. He has at his fingertips, literally and figuratively, all the information necessary to determine the correct syntax of a certain line of code, or the property name for a certain control.

But Visual Basic does not stop at just being the client of the context-sensitive help utility. It can also be the server. By setting the appropriate property of each control to the help file and topic ID, the application being developed can, in itself, become the caller of the context-sensitive help utility. Of course, a help file has to be written and compiled using the Microsoft utilities provided with VB, but once such a file is written it is easily integrated into the application. Thus, the user of the application can set the cursor to a certain list

---

[1] Microsoft promises to provide a compiler with version 5.0. If you value fast development time, this may not be an improvement.

box and press the F1 key and instantaneously get relevant information about the list box.

LANGUAGE CONSTRUCTS

Visual Basic as a language is a robust programming language supporting all of the third-generation language structures in addition to its fourth-generation features. Basic control structures include:

- IF-THEN-ELSE
- FOR-NEXT
- WHILE-WEND
- LOOP-UNTIL
- SELECT CASE
- Subroutines
- Functions
- Classes

It supports all standard data types for constant and variable declarations · including:

- Integer
- Long
- Float
- Double
- Single
- String
- Objects

VB also has a data type called Variant, which can be any of the preceding data types. This is really helpful when developing a routine that can return any number of types depending on the situation.

Additionally, new data types and structures can be defined using the TYPE construct. Thus, an Address type may defined as:

```
Type AddressType

    Name as String
    StreetName as String
    StreetNumber as Integer
    TownName as String
    StateName as String
    ZipCode as Long

End Type
```

Arrays, multidimensional arrays, and dynamic arrays are fully supported. To build a rolodex data structure one should define:

```
Dim Rolodex As AddressType()
```

When a new item is to be added:

```
Redim Preserve Rolodex(UBound(Rolodex)+1)
Rollodex.Name = "John Doe"
Rollodex.StreetName = "Elm Street"
etc.
```

In addition, Visual Basic supports a wide variety of built-in functions that far exceeds the built-in function set of many third-generation languages. I/O reading and writing are superb and many tools are available to open, read, and manipulate files.

Although variables do not have to be formally declared, a development directive can be set to force formal declarations.

ERROR HANDLING

One of Visual Basic's most powerful features is its error-handling utility. Developers do not have to write complex error-handling routines that check for errors after every statement. Instead, the programmer can develop the code as if she expects no errors to occur and let VB trap errors. She directs the application on what to do in case of an error by placing a directive line in each procedure, preferably near the start. Nested procedures inherit the error handling of their callers. So, for example, if the developer wants the program to tell the user when an error occurred, she will write:

```
Sub DoDaDoDa ()

    On Error GoTo ERROR_LABEL:

    ' actual code
    Exit Sub

ERROR_LABEL:
    MsgBox "An error had occurred"
    Resume Next                    ' to continue

End Sub
```

When an error occurs in this example during the normal execution, VB automatically jumps to the error-handling part of the code. Thus, no error checking is necessary for such horrible events as not enough memory, division by 0, lost connection to the database, and so on.

Incidentally, the user can also generate errors by setting the error variable to a number that is not used by the system. A global error-handling routine can then decipher this number, thus, allowing for very simple application-level error handling.

DATABASE PROGRAMMING

Visual Basic excels in providing for database-intensive applications. That is because a database is treated by Visual Basic as just another component, no different than a text box or a list box. Much more will be said about the various methods of accessing the database in upcoming chapters. Here we will cover only the rudimentary concepts behind VB's data engine.

The two most common ways to access a database is by either attaching what is known as a data-aware control to a database or by creating a database object. Suppose you want to have a text box display a certain stock quote from a database for an item matching today's date. If you choose the data-aware control method, you can do so by including the database control in your form, and then setting the database property and connect strings to the database name. In the text box control you will set the DataField property to the stock quote field name.

Alternately, you can type the following code:

```
Dim DB as DataBase
Dim Ss as SnapShot
Set Db = OpenDatabase("c:\databases\db.md")
Set Ss =  Db.CreateSnapshot("Select StockPrice From PriceTable
                                    Where Date = " & Now)
txtStockPrice.Text = Ss("StockPrice")
Ss.Close
Db.Close
```

Needless to say, interfacing with a database in Visual Basic is almost a trivial matter.

Note that Visual Basic can use the Open DataBase Connectivity (ODBC) protocol developed by Microsoft. ODBC allows for seamless interaction between an application and any database for which the vendor has provided an ODBC driver. The advantage of this method is that your application can be developed to talk to any database without having to modify the code. In essence, the application interacts generically with the ODBC program which, in turns, acts as the translator to any one of many compliant databases.

Over the years, I developed several applications that used the ODBC mechanism to talk to several databases including IBM's DB2®, Microsoft SQL Server®, and Sybase Server® depending on the implementation setup. This saved the user much resources in having to develop multiple versions of the same applications depending on the appropriate database.

OLE INTERFACE

OLE (object linking and embedding) is a way of including other applications as objects in your own applications. So, for example, when an application requires a spreadsheet screen, it is not at all necessary to program a spreadsheet application. Instead, one can call in an existing spreadsheet application such as Microsoft's Excel® using OLE technology.

There are two types of OLE implementations. The first involves actually linking and/or embedding another application within the master application. Through such an implementation, the master application relinquishes control to the OLE application whenever the user causes focus to be transferred to the OLE application. An embedded MS Excel spreadsheet can, therefore, be opened into full-fledged Excel for, say, editing, by double clicking on the image of the spreadsheet in the master application.

A second implementation is called OLE automation, which allows the master application to use and manipulate data in the OLE object without actually showing it to the user. For example, you may want to use the MS Excel spreadsheet application as a fancy calculator to determine an internal rate of return of a stream of cash flows. To do so, you can use OLE automation to open Excel in the background, shove in values, and return the result without the user ever knowing that another application just ran.

OLE programming in VB is just as easy as database programming. Using OLE automation, for example, we can access a cell in an Excel spreadsheet like this:

```
Dim objXL as Object
Set objXL = CreateObject("Excel.Application.5")    'Start Excel
objXL.Workbooks.Open("C:\Excel\MyWrkBk.XLS") ' Open workbook
MsgBox _                                      ' Display the value
    Cstr(objXL.ActiveWorkbook.Sheets("Sheet1").Range("$A$1").Value)
objXL.Quit      ' End Excel
set objXL = Nothing
```

Visual Basic version 4.0 provides for ways to make the VB application itself an OLE server. It can then be called from other applications much in the same way described earlier. A portfolio risk manager can, thus, be called upon from the Microsoft Word document that reports to investors on today's risk exposure.

DEVELOPING REPORTS

Although I generally do not recommend hard-coding reports in any application, there are certainly times when such reports are necessary. Here, too, Visual Basic provides an excellent and easy tool to use in report generation.

Crystal Report, the control used by VB, is actually a report-generating system that was developed by a third-party vendor for Microsoft. Now it is shipped with every copy of Visual Basic as a standard feature. Creating a report is a two-step process. First, the developer uses the Crystal Report application to graphically design the report. This process is very similar to the screen design described earlier since it consists of dragging and dropping database fields into the drawing form.

In the second step, the developer includes the Crystal Report control in the application, specifying in the appropriate properties the location of the report designed previously. No coding is necessary unless the application requires some of the report parameters to be modified on the run.

When the program is run, the report as well as the supporting structures automatically become part of the program. The user can, therefore, preview the report on the screen, print it, change printers, change printer settings, and so on.

INTERFACING WITH WINDOWS

Visual Basic interacts with external routines and the Windows environment through what are known as Application Programming Interface (API) routines. These are routines and functions that reside in loaded Windows modules that Visual Basic can call upon.

For example, to read from the SYSTEM.INI[2] file that holds important Windows configuration data, VB applications can define and call a built-in Windows API routine called GetPrivateProfileString. This is done by declaring the routine as follows:

```
Declare Function GetPrivateProfileString Lib "Kernel" (ByVal
    lpApplicationName As String, ByVal lpKeyName As
    String, ByVal lpDefault As String, ByVal
    lpReturnedString As String, ByVal nSize As Integer,
    ByVal lpFileName As String) As Integer
```

From then on, whenever a fragment of data is to be obtained from the INI file, the routine is called as if it were actually defined locally.

The full set of accessible Windows API routines can be found in a file called WIN31API.HLP which is provided with the VB application. VB also ships with an API text viewer that holds within it the correct syntax for each and every routine and variable available in the Windows operating system.

DESIGN AIDS

Visual Basic comes with a visual design guide that details the issues a developer must consider when designing screen elements.

---

[2] 16-bit implementation only.

NEW ADDITIONS TO VISUAL BASIC VERSION 4.0

There are several new features in Visual Basic 4.0 released in early fall 1995. These include:[3]

1. The ability to create DLLs. You can now create OLE dynamically linked libraries entirely within VB4.0. If you do not know what a DLL is, a discussion on the subject will follow later on in this book.

2. The ability to create out-of-process OLE objects that can be shared across the network, not only by VB applications, but within any Windows environment that supports OLE, from PowerBuilder to Delphi.

3. Application partitioning. Through these distributed OLE objects and a variety of object-access and data-access tools, VB4 supports building three-tier client-server applications.

4. Database improvements from replication and FAT cursors to better referential integrity.

5. The ability to create classes, and with them, new controls.

---

[3] Taken from "VB 4.0 Completely Re-Architected," *Visual Basic Programmer's Journal* (October 1995), p. 26.

CHAPTER 4

Those Pesky End Users

Throughout this book, I will be suggesting techniques to deal with many difficult situations, several of which involve the user community. The analysis of these situations and the suggested solutions may lead the reader to mistakenly believe that I condone an adversarial relationship with the users. Let me assure you that although this conclusion is understandable, nothing could be further from the truth.

For years I have battled with my colleagues in the software industry to cease the practice of viewing the user community as the enemy. This is because I truly believe that the *us-versus-them* attitude that prevails in the industry is both destructive and self-defeating. Clearly, no one benefits from the diminished communication and ill feelings that result from the endless fighting between developers and users. On the contrary, there is no more important factor to ensuring a system's success than an amicable and mutually respectful relationship between the two camps.

The fact that in this book I point out difficult situations that involve the users does not, in any way, shape, or form, detract from my belief that a good working relationship with the user community is crucial. In none of these situations do I question the users' sincerity or desire to do what is right and proper. I simply propose some techniques of handling those situations where the users' wishes and intents come in direct conflict with the goals of the development team. That does not mean the users are wrong any more than it means that the developers are right.

Consider the classic example of a user who demands that a new feature be included in a system when the development budget and schedule do not permit such a modification. Is the user wrong by insisting on the feature? Of course not. Is the development team wrong in being reluctant to include the additional work? Hardly. Both sides are operating within their realm of responsibility and the constraints of their available resources. Yet it serves no purpose to turn this situation into a full-blown war. No matter who wins in the end, the users still need the requested feature and the developers still lack the resources to give it to them.

Whatever stress is generated by this scenario can easily be dissipated by approaching the situation as a team. Here one may note that within corporate walls it is much easier for the user to ask for more resources than it is for the development manager. Therefore, if the manager expresses a desire to help the user if only more money could be found, then there is a good chance that the problem will be solved. On the other hand, if the manager stomps his feet and proclaims, as many managers do, that the user does not know what she is asking for and refuses to implement the feature at any cost, then the problem will persist.

Over the years I collected several adages that I have adapted to the information systems industry. You will no doubt find many of these familiar, and some you may consider cliché. Nonetheless, I usually find this list very helpful whenever I am in a difficult situation involving the users.

1. The user is our customer. We must, therefore, treat him or her as we would like to be treated when we are the consumers of some product or service.

2. The user is not here to make our lives miserable. We are here because of the user. Everything we do, therefore, shall be aimed to please and satisfy the user.

3. No one has ever won an argument with a user. If users do not get what they need because we keep on *winning* arguments, they will get it from someone else next time. We will, therefore, eventually lose.

4. The user is never wrong. If you think the user is wrong, see the previous point.

5. If users ask for something we deem unreasonable, we owe them an explanation of why we disagree. If they persist, and are willing to pay the price, it is not unreasonable.

6. Users usually do not know how to program but they have seen Neil Armstrong land on the moon. Never tell them, therefore, that something cannot be done. Quote them a price and let them decide if they need it or not.

7. Users should be active participants in the development process. Do not make the mistake of hiding the development effort from the users and then trying to sell them a bag of goods.

Incidentally, I must admit that, depending on the industry, the relationship between users and developers is improving. In some fields, such as in the investment banking industry, the relationship is approaching the ideal and any animosity between the two groups is hardly discernible. This may be because software developers work in close proximity to the users, sometimes sharing the same workspace or it may just be due to the fact that both the users and the developers are highly paid professionals. Unfortunately, such relationships are still lacking in some more traditional environments.

CHAPTER 5

Why Is It Impossible to Justify a DP Project Financially and What Should Be Done Instead?

Regardless of in which technical environment you choose to develop the project, sooner or later you will have to justify the project financially. The person most likely to want such a justification may be your computer-illiterate boss, your computer-averse boss's boss, or some technically challenged member of the controller's staff. Whomever it is, presenting such justification is going to require more than just technical reasoning. It is also going to require financial justification.

In this chapter I will attempt to describe how to justify software projects in general and the use of Visual Basic in particular. In writing this material I have assumed that you are familiar with at least the rudimentary aspects of financial analysis and that you can calculate such factors as net preset value and return on investment. If you are unfamiliar with these terms, you will be well advised to look these up in any book on project finance before attempting to build a financial case for the project.

Let's begin by admitting that financially justifying any software project is a nightmare. All of us hate doing it mostly because we have been trained and are paid to develop systems, not to count beans. We, therefore, wholeheartedly resent being forced to put on accountant hats and do financial analysis, which we neither understand nor respect.

Moreover, financial analysis subjects us to a vicious irony. Like most MIS managers, we are hardly in control of the resources our systems are supposed to automate and so we are precluded from citing obvious benefits in the financial analysis. To include such benefits would be to gore other managers' oxen and, of course, we need these managers' support for our system to succeed. None of us, for example, would be so foolish as to present to upper management a scenario whereby our system would cause people to be cut from each of their respective organizations. That is because we all know how much senior managers cherish their power and position, which are often directly linked to the size of their fiefdom. So, instead, we usually resort to citing *touchy-feely* benefits such as improved productivity or increased customer satisfaction. Naturally, everyone knows that all such justifications amount to horse apples so we usually get splattered all over the wall when we present it.

But even if we were allowed to include *real* benefits, we are still in a jam because the benefits of software projects are not obvious and often are not tangible. So even the best financial jockeys among us find it extremely difficult to explain to management why millions of dollars should be sunk into developing applications that appear to have questionable benefits. Worse yet, certain applications sometimes seem to affect the bottom line in the wrong direction. For instance, I am still searching for that illusive magic justification for any and all software projects. This is despite my master's degree in business administration from a prestigious higher learning institution, many years spent financially justifying projects, and a reasonably high level of intelligence (at least in my opinion).

So let me state right up front, before we start getting into the nitty-gritty, that a long-ignored fact of software development is: Most software projects cannot be justified using traditional financial methods. That is because there are seldom any positive financial benefits to a software development project. (There, I said it!) Instead, the justification must come from the negative consequences of not undertaking a project rather than from any perceived benefits. Simply put, your company may not become more profitable with a new customer service application, but it will surely not survive if it does not have one!

There is a substantial body of evidence in academic research to prove this point. The gist of these findings—which incidentally does not pertain solely to software applications—is that investment in readily available new technology does not pay off. This conclusion is best illustrated by an example. Suppose you manufactured widgets (don't ask me what they are, I haven't a clue), say, 1 million annually, each costing $1 to produce. You sell the widget for $1.50 for a gross margin of 50¢.[1] All your competitors sell their widgets for the same price, so you assume that their cost structure is similar to yours.

Now suppose new technology becomes available that enables you to make twice as many widgets for the same cost. That is, you can now produce each widget for 50¢. Assume, for the moment, that the technology costs half a million dollars to implement and can be installed in a negligible amount of time. You need not think long to realize that this is a good project. But since

---

[1] Profit before CEO salary, taxes, and other such amounts.

you work for one of those nincompoop companies that needs to justify everything to the nth degree, you immediately sit down to calculate the project's benefits. Your analysis results are as follows:

Project cost:	$500,000
Savings per widget:	$0.50
Annual widget production:	1,000,000
Projected annual savings:	$500,000
Payback period:	1 year
Net present value over 5 years using a 10% interest rate:	$13,000,000

This is not to mention any increase in sales you may achieve by lowering the price, something you can do now due to lower cost.

Any manager would jump at such a project, but should you?

The answer is an unequivocal *"watch out."* On the surface, the project seems to be a great financial bonanza but remember that your company is not operating in a vacuum. In fact, the technology you are proposing to implement is readily available to all your competitors. Naturally, these other players will want to implement such technology as soon as anyone else in the industry does. No doubt, a price war will ensue as the first company lowers its price, and, if economics and past experience are any indicators, the price will quickly settle at below $1 (or somewhere around a price that provides 50% gross margin). The benefits will, thus, disappear and real payback will become negative.

"But why should anyone lower the price," you protest. "If everyone keeps the price at $1.50 everyone will be better off." True, but, game theory[2] not withstanding, trying to have an entire industry maintain a certain price level in a falling costs, multicompetitor environment has been proven to be inherently unstable. This little fact was decisively proven by the Organization of Petroleum Exporting Countries (OPEC) over the last 25 years. And unlike you, OPEC can use monopolistic tactics, permit members to talk to each other about prices, and does not even have any MBAs on board. Since your company does not enjoy any of these benefits and has to conform to U.S. antitrust laws, you don't stand a chance and so prices are likely to drop.

But even if, by some miracle, you succeed in maintaining an artificially high price, you will hardly be better off. That is because maintaining a high price invites competition from players who are not yet in your industry. These people who are currently standing on the sideline soon realize that it will cost them 50¢ to make what you are selling for $1.50 and so they decide to enter the market and undercut your price. Actually, this is the worst of all scenarios as additional producers increase industry capacity, in effect, raising

[2] The theory of how market players react to each other's actions. Something like if they think that we think that they think, *and so on.* Numerous volumes have been written on the subject.

the supply level and causing prices to drop well below what you would expect. Large enough additional capacity will cause prices to collapse down to the 50¢ level. Hey, don't blame me. I am only repeating what Adam Smith taught us a century ago, and he is yet to be wrong.

So why invest in the technology at all? Because you don't have a choice! Your competitors intend to employ the technology whether you do or don't. If you don't deploy the new technology when they do, prices will drop to well below your manufacturing costs, in effect, causing you to have to close down. After all, you cannot continue to operate selling 90-cent widgets at a cost of $1 each, can you? (Unless, of course, you fire the CEO so you do not have to pay his or her salary.)

And if you think that you can prevent the rest of the industry from investing in the technology by wildly waving your hands and pointing to this analysis, think again. Not utilizing readily available technology on an entire industry basis is as unstable a scenario as trying to maintain prices at an artificial level, much for the same reasons.

Software is, and always has been, a readily available technology. You cannot patent software, and even though you can copyright the actual code, you cannot protect concepts and ideas that reside within people's gray matter. And restricting the movement of this gray matter is more difficult than in any other industry, largely because there is such a shortage of qualified personnel. Software professionals are perpetually moving from one company to the next. And the best software professionals are consultants who, by definition, are always on the move. Your software today is someone else's tomorrow.

As if this constant *slushing* of brains across corporate boundaries is not bad enough, many software professionals love writing and publishing information about their code. The end result is that there are no secrets in the software industry, only unread articles. Another outcome is that your much cherished new portfolio evaluation algorithm will be going on line at your competitor's company soon after, if not before, your application is complete. (After all, your competitors need not waste time justifying the project financially as you did. All they have to do is tell their boss that you may overtake their company's lead and, thereby, instantly obtain approval.)

There are many examples of companies that could not or would not invest in software systems because their employees could not justify such systems financially. A recent example is CompUSA, a national chain of retail computer stores that in 1994 almost went belly-up because it lacked a computerized inventory system. Mind you, it didn't lack an inventory. Heavens knows it had more than enough. It didn't lack a system, either, since CompUSA clearly was able to evaluate inventory for tax purposes. The company was only guilty of missing a *computerized* inventory system, the lack of which prevented its management from making timely purchasing decisions.

Few cash benefits could have been realized if the company had decided to develop a computerized inventory system. After all, a clerk is still needed to log receipts and a cashier is still needed to note sales whether or not the system is computerized. Inventory costs would have been lower but when one looks at the cash benefits of lower inventory costs, they hardly justify a huge investment in software. Yet, the lack of such an inventory system caused inventory to bloat to levels above that of the competition, making CompUSA's cost structure uncompetitive. Thus, in 1994, CompUSA was put in a position of either computerizing its inventory system or going into Chapter 11. In a sense, the marketplace forced the company to do what it should have done all along.

Surely, the justification for the computerized inventory system was no different in 1994 than it was at any earlier period: Competitors having such a system can keep a lower cost structure by virtue of more timely decision processes, putting CompUSA at a competitive disadvantage. No financial justification is warranted to reach this conclusion. Unfortunately at CompUSA, as in most companies, such straightforward, common sense justification was not enough.

HOW DO WE OBTAIN FUNDING?

If financial justification is useless as a tool of meriting MIS budgets, and if we agree that corporate culture requires some type of structure in investment decision making, how does one obtain funding for software projects? Clearly, the only answer is to allocate a certain percentage of sales toward MIS projects in accordance with industry standards.

This is not a revolutionary idea. Such allocation is very similar to the way marketing and sales budgets are doled out. No one, including most corporate executives, is so deranged as to request that financial justifications be submitted for every ad campaign or newspaper coupon issue before such marketing efforts are approved. Instead, a budget of say, 2% of sales, is allocated at the beginning of the year and is turned over to the marketing department that, in turn, decides how best to maximize a return. The size of the budget relative to sales is determined by industry average and the company's strategy. A larger budget may be strategically allocated to enhance the company's position. Conversely, a smaller budget than the average may be decided on in an effort to reduce operating costs.

I strongly suggest that you spend the time to convince your company to follow this practice of preallocating your project budget based on average industry spending. Should you fail to do so, you will become one of those MIS managers who is forever trying to explain why the last project undertaken is not paying off as promised. And, of course, unable to explain this discrepancy, you will be perpetually searching the want-ads pages.

HOW DO WE DECIDE WHERE TO INVEST?

Having explained in detail why financial justification is pretty much useless when it comes to justifying software projects, I must now turn to a perfectly legitimate use of such analysis. Namely, financial analysis is an excellent tool in prioritizing projects.

Like most companies, yours probably does not have unlimited resources. Your department, in turn, also has far too many projects chasing not enough dollars. So how do you decide where to put resources? Compare the investments to the benefits, of course. Note, however, that unlike the financial analysis I railed against earlier in the chapter, this is an internal analysis constructed to compare projects to each other for the sole purpose of prioritization. Thus, such analysis need not actually meet the criteria of corporate-wide financial justification since the results, in and of themselves, are inconsequential. The fact that project A has a return of a negative $3K and project B has a return of a negative $5K does not mean that neither project should be undertaken, as traditional financial theory would suggest. Rather this comparison simply says that project A should be allocated resources first and only then, should any resources be left, should project B be undertaken.

A few ground rules about financial analysis when it is used for comparison purposes are in order.

Rule #1: **Don't always ignore sunk costs.** Sunk costs are any costs you have incurred prior to the date of the analysis which cannot be recovered if the project is terminated. Many experts adamantly insist that in order for you to do a correct financial analysis you must ignore sunk costs. This is based on the theory that you do not want to throw good money after bad. If the project is failing, it may be worthwhile to cut the losses and put the resources somewhere else than to continue to sink those resources into a failing effort. Thus, if you invested $1 million in project A and need to invest another $250K to complete it and you compare it to a new project, project B, that requires only $100K to complete (assume equal financial benefits), you should ignore the sunk investment and compare only the future costs. Accordingly, you should proceed with project B ($100K versus $250K with equal benefits—not $250K versus $1,100K as you may be tempted to do by adding the scrapped costs into the cost of the new project.)

I call this the golden rule of project analysis because it is so strongly preached by the high priests of finance. Admittedly, it is a very important rule. Clearly, you do not want yesterday's wrong decisions to drag your efficiency. Taking an example from day-to-day life, if you invested in a certain stock and its value dropped by 50% since you bought it, you should not consider this loss in deciding whether to hold it or sell it. Such a decision should be solely based on where you think the stock is going in the future.

However, many people apply the sunk costs rule the wrong way. In the foregoing example, there surely is $1 million of sunk costs that are not recoverable. But, if project A still must be completed sometime in the future, the analysis should *not* ignore the fact that the future cost of project A will be $1.25 million and not just $250K (if you consider that scrapping the project will force you to start from scratch later on). In other words, you may only ignore sunk costs if the project can truly be scrapped, buried, and forgotten.

Otherwise, you will still need to make the investment at a later date and, therefore, sunk costs will have to be invested again.

Rule #2: **Consider only cash costs in the savings column.** The second rule of project analysis is to consider only cash costs and cash benefits in cost-cutting justifications. I call this the "don't-fool-yourself" rule. Many people will come up with benefits that are not tangible and cannot be realized even if the project is undertaken. For example, such benefits may include 2 person-hours saved daily, reduced defect rate by 1 part per 20, and so on. These appear at first glance to be true savings that can be translated to cash but in reality they may not be.

This is plainly obvious when one examines the situation more closely: A person works an 8-hour day doing certain tasks. If you succeed in shaving 2 hours off that person's day, you still need someone to do the other 6 hours worth of work. This means that you will not be able to eliminate the position and, therefore, will not save any money as a result.

Some people protest vehemently against this analysis. They say that their project may not eliminate the position entirely but several such projects may, together, do so in the future. Furthermore, a part-time position can be created in lieu of the reduced work position, saving money in the process.

Indeed, if you can prove to yourself that such savings are realistic, by all means, you should include them in the analysis. However, my experience has shown that these savings are seldom possible. People rarely work 8-hour days any more and so your system will most likely save only the extra time they put in. Also, in many settings, only one person is left to do a job after several rounds of cost cutting and layoffs have eliminated the rest of her team. This person cannot be made into a part-timer as she is a valuable resource to the company. As for the multiple projects that together cause positions to be eliminated, I would suggest you include such savings with the last project completed rather than try to allocate the benefits between different projects. This way, if the last project is scrapped, you have not included bogus benefits with the initial projects.

The "don't-fool-yourself" rule means that you should consider only two types of benefits symbolized by Paychecks and Purchase Orders. If you can list next to the benefits column of your analysis the value of the Paychecks and Purchase Orders that will be no longer necessary or that will be reduced as a result of your project, you should include such benefits. Otherwise, if the number is nonexistent, don't include it as a cash benefit.

Rule #3: **Include all cash values of the benefits.** The flip side of the previous rule is that you should not forget to include all real benefits but make sure you list the benefit in cash. Improved quality, increased customer satisfaction, and reduced inventories are all lofty goals but they provide no information, as stated, for a financial analysis. Try to find out how much scrap will be eliminated due to improved quality and put a cash value on it. Likewise, try to get marketing to tell you how sales figures will increase if customer complaints drop by 25% as a result of your project. Include this increase in profit as your cash benefits. Finally, calculate the cash benefits of reduced inventories in terms of the interest that could be earned on the money were it to be sitting in the bank as opposed to on the warehouse floor.

Since you are not using the result of the analysis to justify individual projects, the analysis does not have to be precise. It must, however, be consistent across all projects. In other words, if you determine that the 25% in reduced customer complaints as a result of project A will translate into $2 million of additional profits, make sure you count on a larger profit for project B that claims to reduce complaints by 50%. (Note that this number may not necessarily be double depending on what the marketing department thinks the marginal effect of the last 25% will be, but it should be consistently larger than smaller benefits.)

Rule #4: **Diversify your risk.** This is also known as the good old "don't put all your eggs in one basket" rule. Just as you would with your private investment portfolio, you want to spread your resources across several projects, each having a different chance of success. This way, if one project fails, your entire portfolio may still have a reasonable return rate. If, on the other hand, you invest all your department's resources in one risky project with a promise of a high payback and the project fails, you are left with a big loss.

Always remember that the highest return is usually associated with the highest risk. A revolutionary new decision support application using the latest artificial intelligent techniques may promise great cash benefits due to improved decision making, but the untested technology may also prove to be unworkable. Be prepared with other success stories so that, in the event of such a failure, your department can show an overall positive return on the company's investment.

In a sense, you may want to forgo the large projects and stick with many smaller projects even if the payback analysis suggests you put all the resources with the mother of all projects. That is not to say that you should never take on big projects. Sometimes it is necessary to revamp the company's general ledger or payroll systems, or other such monsters that may take many months to complete. In such an eventuality, make sure that over the life of this big project you also complete many other smaller applications. Always resist the pressure to throw everything you have at a single effort no matter how much the client department yells and scream.

RISK-ADJUSTED PROJECT EVALUATION

	Cash Flow	Probability	Probable Cash Flow
Year 0	(150,000)	100%	(150,000)
Year 1	50,000	100%	50,000
Year 2	50,000	80%	40,000
Year 3	50,000	60%	30,000
Year 4	25,000	40%	10,000
Year 5	25,000	20%	5,000
Net Present Value	6,310		(35,467)
Internal Rate of Return	12%		−5%

This project appears to have a positive return until the risk associated with it is included.

CHAPTER 6

Why Correct Scheduling Is Crucial and How to Schedule a Visual Basic Project

Perhaps of all aspects of project management, scheduling presents the most caveats. Certainly it is no secret that projects that flop do so hardly because of technical difficulties. More often than not, such failure is caused by the inability of the project team to meet the promised timetable. Missed deadlines invariably cause upper management as well as the user community to grow nervous. Questions start popping up such as: Do we have enough money in the budget to continue? Are we getting bogged down in a quagmire? Do we have as capable a team in place as we were told? Shouldn't we outsource this project to *our favorite* consulting company?

These examinations sound reasonable enough to the casual observer. After all, who would not raise such issues faced with a missed deadline? And, indeed, in any other situation such squeamishness would be perfectly justified. For example, were you to contract a builder to construct a house and were told the project would take three months you would surely be surprised, to say the least, if you visited the construction site three months later and saw that very little has been accomplished. Under such a scenario you have all the right in the world to become very upset. Actually, I strongly recommend that you do.

But software development is hardly similar to building a house or constructing any other tangible structure. There are several distinctions that make software scheduling much harder to plan, monitor, and report. To list a few of these differences:

50

1. We have been building houses and constructing bridges and roads for thousands of years. As a result, everybody and their IRS agent know what it takes to complete these things. Any self-respecting engineer has ready access to scores of reference books listing in detail the various acceptable and reasonable standards of project scheduling: 2 person-days to pour a foundation, 3 person-hours to machine a screw, and so on.

   But even if we set out to build a new structure that varies somewhat from what is described in our collective knowledge base, we still have enough experience to be able to estimate, within a reasonable range, how long it would take to complete.

   Software development, on the other hand, is a relatively new endeavor. Serious software development has only been around for the last 30 years or so. It is, therefore, safe to assume that most people who have ever worked in the field are still doing so. As such, the database from which project managers draw to estimate the length of time it would take to complete development is extremely shallow. In preparing to write this book, I was astounded to find out that the number of publications covering the issue of software scheduling is exactly zero. In other words, there is little reference material for a manager to draw upon other than his or her own experience. Consequently, unless a manager is being asked to plan a project she has already completed before, the chances of her arriving at a reasonably accurate time line is somewhat less than certain.

2. Until the day the application is actually delivered, software is not normally viewed as a tangible object and, thus, progress is not easily observed by outsiders. When a bridge or house is being constructed, it is easy to see the results of the efforts expended so far. In the case of the house, for example, at the end of one week one can observe that the foundation has been poured; at two weeks, the frame is up; at three, the roof is completed, and so on. Software, on the other hand, is bits and bites inside the computer. These cannot easily be visualized and so few people outside the project team are capable of comprehending what progress has been made. Consequently, when the project manager reports that the delivery date may be pushed a bit, he is alarming people who have no concept whatsoever of what has already been accomplished.

3. A large percentage of the user community as well as upper management do not view software development in the same light as they view any other type of development. Software is looked upon as some kind of black magic. It is, therefore, assumed that the development team can simply wave their magic wand in the air and say a few *abracadabras* and, *poof*, software appears. At one point in my career I worked for a robot manufacturer. I always got a kick from the project plans that passed across my desk. The planners would allocate six weeks for equipment delivery, four weeks for placement design, three weeks for installation of the equipment, three weeks for testing, and, almost as an afterthought,

one week for software development. Needless to say, we never came in on time. Yet most planners could not get it through their skulls that there is really very little difference between the time it takes for design and development associated with hardware and that associated with software.

4. Upper management and the user community have trouble understanding the impact specification changes have on the schedule. It is a baffling experience. The same person who would understand perfectly well that asking to add a room to a house being built would surely delay completion has tremendous difficulty comprehending that adding a new feature to an application affects the delivery schedule. How many times have we all been exposed to this peculiar double standard? A user raises holy hell about a feature that absolutely, positively must be included in the application or it would never fly. Two months later, the same user comes back and threatens to start World War III should the project deviate even one fraction of a second from the agreed-upon delivery date. Somehow, the connection between the added feature and its effect on the delivery schedule just never factors in.

The use of a component-based development environment, such as Visual Basic, alleviates some of these problems. VB turns at least some of the original, never-before-done work into assembly tasks. And since assembly time is more easily estimated than original craft work, it is easier to figure out what it takes to complete a project. In essence, by componentizing development, one can develop a building-block approach to scheduling.

From my own experience, for example, I have learned that it should take about one day to program a single input-output Visual Basic screen (form). This includes retrieving data from the database, displaying them on a screen, prompting for user input and/or action, and restoring the data to the database. Adding a day for specification and design, and a day for testing and approval, we derive the figure of 3 person-days per screen. Padding this up a bit to add contingency time for variations, complications, scope creep, and unforeseen circumstances, we conclude that 4 person-days should be allocated for each application screen.[1]

Using this estimate, one can easily scale it up to a full application simply by counting the number of screens and dialog boxes and then multiplying this figure by the 4 person-day number we derived per each screen. Accordingly, an application that has 30 screens and 15 dialog boxes should take about 180 person-days to complete. That is:

---

[1]Under no circumstances, should one read this sentence to mean that the schedule should be padded. A schedule should and must be as lean as possible so as to truly compete in the marketplace against other people who offer to build the system. The contingency figure I am suggesting here has to do with the variability between different screens and the normal incidentals such as doctor appointments and such that are likely to occur during the project.

$$(30 + 15) \times 4 = 180 \text{ workdays}$$

If you have budgeted for two programmers, the application can be programmed in about four and a half months.

$$\frac{180}{2} = 90$$

90 workdays are approximately 4.5 months if you assume that there are 20 workdays per month. Remember, of course, to add holidays and vacations as needed when you calendarize this figure.

SOME TYPICAL ESTIMATES FOR A VISUAL BASIC PROJECT

Planning Item	Typical VB Time Estimate[a]
Gather data specifications and edit and validation rules.	1 hour per 5 data fields.
Database server setup (allocate memory, define database, setup logs, etc.).	1 day.
Design and construction of the database (define tables, define fields, define indexes, etc.).	1 day per 15 tables.[b]
Gather data/transaction entry screen user requirements.	1/2 day per user.
Prototype data/transaction entry screen and review with the user.	1/2 day per screen per user.
Code data/transaction entry screen including data storage and retrieval and edit and validation rules.	2 days per screen.
Data/transaction entry screen unit testing.	1 day per screen.
Gather reporting requirements.	1/4 day per report per user.
Code reports.	1/2 day per report.
Additional time for analytic, audit trails, and extra security systems.	Varies but generally another 1/2 day each per implementation point[c] including unit testing.
Integrate modules.	1/4 day per module.
Unit testing of entire project.	1/2 day per module.
Installation.	1 day per user.
Documentation.	1/4 day per screen.
Beta testing.	1 day per screen.
Training.	1 day per user per 10 screens.

[a]These estimates are for database entry and retrieval systems (a marketing database, for example) or transaction-based systems (inventory, security trading, etc.) Other applications would have slightly different estimates.

[b]Assuming you use a CASE tool such as ERWIN ERX that converts database design to SQL code.

[c]Implementation point is the place in which the function will be used. That is, a net present value calculating function may be used only once in the program. On the other hand, a security mechanism may be used every time a user wants to access a protected field.

An interesting observation about this planning methodology is that contrary to intuitive beliefs, the number of items on a data entry screen makes little difference in the estimate. In other words, a mini-project consisting of a screen that contains four text boxes still takes nearly as much time to build correctly as a mini-project of a screen with 25 different text boxes. The reasons for this are too technical for the scope of this book but it may be worthwhile to draw an analogy that illustrates this point. If you intend to plant tulips in your back yard, how would you compare the time it takes to plant 20 bulbs to that taken to plant 40 bulbs? Well, if you consider the entire task—going to the garden supply store, taking the tools out of the shed, planting, washing the tools, returning them to the shed, and cleaning up—the time taken to plant an additional 20 bulb becomes marginal, at best. Likewise, the number of screen/data items per planning unit is not very important to your estimate.

Finally, a disclaimer is in order. Although I am a strong advocate of the methodology of this chapter, I recommend against using my estimated figures blindly. That is because there is no realistic way I could predict the specific aspects and requirements of your own project. Nor can I foretell without any further analysis the skill level of your team, the benefits of the tools you use, or the effects of the environment within which your project is to take shape. Subsequently, you would be wise to check my figures before you attempt to apply them to your own project plan.

Also note that these numbers work for me again and again because I usually try to minimize the variability between one project to the next. I can, thus, use my experience to predict future performance. You can likewise use this methodology very successfully if, and only if, you . . .

1. take the time to document how long it takes your own organization to develop each user functionality, *and*
2. can isolate and eliminate variability between projects. (Use the same people, same or better hardware, same software, etc.)

THE IMPORTANCE OF REALISTIC SCHEDULES

In his book *Debugging the Development Process*, Steve Maguire of Microsoft points out a very important rule of thumb that I strongly recommend you use with the planning method I just described: "Make sure your schedules are attainable but aggressive enough to keep team members focused on steady progress."[2]

If you put too much slack in the project, your team members will not be challenged and will soon move on to more formidable tasks such as playing their favorite computer games. On the other hand, if the schedule is viewed by the team as unachievable, they will despair and instead of working hard

---

[2]Steve Maguire, *Debugging the Development Process*, (Redmond, WA: Microsoft Press, 1994), p. 97.

on completing the project will turn to, you got it, their favorite computer game.

USE SCHEDULING TOOLS

There is much more to project scheduling than just determining the amount of time between two points. And so, simply arriving at an overall estimate of the project length is not enough. Individual tasks must be prioritized and the order in which they are to be programmed has to be determined. Suppose, for instance, that you are managing two programmers in a multiscreen application. Further assume that screens 1, 2 and 3, must be completed by the time screens 4 and 5 are started. If you assign one programmer to the first three screens and another to the last two, then the first will be working hard while the other is idle for the first part of the project while during the second half, they will reverse their workload. Clearly, this is not a very efficient use of resources. Correct scheduling can ensure that not only are tasks completed in order but that the workload is spread across all resources.

Furthermore, correct scheduling provides a manager with the critical path—the set of tasks that absolutely, positively must be completed on time to ensure timely delivery. For example, if task 3 can only be started after task 2 is complete, and task 2, in turn, can only be started after task 1 is done, any slippage in task 1 will cause task 3 to be late. This ripple effect then causes the entire project to slip. On the other hand, a task that has no other task depending on its completion may be allowed to slip without any significant effect on overall project delivery.

Finally, a good schedule should contain milestones or a set of subgoals against which the progress of the project can be measured.

There are several tried and true methodologies that incorporate all of these issues and, therefore, assist in the task of devising a complete plan. The best known of these use either the Gantt (see Figure 6.1) or PERT (see Figure 6.2) charts to model the schedule and ensure correct resource allocations. Describing the intricate details of these two schedule modeling techniques would, obviously, be beyond the scope of this book. So if you have never heard of either PERT or Gantt, then this is an excellent time to sign up for a project management course. At the very least, visit your local bookstore and ask the nice person beyond the counter for the engineering section. Look for and purchase any book that covers these two methodologies and study it thoroughly. But whatever you do, do not attempt to schedule the project or allocate resources without such knowledge tucked away safely in your gray matter.

On the other hand, if you are familiar with these methods and understand them well, I strongly recommend their use in planing a schedule of the project. There are quite a few excellent off-the-shelf computer applications that run on just about every type of operating system there is that will automate the whole process and help monitor project progress. One such a tool is Microsoft Project®, for example.

ID	Name	Duration	Scheduled Start
1	Database Training	143d	9/9/92 8:00am
2	Move to new database s	5d	9/9/92 8:00am
3	Install software	3d	9/16/92 8:00am
4	Install test drive	20d	9/21/92 8:00am
5	Set up terminals	10d	10/19/92 8:00am
6	Work software tutorials	30d	11/2/92 8:00am
7	Develop training class pro	30d	12/14/92 8:00am
8	Phase I training	20d	1/25/93 8:00am
9	Phase II training	20d	2/22/93 8:00am
10	Data conversion table	5d	3/22/93 8:00am
11	Complete training	0d	3/26/93 5:00pm
12	Project Planning	152.83d	9/9/92 8:00am
13	Capacity test	1d	9/9/92 8:00am
14	Usage time map	5d	3/29/93 8:00am
15	Network capacity test	1.5d	4/5/93 8:00am
16	CPU capacity test	1.33d	4/6/93 1:00pm
17	Capacity acceptance	2d	4/7/93 3:40pm
18	Capacity plan complete	0d	4/9/93 3:40pm
19	Interfaces	57d	4/9/93 3:40pm
20	File downloads and convi	20d	4/9/93 3:40pm
21	Test plan	12d	5/7/93 3:40pm
22	Acceptance document	7d	5/25/93 3:40pm
23	Modify requirements	4d	6/3/93 3:40pm
24	Implementation plan	14d	6/9/93 3:40pm
25	Project Complete	0d	6/29/93 3:40pm
26			
27			
28			

Figure 6.1 *An example of a Gantt chart*

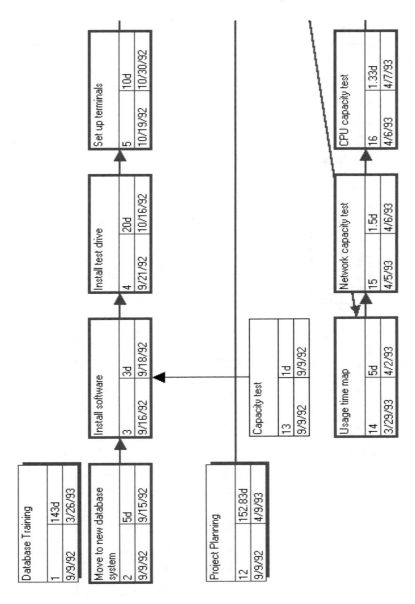

Figure 6.2 *An example of a PERT chart (part 1 of 3)*

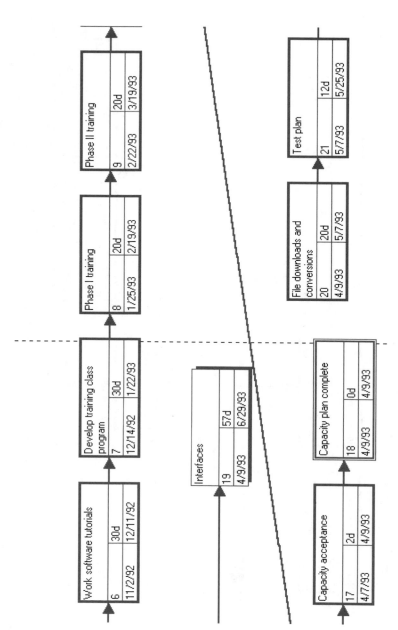

Figure 6.2 (cont.) *An example of a PERT chart (part 2 of 3)*

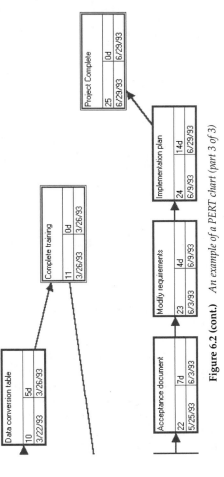

Figure 6.2 (cont.) *An example of a PERT chart (part 3 of 3)*

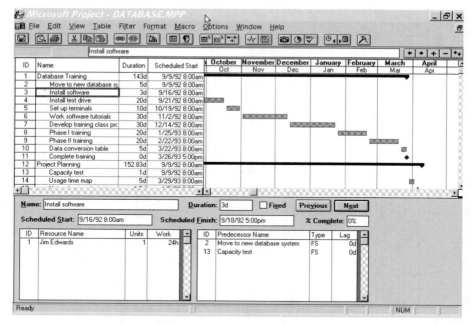

Figure 6.3 *The Microsoft project task entry screen*

The reason I am so adamant about using the PERT/Gantt tools is because I truly believe that schedule modeling instills discipline into the planning process that is impossible to achieve otherwise. Many a time, for example, I made the mistake of planing a project using the back-of-the-envelope method (not covered here) only to find out later using formal scheduling techniques that I had overallocated resources or misidentified the critical path. The simple truth of the matter is that the act of scheduling requires us to hold and joggle in short-term memory more than our mere mortal brain can accommodate without the help of visual aids and computers. The bigger the project, the more tasks it contains, the more joggling is required, and the bigger the chance of a screw up. My approach to this dilemma is to not trust my humanly constrained gray matter and to employ the aids of simple, kindergarten-type charts and computers. This works wonderfully well and so I strongly advise it. See Figure 6.3 for an example of Microsoft project task entry screen.

SIGN OFF ON SPECS

Now that we have covered the mechanics of constructing a schedule, we should move on to review how to deal with some of the pitfalls that could prevent you from adhering to the schedule. The first and biggest obstacle to meeting a deadline is a set of specifications that is not completed and agreed upon at the time the schedule is set. This is because once a manager commits to a delivery date other managers make decisions based on this date. Customers are promised the application, vendors are told of pending changes, hiring is speeded up or slowed down, and so on. Yet the subsequent changes in specifications may cause the project to grow beyond the original scope and thus stretch the delivery date well beyond what was promised. It may be too late, at that point, to turn around and tell your customers, whether they are upper management or the user community, that the delivery date must be moved. At the very least, attempting to do so will cause the customers to lose faith in your management ability and, worse, to question the very justifications that made them go along with the project in the first place.

A schedule derived from incomplete or unapproved specifications is a structure built on proverbial quicksand. Therefore, no matter how tempting it is, no matter how much pressure you are put under by your boss, never provide estimates of time and material until you are presented with a complete set of requirements. And these specifications must be approved by every user and manager who is likely to hold your feet to the fire should you fail to meet the delivery date.

If you must provide some kind of an estimate, assume the absolute worst-case scenario. Assume that you will be asked to build the mother of all software systems and estimate accordingly. And don't be alarmed if you are told that some consulting company has agreed to complete the project at a fraction of the time you quoted. Let them have it and I will guarantee you that you will be soon asked to assume responsibility for the project when it becomes apparent that the consultant cannot meet the deadline. That is much better than if it were the other way around, wouldn't you say?

SCOPE CREEP

A close relative of fuzzy specifications is scope creep. This is the process by which the specifications are changed on the fly while development is in progress. Usually this happens in the beta test phase of the project when the users are first exposed to the newly developed system only to find out that what they asked for is not exactly what they needed. What happens next is a process through which the users submit a set of change requests that, in turn, trigger other change requests as the discovery is made that the new changes still do not really fit the bill. This process is often called the furniture moving phase of the project since it is reminiscent of the little old lady who has just received a new couch. She persistently and repeatedly asks the two sweaty and tired movers to move the couch around the room so she can tell where she likes it best. Sooner or later the couch ends up visiting the same corners several times while the lady is still not completely sure and the movers contemplate thoughts of a gruesome homicide.

Scope creep causes schedule slip-ups in a way that is not easily detectable during development. Many project managers' careers are dependent on the satisfaction of the user community and so they try to please users whenever possible: "How long will it really take to move a text box from one screen to another anyway? Go ahead and do it if it makes John happy." Little do these managers realize that these little two-hour projects mount up and before they know it, the entire set of specifications has been rewritten. Moreover, every instance of scope creep triggers new bugs and requires a new phase of testing. What at first seems like a small two-hour modification soon turns into three days of testing, documentation changes, ripple-effect bug fixes, and a whole new set of headaches. These all add up to major delays in deliveries.

The worst part of it all is that nobody remembers these change requests when the revelation is finally made about the slip-up. All of a sudden, the very same user who begged and pleaded for that *one-more-small-little-change-and-then-I-will-shut-up* modification now develops a memory block and joins in the chorus to hang the project manager from the highest window. And so, we must draw the analogy and say that scope creep is to deadlines what the cookie monster is to a batch of freshly baked cookies of the chocolate-chip variety.

But scope creep is not inevitable. A manager can satisfy his desire to meet customer needs while protecting the schedule at the same time. The preferable way to do so is to document each and every change request along with the estimated delay the change is likely to cause. This document should then be sent for approval to anyone who may have an issue with a delay. Only upon approval should the work commence to make the changes.

If you follow this method, you will soon find out that not all changes are really show stoppers, as the indecisive *furniture movers* have surely claimed. In fact, you may be surprised at the low number of change requests that will be logged after the first or second time you go through this process. This is because, as a result of your memo, the poor souls who made the requests probably ended up getting their heads bashed in by their managers who "could not believe they did not think of these issues during specifications. Now the whole world will blame us for being late." Of course, this decrease in feedback may not always be desirable since a high level of customer satisfaction is still required to entice the user to actually use the application, but at least it solves scope creep.

DO NOT TRY TO MEET A RIDICULOUS SCHEDULE

No matter how careful we are and no matter how diligent we try to be in arriving at a reasonable schedule, sooner or later all managers find themselves in a situation in which the delivery date is discovered to be simply unachievable. Perhaps it is because we had been asked to take over a badly planned existing project. Maybe it is because an unfortunate set of circumstances, such as layoffs or a natural disaster, caused the project to slip well beyond any chances of recovery. Or perhaps it is because there were a considerable number of legitimate changes that were identified by the user only after the system was released to beta. Whatever the reasons may be, a manager must sometimes have to deal with salvaging a plan that has gone awry.

But there is also another reason why a project may not meet the deadline. Some managers (not us, of course) use an overly aggressive schedule right from the start in an attempt to get as much out of the team as possible under the disguise of an overlooming deadline. These managers believe that unless they schedule aggressively, say 80 hours per person per week, the team will slack off and play computer games rather than be productive.

If you find yourself in a slip-up situation or if you are one of those managers who likes to plan aggressively, you will be wise to heed Microsoft's Steve Maguire's advice: "Never allow the schedule to drive the project or to demoralize the team"[3] and

> [n]ever allow team members to jeopardize the product in the attempt to hit what might be, after all, an arbitrary deadline.[4] The schedule can have a devastating effect on a project if it creates slip-hysteria and causes team members to make bad trade-offs in order to hit arbitrary deadlines. If you create a schedule that has unattainable goals in hopes of extracting as much overtime as you can get out of each developer—you're creating a situation that will demoralize the team. Once the team members feel they're in a hopeless position, you're going to get anything but optimum work from them, and once the project is finished—maybe sooner, they're going to look elsewhere for work.[5]

Remember that as important as it may be, meeting the schedule is not the most important goal of your project. On the other hand, providing the users with a reliable and usable application is. If you need to sacrifice something, miss the deadline instead of demoralizing the team and releasing shoddy code.

MONITOR THE SCHEDULE
AND SEND PROGRESS REPORTS

So now we know how to schedule and what we must not do in order to meet this schedule. But how do we prevent management and the user community from perceiving a problem when one does not exist? That is, how do we make what is otherwise an invisible process plainly apparent to the casual observer?

---

[3] Ibid., p. 94.
[4] Ibid.
[5] Ibid., p. 105.

The way to turn software development into a process that more closely resembles building a house is to advertise to the whole world where you stand at any given time. Monitor the schedule closely and watch those milestones. Every time a major milestone is met send out an e-mail message to the entire user community and to the appropriate managers announcing that yet another phase is completed, on time, of course, and that the team is well on its way to a timely delivery. By the same token, when the team encounters a snag, send out a memo explaining the problem and the exact impact on the schedule. Do not wait until the end of the project to tell people about it.

The purpose of all this correspondence is to create a mental picture in the mind of your customers—users or managers—of how much is completed, how much is still left to be done, and when the delivery date is likely to be. This gives the agents of your system—salespeople, superusers, *and so on*—the opportunity to protect themselves against any potential impacts. It also allows for correct budgeting by those people who are responsible for funding your project. If people know three or four months ahead of time that the project may be late by a week, they can budget for the extra resources. The team will, thus, not be left without funds when the decision is to be made of whether or not to continue the project.

And budget is the subject of the next chapter.

CHAPTER 7

How to Budget for a Project Including How to Deal with Accountants

It should hardly come as news to anyone reading this book that unlike traditional engineering projects—bridges, plants, roads, machinery, and so on—software projects do not require a large investment in material. Instead, the cost of software development is essentially driven by its labor-intensive nature. Expenditures highly correlate with the number of hours spent in the entire development cycle. And so, except in some extreme cases where hardware is a part of the project, budgeting for a software project is pretty much a direct outcome of scheduling.

But the fact that software budgeting is somewhat easy for any single project does not make the issue of budgeting trivial. In fact, errors in budgeting typically have disastrous consequences. On the one hand, overestimating the cost of a project may very well mean that the project ends up in the no-starter category. On the other hand, underestimating and the resulting cost overruns almost always mean trouble. If you think of scheduling slip-ups as the events that trigger a review of the project, budget overruns often cause the project to die a quick yet painful death. Budgeting accuracy is therefore essential.

There is another aspect of budgeting that is often missed. That is, the size of the budget determines the project's visibility. The side effect of such visibility is that high-budget software projects are constantly being viewed as cost-cutting targets. There are several reasons for this unfortunate situation. First, a large portion of competing hardware projects is undertaken to replace an existing structure or machinery that is about to collapse in the absence of such effort. Thus, canceling a hardware project has much bigger cost consequences than canceling a software project. Second, unlike any hardware projects where certain costs such as clean-up and disposal continue well after the project is terminated, software development costs can be quickly eliminated simply by firing the development team. Finally, absent rare situations such as a regulatory change or a sudden discovery of a bookkeeping error, software is viewed as nonessential.

We already talked about the fact that software cannot be justified financially and so, in the short run, it is, by definition, expendable. This is especially true to a company that is struggling to survive. For instance, I have heard, many times, managers question the need for a certain development when "we are doing just fine with our current paper systems. Why do we need this high-tech stuff anyway?" And, to be honest, given a financial crisis I too cannot think of a good reason. Surely you may also agree that any of the long-term reasons we can all come up with just do not apply when the company is about to go under.

It is best, therefore, to keep budget small and lean.

THOSE HATEFUL BEAN COUNTERS

Before we attempt to define the budget process, we must first cover a touchy issue. We technical people have a very hard time communicating with the people whose job it is to approve and monitor our budget, namely, the accountants. I, for one, have yet to witness a project development effort in which the animosity between the technical staff and the accountants was absent. Evidently, every engineer and software developer instinctively hates all accountants and vice versa.

The cause for this heartfelt abhorrence is not difficult to identify. It is mainly due to the communication gap that exists between the two camps, which in turn is caused by a difference in training, methodologies, and organizational mission. Except on some very rare occasions, accountants have no technical training, they do not talk our language nor do they comprehend certain technical concepts that are well understood by even the most junior members of the development staff.

Likewise, developers have trouble understanding accounting concepts and financial control issues. On the same token that accountants do not understand why a developer may need some additional memory chips to complete the job ("my son tells me 2 Megs are enough"), very few development managers understand the devastating effect uncontrolled purchases have on the company's immediate cash flow. And so by allowing accountants to communicate directly with development personnel, we have created a situation that would be comical were it not for its seriousness.

This communication gap is not easily bridged but we can drastically reduce the frustration levels that are mutually encountered by both sides if we make the effort to at least understand the other side's motivation. Since this book is written for development managers allow me to try to explain the bean counter's point of view:

> The most immediate danger any company faces in the short run is the possibility of running out of cash. In fact, most companies declaring bankruptcy do so not because they are unprofitable but because, to put it simply, they had let their checking account dwindle to nothing.
>
> In the longer term, profitability is very important. And so, correct financial reporting and budgeting is crucial to profit and loss (P&L) decisions. Once such decisions are made, the underlying assumptions should remain constant or the decision process must be reopened. For example, a company may decide to undertake a $1 million project in order to be able to reap an additional $2 million in profits. If the cost of the project increases above the $1 million figure, the decision may no longer be valid.
>
> The accountants are, therefore, given the mission of ensuring that (a) the company does not run out of cash and (b) that expenditures adhere to the agreed upon figures. They accomplish their mission by doing two things. First, they monitor and report cost and revenue figures, a task that, by itself, is harmless enough. Second, depending on company policy, they are given approval authority over some or all purchasing and expenditures. (Incidentally, exercising this very authority is usually the cause of endless friction since accountants are asked to make technical decisions even though they are not qualified to do so.)

If we understand this point of view, and if we ignore the horrifying analogies with the defense of certain Gestapo officers after World War II, then, clearly, the accountants are only doing what they have been told. In other words, when they refuse to approve the hiring of an additional developer they are fulfilling their duty. We may argue endlessly about the damage to the company their denial causes but, remember, they are not the decision makers. They are simply the enforcers: "If the additional person is really necessary, then surely it must be budgeted for . . . *blah, blah, blah, blah.*" The bottom line is that as hateful as they may be, bean counters do serve a very important organizational function. Thus, understanding their point of view may go a long way in improving communication.

ACCOUNTING TERMS

Another helpful way to span the communication chasm between gear-heads and accountants is to attempt to understand the accounting language. The following is a list of some important accounting terms and an explanation of how they affect the budgeting process:

Account: A single accounting line item that acts as a bucket collecting costs or revenues. For example, a payroll account collects all the costs of paying people's wages and salaries.

Double-Entry Accounting: This is a centuries-old system of ensuring all funds are accounted for or balanced. Without going into unnecessary details, double-entry accounting means that every dollar allocated to a certain account has to come from another account. For example, the $4,000 spent in cash to purchase a work station could be annotated in the accounting system as:[1]

	Increase	Decrease
Plant and Equipment	$4,000	
Cash		$4,000

That is, the funds to buy the computer were taken out of the Cash account and an equivalent cash value item was placed in the Plant and Equipment account.

The implication to project management is that account name and numbers are important. If you budgeted $40K for computer equipment, make sure that when you actually purchase the computers you indicate on the purchase order that the money is to come from the Plant and Equipment account. Otherwise, you will have to explain why, at the end of the project, you still have $40K in the Budgeted Plant and Equipment account while some other account is overspent by $40K.

Direct and Overhead Costs: A direct cost is any expenditure that can be directly attributed to the project. Overhead is any expenditure that is not directly associated with the project. For example, the salary and benefits of a programmer who is working on only one project is considered a direct cost of the project since it cannot be associated with any other ongoing effort. On the other hand, the cost to lease and operate the building in which the project is being developed is considered overhead because it is not directly incurred due to any particular project.

Because overhead is not directly associated with any given project, it is allocated by various methods to the different entities that use it. For example, the cost of electricity to light the building may be allocated to your project based on the share of floor space your team takes up.

When budgeting, never forget to budget for overhead costs.

Allocation: This is the method by which overhead costs are assigned to the project. Project managers may want to question the allocation method if they find that they carry a larger than reasonable share of certain overhead cost. For example, unless you are a one-project firm, you definitely

---

[1] Increase and decrease are used in this example instead of the more traditional debit and credit for simplicity.

have a problem if you find that your budget includes 90% of the CEO's salary.

Variable and Fixed Costs: Variable costs imply the cost is directly correlated with the level of effort expended, while a fixed cost remains constant along a wide range of operating variables. The hourly cost of a contract programmer is variable since the more hours he or she works, the more cost is incurred. On the other hand, the cost of a site license for a certain development tool may be a fixed cost since it does not change according to the number of projects.

Up to very recently, all overhead costs were considered fixed costs while many direct costs were thought of as variable. This is no longer true. Accountants had figured out that many overhead costs are really variable but that the relationship with whatever it is that drives them is not easily identified.

In budgeting, any cost that is directly related to the length of the project, the number of workstations involved, or the number of team members should be considered variable. These costs should be closely monitored as they are more likely to increase with schedule slip-ups and scope creep.

Variance: The difference between the amount budgeted and the amount actually spent is a budget variance. The difference between cost incurred this period compared to another period is a period variance. Sane companies construct their accounting systems in such a way that a negative variance is always a bad indicator while a positive variance is always good. This means that if the variance (difference) between your actual floppy disk spending and the budgeted amount is a negative $100, then you have overspent your budget by that amount or, in other words, bought $100 more floppy disks than planned. If, on the other hand, there is a positive variance of $100, then it is time to go shopping.

Unfortunately, this standard is not always true. Many companies use an accounting system in which the sign in front of the variance means absolutely nothing. In one account a negative variance is good, in another it is bad. There is, believe it or not, a method to this madness but you need to understand accounting to comprehend what this method is. To the rest of us, this convention is very confusing since one cannot easily tell by looking at the current budget comparisons how well one is doing. So if you work for such a company, I strongly recommend that you sit down with the accountants at the beginning of the process and write down the variance convention for each budget account.

For simplicity's sake, in this chapter overspending is a negative variance and underspending is a positive variance.

Adjustments: Correcting a mistake in the accounting records is called making an adjustment. That is because, for audit trail purposes, accountants cannot just erase a bad entry. Instead, they must create an equal and opposite entry, or an adjustment.

If you find a mistake in your cost figures or in the budget variance report, do not get upset if you are told the mistake cannot be removed for this reporting period. You will most likely see an adjustment made during the next reporting period. Now if we could only fix software bugs this way. . . .

Fiscal Calendar: For various reasons many companies start their budget cycle on a date other than January 1. As a project manager, you need to know when you will be expected to submit your budget proposal so you can prepare for it well in advance of the two and a half hours you will typically be allocated to accomplish this task.

Fiscal calendars also have a crucial role in games *some people* play so they meet their budget. These are dirty, rotten, slimy practices and I will not be part of such tricks in this book. See me after class and we will talk.

General Ledger: All accounting transactions are recorded in chronological order in the general ledger as they are incurred. At the close of the reporting period, the transactions are sorted into and summed in the appropriate reporting account.

The limited implication of this term to project management comes into play when a mistake is discovered. The general ledger is the first place one should look to find out if the transaction was recorded correctly.

Depreciation: Even though every purchase made is normally paid for within a short period of time, the U.S. government does not allow corporations to expense some of these purchases immediately. Basically, the thinking is that if some machinery has a useful life of ten years, then the appropriate share of the cost, the depreciation, should be incurred against revenue each year. This way, if the machine is no longer needed, it could, presumably, be sold for its cost less depreciation.

YTD: This is an abbreviation for Year to Date. It means all costs incurred up to now starting with the beginning of the <u>fiscal</u> year.

MTD: Abbreviation for Month to Date.

P&L: Profit and Loss.

THE MECHANICS OF PREPARING A BUDGET

Whereas the importance of budgeting correctly is crucial, the actual mechanics of preparing a budget are rather simple, as the beginning of this chapter might have hinted. The following methodology enumerates the steps by which a software budget can be constructed.

1. Completely specify and schedule a project or a portion of a project that can be justified as a stand-alone entity.
2. Research prevailing contract rates and salaries for the caliber of talent you wish to hire or divert to your project.

3. Determine the period for which you are budgeting. If a project is scheduled to last longer than a year, you may be required to budget only for the fiscal year.

4. Determine your company's budgeting and accounting conventions. What are the account names? How are account numbers denoted? How should they be aggregated? Should numbers right of the decimals be dropped? The best way to do this is to obtain and study a few samples of other projects' budgets.

5. For each line item fill in the projected spending. Here are some examples:

People Costs	
Employees	Multiply the fully loaded, prorated hourly equivalent employee rate you get from accounting by the hours each will work. Some companies split the actual salary from the benefits and then budget this cost on two separate lines.
Consultants	Multiply the prevailing hourly rate for each class of consultants by the number of hours scheduled. Remember that you may have to pay overtime on an hourly basis.
Business analysts and other high-level salary personnel directly assigned to the project	Find out the prorated, fully loaded hourly equivalent of *each* person and multiply by the entire project length.
Your own salary and that of the managers reporting to you	Determine your fully absorbed, prorated hourly rate and allocate according to the amount of time you are expected to spend on this project.
Relocation costs	If you intend to hire anyone from outside your geographical area, make sure to include the estimated relocation costs. A good estimate can be obtained from the accounting department.
Hiring costs	If you intend to hire new employees, budget for the cost of advertising and hiring agencies to recruit.
Bonuses and incentives	If your company gives bonuses, do not forget to include the share of the bonus that is attributed to your personnel. Also you may want to employ an incentive system regardless of your company's policy. Budget accordingly.
Development-Related Software and Hardware	
Workstations	If these are not depreciated, only include the costs of new hardware. If a developer already has a workstation, chances are it was already expensed to another project.

Software and licenses	List all the software and software licenses you need and sum up the total amount of money you will need to purchase them. Remember, disregard existing software and licenses as those have most likely already been expensed unless they must be depreciated.
Allocation of other departments' computer and support costs	Departments such as mainframe operations and PC support often must charge out all their expenses to the clients who use their services. Determine what the fully loaded hourly rate they charge is and budget according to the number of hours you anticipate employing their services.

Training, Meals, and Travel Costs

Training costs	Decide what classes you wish your employees to attend or what training sessions you want to hold in-house. Determine the cost and include it in the budget. Note that, in some companies, the salary costs for the time spent in training should also be included in training costs.
Conferences, travel, and meals	Try to predict ahead of time the cost you will be incurring as a result of your traveling or sending your employees to client sites or conferences. Also remember to include meal costs associated with any celebration you intend to sponsor as a result of meeting a deadline or reaching milestones, not to mention holiday parties.

Office-Related Expenses

Allocation of secretarial services	If you share a secretary, you will most likely have to carry some of his or her payroll.
Office supplies	You know: all the paper and paper clips you will be using? You got it.
Fax and copy machines	Some of this equipment is leased and most requires extensive servicing. Determine if your project must carry some of these costs and budget accordingly.
Telephone usage, beepers, and cellular phones	Budget for all of these by looking at historical standards. Accounting should be able to help you with this number.
Maintenance, repair, and upkeep	If a pipe breaks over one of your people's cubicles, chances are you will be the one that will pay for the repair. Put in a contingency number.

Overhead Allocations

Building and utilities allocations	Determine the amount your project will be allocated for lease, electricity, water, heating and ventilation, and janitorial services. Budget accordingly. (In most companies, this portion of the budget is completed by the accounting department but do not assume so.)

Depreciation	Some existing equipment and software licenses are being depreciated over time. Your project may be allocated some of this depreciation for equipment that was already bought in the past. Again, this line item should be completed by accounting but not always.

6. Be prepared to explain and defend each line item in the budget approval process. Keep all supporting material and any worksheets you may have used to arrive at the figures.

One last point: In many companies the fact that the budget is approved does not mean that the hiring and purchase requisitions are approved. This means that you may have a budget approval to hire six people but when you actually attempt to put the paperwork through, you discover that you may hire only five people. You may even be asked to rejustify your requirements in yet another gut-wrenching process. There is no rational explanation for this behavior other than that the accountants are sometimes the complete nincompoops we have always said they were. If this happens to you, make sure you revisit your assumptions and let everyone know the implications of the shortfall.

But the fact that the budget is not the final approval step should not stop you from fighting to include it in the budget. Remember, if an item is not in the budget, chances are you will spitting blood before you are allowed to obtain it.

HOW TO SURVIVE A BUDGET REVIEW

A budget review is like an IRS audit only it is a certainty as opposed to a mere chance. A budget review does not necessarily happen every month but it does happen at regular intervals. During the review, every account is examined and the manager in charge is asked to explain the variance between actual spending and projected spending. Any cost overruns are usually identified during this process. Typical attendees at budget reviews include the project manager and his or her boss and accountants and their managers.

The events leading to a budget review are as follows: At the end of every cost period, usually a month, the bean counters collect all the beans and assign them to the different accounts. They then distribute a report for each project and/or cost center showing for each account the projected, or budgeted, figures in one column and the actual spending in the next. A third column shows the variance or difference of actual costs from projected costs. These three columns are repeated for the year-to-date figures. A meeting is then called to parade the various project managers through to review the reports.

Unlike what you might expect, these are very civilized meetings. Variance explanations are usually noted down without a comment and the meeting goes on. The fireworks start after the meeting when certain explanations are deemed to be unacceptable. Therefore, it is very important to say and do the right things during the review. These are my suggestions:

1. Act like a Boy/Girl Scout and *be prepared*. Don't assume that just because you came in under budget for the given review period everything is fine. There may be erroneous charges made against your budget but unless you take the time to review all accounts you will not figure that out until you actually go over budget.

2. The magnitude of a variance does not really matter. One dollar in overspending is just as bothersome to the bean counters as $1 million. Therefore, have explanations for *every* variance, no matter how small. You can obtain the costs that went into the account from the general ledger.

   Possible explanations for common variances that are not due to true overspending include:

   - Calendar: A certain cost such as a computer purchase was calendarized in the plan to be incurred at 1/12 its budgeted amount every month. In reality, the entire set of computers was purchased in January. A large negative variance therefore appears in January while a positive variance shows up for the remaining eleven months.
   - Price Variance: The telephone company raising the phone rate shows up as a negative variance on your budget for telephone usage. There is nothing you could have done about it, so make sure it is not viewed as overusage of the phone privileges.

   Note that accountants tend to concentrate on items they understand while ignoring matters about which they know little. I have often witnessed cost reviews in which the accountants spent two hours grilling a manager about a minor negative variance in the office supply account while completely ignoring a cost overrun of a few thousand dollars in equipment purchases.

3. Even though accountants are not differential to the *magnitude* of the variance, they do care about the *sign* of the variance. They tend to concentrate only on the negative variances. In other words, you earn no kudos for underspending. Remember that the job of the accounting department is to ensure an adequate cash supply and adherence to financial commitments. They could care less about the fact that you are not spending as much as you said you would. Be careful, though. In some settings, your current period spending plays a large role in next period's budget. In particular the accountants often want to know why you are budgeting a number that is so drastically higher than what you have actually spent in the past.

**TOTAL PROJECT BUDGET FOR DESIGN AND DEVELOPMENT
OF THE X TRADING SYSTEM**

	Account item	Units	Unit Cost	Total Units	Total Cost
10	*Employee Costs*				
10-0100	Programmers (employees)	hrs	$51.26	2,500	$ 128,150
10-0200	Programmers (consultants)	hrs	$100.00	1,500	$ 150,000
10-0300	Testers (employees)	hrs	$43.85	750	$ 32,888
10-0400	Testers (consultants)	hrs	$75.00	750	$ 56,250
10-0500	Documentation (employees)	hrs	$ —	—	$ —
10-0600	Documentation (consultants)	hrs	$ 75.00	350	$ 26,250
10-0700	Business Analyst (employee)	hrs	$60.25	1,250	$ 75,313
10-0800	Management	hrs	$63.20	1,250	$ 79,000
10-0900	Relocation Costs				$ 25,000
10-1000	Hiring Costs				$ 12,500
10-1100	Bonuses and Incentives				$ 30,000
	Total Employee Costs				$ 615,350
20	*Development Hardware and Software*				
20-0100	Workstations	ea	$6,540	4	$ 26,160
20-0200	Software and Licenses	ea			$ 3,278
20-0300	Allocation of PC Support Dept	hrs	$50.00	500	$ 25,000
	Total Development Hardware and Software				$ 54,438
30	*Training, Meals, and Travel*				
30-0100	Training Costs				$ 13,254
30-0200	Travel Expenses				$ 7,500
30-0300	Meals and Entertainment				$ 3,250
30-0400	Conferences and Meetings				$ 1,005
	Total Training, Meals, and Travel Costs				$ 25,009
40	*Office-Related Expenses*				
40-0100	Allocation of the Secretarial Pool				$ 5,700
40-0200	Office Supplies				$ 2,300
40-0300	Allocation of Copy and Fax Service and Supplies				$ 3,600
40-0400	Telephone Usage				$ 10,500
40-0500	Beepers and Cellular Phones				$ 4,750
40-0600	Maintenance, Repair, and Upkeep				$ 14,300
	Total Office-Related Expenses				$ 43,850
50	*Building and Utilities*				
50-0100	Allocation of Building Lease				$ 124,300
50-0200	Allocation of Heating and Ventilation				$ 31,500
50-0300	Allocation of Electricity				$ 32,000
50-0400	Allocation of Water Usage				$ 250
50-0500	Allocation of Janitorial Services				$ 12,400
50-0600	Insurance				$ 689
	Total Building and Utilities				$ 201,139
60-0100	Depreciation				$ 41,256
	Total Project Cost				$1,596.392

CHAPTER 8

Outsource, Buy Off the Shelf, or Grow Your Own?

The rise of Visual Basic and other rapid application development tools (RAD) prompts us to revisit the age-old dilemma of who we should entrust with the development of the project. Usually we are faced with three clear options: outsource, buy off the shelf, or develop in-house. Let's review these as they stood prior to the introduction of RAD tools and then see how Visual Basic changes the picture.

OUTSOURCE

This means turning over the development of the application to a system house on a fixed-price contract basis. To make this work, it is required to author extensive specifications covering every little detail of the system as well as the delivery and payment schedules. Outsourcing is viewed as a good way to reduce financial risk since, from the project's inception, everybody knows what it is going to cost. The drawbacks, however, are considerable.

First, outsourcing is a very rigid paradigm. Once the specifications are agreed upon, no changes are allowed. If the users discover later on, as they usually do, that the system does not fully answer their needs, there is little that can be done about it. Additional contracts must be drawn for additional costs.

Second, dealing with misunderstandings about the contract or deliverable is a messy undertaking. Often correcting such problems involves lengthy negotiations between management of both sides. When the differences cannot be resolved, additional funds must be expended to revise the contract or to initiate litigation. Not surprisingly, outsourcing often results in bad feelings and lost friendships, not to mention quite a few firings.

Third, there is the question of who owns the source code. Even if the contract stipulates that all source material is to be turned over to the client, the contractor cannot be made to forget the proprietary knowledge learned during the project. As such, the contractor is liable to use this knowledge in developing a competitor's application or an off-the-shelf package.

Finally, outsourcing creates a perpetual dependency between the client and the contractor. Even if the source code is owned by the client, it is doubtful that anyone at the client site is able to maintain it. Hence, the client must turn to the contractor for minor fixes and enhancements, expending additional financial resources in the process. The bigger the dependency, the higher the price *extorted* by the contractor. And, of course, if the contractor goes out of business, the client is left holding the bag.

BUY OFF THE SHELF

This is the practice of buying a commercially available package that was developed by somebody else. In many instances, buying an existing package is a preferable solution to developing from scratch. Implementation is fast, since the code is already written. Problems are few, since presumably the vendor has debugged the application earlier on somebody else's installation. And the price is lower because development costs are spread among numerous clients.

Because of these benefits, the majority of personal computer applications are purchased this way. No one, for example, is so insane as to develop their own e-mail, word processor, or spreadsheet applications. A plethora of such products is available for a very low cost. They were developed by several well-known vendors, who had long perfected the features and functionality of each. Rebuilding such applications is, therefore, as senseless as building one's own car from scratch rather than buying a ready-made one off the lot.

Yet, for business applications, off-the-shelf products may not always be the ideal solution. Any business that depends on technological innovation to compete against its rivals usually opts to develop selective applications in-house or through outsourcing. They do so even when a shrink-wrapped application is available to purchase because using a commercially available application does not provide any competitive advantage. A commercial stock market analysis system, for instance, may do the job just fine. But if you are an investment banker who wants to beat the market's performance, not just match it, you may want to incorporate some proprietary algorithms. Likewise, if you identify client relations as a competitive advantage, you may want to include in your sales database information that can make you a better vendor. Off-the-shelf applications may not permit you to enter such data.

HOMEGROWN

This means, of course, developing your applications in-house. It is the most flexible approach but it is also the most expensive. Typically, the user community is most satisfied with this option, since users are often asked to participate in developing the system from the beginning. Naturally, you need to employ an army of programmers, testers, business analysts, and data processing managers to make this work. But this approach does alleviate some of the problems of outsourcing since you need not go to court over minute details. Instead, you may simply fire anyone who refuses to do what the users want. And the knowledge base stays home provided, of course, that you can keep your development team happy and away from the help-wanted pages. Consequently, there is no better choice if the application is meant to provide a competitive advantage.

ENTER VISUAL BASIC

The ability to quickly prototype and develop applications notably tilts the scales against outsourcing and toward developing in-house. Even though VB and other RAD tools can cut the cost of outsourcing substantially, practically speaking, such is not the case.

Let's more closely examine this statement: One important way in which VB speeds up development is by substantially reducing the scope of specifications and the cost of prototyping. This advantage cannot be capitalized upon in outsourcing because of the nature of the relationship between the client and third-party contractors. Thus, full specifications, a formal sign-off, and a rigid deliverable schedule do not permit rapid application development to be fully implemented.

Of course, once specifications are complete, development is speeded up with Visual Basic whether done in-house or through a contractor, but by that time much of the time savings are lost. Also such speeding up is experienced by the in-house team with the same magnitude as the outsourcing vendor. It can, therefore, be done less expensively in-house where a profit margin is not collected.

I suppose that if we were to live in a less litigious society, one in which building long-term relationships is viewed more highly than quick profits, VB could actually help make outsourcing more attractive. Under such utopian conditions, the vendor could work closely with the client to develop a prototype and then, on faith rather than by contract, proceed to generate the system. However, such is not likely to happen anytime soon, nor is it clear that it could, given human nature and corporate governance as we know it.

SO WHAT SHOULD ONE DO?

I strongly recommend that you purchase commercially available packages whenever possible. This option provides the best cost-to-performance ratio of any of the other options. However, if you wish to build or maintain a technology-based competitive advantage and so need to develop systems anew, you would be better off building these in-house rather than outsourcing them to a software contractor.

You may be interested to note that I hold this opinion even though my own company would stand to profit substantially from outsourcing.

---------- CHAPTER 9 ----------

How to Hire the Best
and the Brightest Programmers

Most MIS managers know that the competency of their technical staff is a critical factor in any project's success or failure. But even if you had never really thought about it before, this should come as no surprise since software development is primarily a labor-intensive process. More important, it is brain intensive. From this perspective, Visual Basic is no different than any other development effort. Staffing for a VB project is the most important single role a manager plays.

The difference is that in addition to the normal technical challenges of any development effort, Visual Basic presents a new development paradigm and is, therefore, very threatening to the establishment. So by hiring the best and the brightest, a manager ensures the project's success not only on the technical front but also on the political front. This is because an able programmer can easily defeat any naysayer's arguments against using VB.

To help you with the task of hiring the right people, I compiled some recruiting do's and don'ts. These suggestions are divided into two groups: The first group lists general programming requirements that fit any development project. The second group covers those skills that are specific only to Visual Basic.

GENERAL REQUIREMENTS FOR ANY SYSTEM DEVELOPMENT EFFORT

Do HIRE SMART PEOPLE. Sheer brain power is by far the most significant trait of a prospective programmer, as it surely is in most other intellectually challenging jobs. Yet many managers make the mistake of rejecting applicants who display superior mental ability. Sometimes this is due to the hiring manager's own inhibitions and insecurities. But most other times, managers are reluctant to hire brainy prospects for fear that the employees will be bored with their work assignment or because they may appear to be overqualified for the job.

These beliefs seem reasonable, at first, but they fall apart under close scrutiny. If yours is a client-server system utilizing a database server and a fourth-generation language, you are already tackling some of the most challenging and interesting technologies in existence today. That is precisely why some of the smartest programmers in the field are knocking on your door instead of on the door of your mainframe-based competitors. It is, therefore, highly doubtful that you will fail to provide enough of a challenge to keep such people interested.

As for the notion that an intellectually superior, well-educated candidate may be overqualified to work on business applications, there too you may be misjudging the situation. Let me state your position a little differently than you may see it: No matter how simple to build, when implemented, your application will be handling millions of dollars in transactions, will provide information to top management based upon which they will be making important decisions, and will, most likely, ensure customer satisfaction and continued loyalty to your company. Do you really think that there is anyone among the candidate pool who is *overqualified* for such responsibility?

Consider some analogous situations: Suppose you are managing a professional baseball team. Do you want the season to depend on a bunch of .250 hitters? Or maybe you are commanding an army in battle. Are you going to rely on soldiers with an average physical ability? Or maybe you are designing the next space shuttle. Will you trust the lives of the astronauts to the hands of third-rate engineers? The answer to all three of these questions is of course not. But surely you realize that your particular project is not any less important or any less demanding than a baseball game, or a war, or a space vehicle design. To succeed, therefore, you must hire the best and the brightest people you can find.

Do hire people who display a can-do attitude. Computer programming requires much resolve and determination due to the fact that there are many ways to accomplish similar tasks. It can sometimes be very frustrating when a certain algorithm does not work correctly. Too many people deal with these frustrations by throwing their hands up in the air and pronouncing the proverbial "you cannot get there from here." I cannot tell you how many times I have heard the following statement made by coworkers: "There is a known bug and the vendor finally admitted it." The implication, of course, is that we must scrap the ailing feature because there is obviously no way to get it done.

Based on the old adage stating that a good craftsman never blames his tools, you would do well if you did not hire the programmer type just described. Instead, concentrate your efforts on those people who believe nothing can stop them from achieving their goal. These programmers know that there is more than one way to skin a cat and so they welcome the challenge a problem presents. They set out to overcome the obstacle first before they start complaining about it. (And complain they will. They will even use their ingenious solution to proclaim their cleverness and their ability to overcome adversity, a claim you will better affirm a thousand times or you risk living in prima donna hell.)

Such resolve and determination make all the difference to project success and are especially valuable at two o'clock in the morning before a deadline. Remember that the nature of the software business, unfortunately, is such that the tools your team depends on may have been released with some obscure bugs. According to Murphy's law, you will discover one such show-stopping bug the day your program is about to be put into production. When such a disaster occurs, and you are awakened from a much needed two hours of sleep, would you rather hear "it's the vendor's fault" or "you wouldn't believe what I had to do to fix the problem"?

Incidentally, it may seem to some that I am unnecessarily dwelling on what is very obvious. After all, who would not want a bunch of can-do crack programmers working on their project? Unfortunately, such is not the case in the real world. So many managers, who themselves belonged at one time to the confident group, hire, or worse, keep those who are unable to solve tough problems. This is precisely because these managers enjoy solving problems themselves. They hardly mind having an army of low-level programmers who work on the boring stuff and who then let them get involved in the tough challenging work. That is why my point of hiring a can-do staff is so critical. A manager's duties and responsibilities are purposely different from that of his or her employees. Managers are not paid to program and they should not waste your company's money doing so. They should hire good people so they can be free to do their real job.

So how can you tell which group a candidate falls into? Ask the prospective employee to tell you about a recent problem he encountered and what he did to solve it. The person you want is the one who tells you at length about a tough bug he found and proudly tells you how he used an ingenious method to solve it.

DO HIRE VETERANS AS WELL AS ROOKIES. The best teams, whether in sports or in software development, combine seasoned veterans with green rookies. In sports, this mix is necessary for obvious reasons: Rookies contribute to the team's speed and enthusiasm while experience and level-headedness are provided by the veterans. Moreover, sport teams who strive to build dynasties use the age mix so their rookies can take over for the veterans when they retire and, thus, retain the knowledge base the team depends on.

Of course, physical ability is hardly necessary in software development, but the analogy is not so far-fetched. The steep learning curve of computer science means that an experienced programmer may be able to provide a solution in a fraction of the time taken by a new recruit. Alas, the experienced programmer is not as enthusiastic for the job and, with a family and a house to care for, is more apt to leave work at normal hours and less likely than a greenhorn to make personal sacrifices. Together, however, they make a wonderful development team, with aged veterans guiding enthusiastic young rookies, minimizing mistakes, and maximizing productivity in the process.

As an added bonus, the correct age mix allows you to develop a healthy bull pen of young programmers who retain the knowledge obtained from the veterans when they later retire or move on.

DO PAY YOUR PEOPLE WELL. With hiring as with many other aspects of business, you get what you pay for. If you pay your programmers below market rate, chances are you employ less than the best. Likewise, if you reward your people well, you attract and retain the best and the brightest.

If you have doubts about the truth of this statement, consider this: Why would any programmer agree to work for you if you do not pay them at least average market rates, especially in view of the tremendous shortage of qualified people? One reason may be because she is a loyal employee and is willing to make personal sacrifices for the company as long as she is treated well. Not! If you believe anyone in today's cost-cutting, right-sizing, reengineering, downsizing world still has any notion of loyalty toward any company, either you or they probably also believe in the Tooth Fairy and the Easter Bunny. Lets face it: For better or worse, such values are long gone.

A more likely reason for someone to be willing to accept below-standard wages is because he cannot do any better anywhere else. That is, either his skill level and his qualifications are inferior, or maybe he has some other problem such as being hard to work with or a lack of a valid work permit. No matter what the reason, you lose. Even if you get lucky and are able to hire a super programmer for less than normal rates, you will probably not be able to retain her very long. Evidently, there is such a shortage of good programmers that it is not unusual for people to receive several recruiting calls a week. If you do not pay well, you provide hardly enough incentive to keep your programmer from the temptation others provide.

If, on the other hand, you do pay well, you attract a large candidate pool from which you can select the best and the brightest programmers. Once they join, they will be bound to stay on by virtue of the proverbial *golden handcuffs*. That is, they could not be lured away with better compensation offers somewhere else. And as much as people say that the money is not the most important aspect of their job, it often is. After all, we all have mortgages, cars, families, and hobbies to support and most of us will put up with a lot of frustrations before we turn a blind eye to a fat paycheck.

High compensation also has a side effect of keeping spirits high and providing a short-term motivational boost. People who do not have to worry about where their next mortgage payment will come from are more likely to turn their full and undivided attention toward their work. The drawback, of course, is that high pay, by itself, does not provide an ongoing incentive.

Sooner or later, programmers, no matter how well paid, will look for approval and feedback in the form of a raise. In the absence of such a raise, their motivational level decreases and morale sinks. But all is not lost. Remember that even if you are unable to provide such raises, you will not lose very many programmers if the base compensation is high.

Finally, note that if you employ consultants through an agency, the consultants may only be compensated a small fraction of what you pay the agency. If that is the case, you are throwing your money away by enriching some person who is not contributing in the least bit toward the success of your project. At the same time, the consultants are likely to be demotivated, depressed, and in search of other opportunities. Insist, therefore, that the consultants you hire be paid at least 80% of the contract rate, and put that in writing.

DO HIRE CONSULTANTS AS WELL AS EMPLOYEES. For some readers the immediate response to the earlier suggestion of hiring veteran programmers and paying them well is likely to be: "I would love to hire experienced programmers but my company's personnel department does not allow me to pay them the desired salary." Indeed, reluctance to pay programmers their worth is a huge problem in today's corporate world. The roots of the problem lie in increased government regulations and ever growing threats of lawsuits, factors that have gained personnel departments a tremendous amount of power. These departments, thus, exert their influence in areas where they could not do so in years past such as in the hiring of programmers and other technical personnel.

Specifically, most personnel departments see it as their God-bestowed mission to protect the corporate wage structure. They fight against and often win any attempt to pay a new hire above the salary cap set for the specific position by whatever marketplace study they happen to hold, never mind that the study was commissioned back in 1954. This zeal has worked wonders in keeping the compensation of certain occupations below the poverty line but has proven a disaster for technical departments' hiring and retention ability. In holding down salary offers, personnel managers, of course, miss two points: First, there is a tremendous shortage of good programmers, and, second, programmers do not have to work for starvation wages. But then who are we to inflict Adam Smith's rules of capitalism, supply and demand, and other economic factors on such well-meaning morons?

Alas, all is not lost. You can still hire good programmers by bypassing the personnel department altogether. You can do so by purchasing programmers just as you do machines and equipment—with a purchase order. In other words, hire contractors rather than employees for positions for which your company is not willing to pay going market rates to fill. In most companies, a purchase order does not undergo the wage scrutiny of an employment requisition. Furthermore, it is perfectly acceptable by corporate standards to pay a consultant two or three times the amount you can pay a comparable employee and so you are no longer constrained by compensation issues.

As an added benefit, of course, you are not restrained by labor law should you have to fire a consultant for poor performance or lay consultants off for lack of work. In contrast, employees are much tougher to fire and laying employees off is devastating to morale.

Do hire people who know something about the application. If you are building an insurance claim system, a programmer familiar with insurance applications can bring to the team some much needed user perspective. Even if he or she is not a user and never has been, by virtue of past experience, the programmer intuitively knows what is expected of the applications.

On the other hand, do not overplay the importance of this requirement. I have seen managers who are so adamant in their business application requirements that they routinely pass on a chance to hire some great programmers. Remember that a good systems engineer who lacks the appropriate business experience is likely to pick up whatever is necessary. On the other hand, a bad programmer with business experience could never make up his or her deficiency.

For example, if your application is an insurance claim processing system, you do not need to find someone who has experience with claim data entry. A programmer with <u>any</u> previous insurance system background who is also a homeowner, owns a car, and has visited a doctor or two in the last few years knows what an insurance claim is. Such a person, therefore, has 95% of the needed information to become part of your team. Narrowing the hiring requirements any further will exclude a major chunk of the candidate pool and, at best, you may gain only the remaining 5% of the required knowledge.

Do hire people with good communication skills. American technical colleges fail miserably in teaching programmers the ability to communicate with each other as well as with the user community. This problem leads to missed deadlines and much frustrations among users as what they believed they were asking for turns out to be useless features in the final product. In fact, whatever other skills the programmer may display often become ineffective if he or she applies them toward the wrong end due to misunderstandings and miscommunications.

You can easily determine if a candidate has a communication problem through your interview process. If you ask a question about one subject and get an answer about another several times during the course of an interview, chances are the candidate has a problem. Think twice about hiring such a person.

Don't keep bad programmers around. Don't hold on to people who are hurting your effort just because you feel some loyalty toward them or because you are afraid to fire them. There are a couple of reasons for this rule. First, you are wasting your company's resources by employing someone who is not providing a return on his salary. Second, and perhaps more important, a bad employee sucks up other team members' resources and reduces morale. In other words, other team members resent having to cover up for someone who is not able to carry his own weight.

If over a sufficiently long period of time (6 to 12 months), an employee has proven beyond any doubt that his or her performance is substandard, or that he or she is otherwise undermining your project, it may be time to let the employee go. Before you initiate any proceedings, however, try to determine why the person's performance is so poor. It may be that the employee has a personal problem or a temporary disability or is worried about a sick family member. If there is a good reason for the problem, you will be well served to do whatever you can to help. At the end, the employee will be forever grateful and may turn out to be a star performer.

DON'T ASK HUMAN RESOURCES TO HELP IN THE HIRING PROCESS. A huge mistake some companies make is when they delegate to the human resources (HR) department the responsibility of uncovering candidates for technical positions. This is because the typical HR recruiter would not know a programmer if he were married to one, nor could he judge a candidate's skills and ability any better than could an oak tree.

Most HR personnel, even the so-called expert technical recruiters, have been trained in such important software-related subjects as organizational behavior, corporate psychology, labor law, and job design. Obviously, other than the fact that they often use a computer to produce a mountain of policy documents, they have no clue as to what programmers do or what makes someone a good technologist. Nonetheless, they ferociously guard their *right* to be the gatekeepers of the organization by conducting all screening and preliminary recruiting functions. If you are lucky, the resulting list of *qualified* candidates they present to you is no worse than a random selection from the candidate pool. If you are not so lucky, you end up in the shallow end of the pool (without a paddle, of course).

Since human resources recruiters know little about your project or your needs, they often require you to fill out a job description form (in fact, several, one for them, one for the file, one for the Americans with Disabilities Act, one for the Equal Employment Opportunity Commission, etc.). They then take this document and ask the most incompetent secretary in the department to type it up. The document is then copied several times until the letters are no longer discernible to the average reader. Finally, the document is given back to the secretary to be placed as an advertisement in the local paper. The result often looks like this:

Equity trading department of a large, Fortune 300 company seeks a systems analyst with 10-12 years of Virtual Basic experience developing stock trading applications. Windows 4.9.2, SOL Server a must. Should have programmed in SDK. Experience with C, C++, COBOL, Pascal, Assembler, DB2, IBM, PC, DEC, HP 3000 a plus. Good communication skills. Send resume and salary requirements in strict confidence to P.O.Box 1313, Good Luck, PA. No phone calls please.

First lie: The company is not large. It is huge.

Visual, that is. Only been in existence for 5 years.

There is no Windows 4.9.2, but maybe they mean SQL Server 4.9.2.
Windows Software Development Kit is not a programming language (very tough to convince people of this fact). . . .

. . . No need for any of these languages or hardware. It is copied directly from the buzz word list and serves the only purpose of becoming the basis for rejection.

Well, you see the point. Take the time to perform the entire hiring process by yourself. You will not regret it.

SPECIFIC REQUIREMENTS TO
A VISUAL BASIC PROGRAM

Do hire generalists. On the theory that a hammer tends to see all problems as nails, you do not want to hire a specialist of any one language. Such specialists often attempt to program Visual Basic like their language of expertise, missing most of the productivity tools of VB in the process, and getting frustrated by an imaginary *VB wall*. Rather, do hire people who have had a long career working with many different languages and platforms.

Generalists—those who can program in any language—have spent their entire careers discovering the abilities and limits of several different tools. Such people are more apt to have mastered Visual Basic's new programming techniques just as they had done with other languages because they are not inhibited by their preexisting knowledge base. Furthermore, generalists tend not to be constrained by the medium with which they work. They often are able to see past the programming language right down to how the operating system works and then mold the language of the moment to the operating system and peripheral devices.

Note that a generalist is a much better choice than even a VB specialist. A person who knows no language other than Visual Basic may be missing the understanding of how VB operates behind the scenes. This understanding is crucial in an event-driven environment to ensure that, for example, one part of the code does not step over another. Then, again, a VB specialist is still better than any other single language specialist.

DON'T ASK DICTIONARY QUESTIONS IN THE INTERVIEW. Many interviewers make the mistake of asking candidates to list or name certain elements of a language or a system with which the interviewer is familiar. The theory behind this line of questioning is that if a candidate is an expert in the use of the system, she should clearly be able to spit out the definitions in short order. I call interviews that use this method *dictionary interviews* because they require the candidate to recite words and definitions.

Dictionary interviews are ludicrous since they provide little or any information about the candidate's skills or ability. On the contrary, the more a candidate knows, the worse he will do on a dictionary interview. Why is that so? There are literally thousands of terms, functions, API calls, variables, and constants in the Windows environment and all its applications including Visual Basic. The human mind cannot possibly hold such information, and any attempt to memorize even a small subset of such data is futile. The environment is so diverse that even the best programmers routinely forget the syntax of common elements in VB if they do not use them for a couple of weeks. And, naturally, the more a person knows the more he forgets.

Luckily, VB, Windows, and many other good Windows applications provide a wonderful tool called context-sensitive help. With the click of a single key, a user can view the definition for the term in question, jump to related subjects, view an example of how it is used, or even search the entire database for other terms. With such a tool, no one ever needs to remember anything but the most fundamental aspects of the development environment. Indeed, good Windows programmers can tell you that they often use the help utility more than any other feature of their application.

Allow me to illustrate how a dictionary interview defeats the purpose of determining a candidate's qualifications: I once went through an interview where the interviewer asked me to list several types of joins (a method by which several data tables are linked in a query). I listed left joins, equi joins, and right joins. It turns out that the interviewer was looking for inner joins and outer joins. We were both correct, of course, depending on the application and the context, but the entire question seems ridiculous. No technologist I know communicates using such terms nor does anyone need to do so. That is, no one says something like "If I want to obtain employees' names in the department should I use a left or a right join?" Instead, they construct SQL statements that, by definition, are a specific type of join. As a result of asking such a dictionary question, the interviewer probably thought I knew little about database technology when in reality I demonstrated that I knew something he did not. Furthermore, after the interview was over I realized that if the tables were turned, and I were the one asking him the same question, he would have also failed to answer the question to my satisfaction.

An analogous situation from the nonprogramming world would be the process of hiring a technical writer. Imagine that rather than spending the interview trying to determine general communication skills and writing ability, you ask candidates to define such words as *dexterous* or *omnipresent* or . . . well, you get the idea. By the end of the interview you tally up how many words the candidate got right and make your hiring decision accordingly (kind of like the way American colleges choose their students! But that is a subject of another discussion).

This may appear to be a ridiculous example, yet that is exactly the way programmers are often interviewed. In the software development world, as in this example, even if a candidate answered all the questions flawlessly, you would still not know a single thing about her ability to perform the task at hand. Conversely, the fact that the candidate may not be able to recite some of the definitions does not make her a bad prospect. Hence, dictionary interviews are a waste of time. Just because a candidate does not know the name or definition of an item that you happen to remember because you have just worked on it the morning of the interview does not make her a bad programmer.

A much better way to determine a candidate's technical ability is to ask him to bring in a sample of code. Another way is to ask a lot of *how* and *why* questions: How would you obtain employees' names from a department table? Why would you do it in this way as opposed to. . . ? How would you write the result set to a file? and so on. Answers should be structurally and logically correct and not necessarily syntactically accurate. Remember that syntax accuracy is trivial in a world of automatic syntax checking and context-sensitive help.

DO HIRE PEOPLE WHO HAVE A HEALTHY ATTITUDE TOWARD VISUAL BASIC. One of the best indicators of how well programmers will perform in the VB environment is their level of enthusiasm for the product. Most people who are great Visual Basic programmers also think the language is the greatest invention since the do loop. They just cannot stop talking about the benefits of the product and its abilities. They often welcome both verbal and technical challenges to prove that VB can do anything other languages can do, faster and better.

People who are less than enthusiastic about VB tend to be novices who have not yet figured out how to properly use the tools that the language provides. These programmers much rather prefer to work with their favorite language that allows them to show off their ability much more easily. If they are forced to stick with VB, they are liable to point out alleged shortcomings at every turn and proposed to *fix* these problems by importing routines from their specialty language.

A good way to determine whether a person is enthusiastic about VB is to ask him what he thinks about the language. If the candidate's eyes light up, his tone of voice rises by a couple of octaves, and he begins a half-hour dissertation about how great VB is, continue to interview. If, on the other hand, the candidate begins his answer with some phrase such as "VB is OK but it has its limitations," thank him for coming and end the interview right there and then. No sense wasting any more time.

DO HIRE PEOPLE WHO HAVE MICROSOFT WINDOWS BACKGROUND. Ignoring for a minute the fact that VB can be used with DOS (read: Dead Operating System, one whose time has come . . . and gone), one of the greatest cost savings you can achieve with VB is by conforming to Windows standards. *That is,* by making your program look and feel like other Windows applications, you can substantially reduce training costs. This is because users can easily pick up the methodology of your program by drawing analogies to their other Windows applications. For instance, one way to cut and paste in Windows is almost universally accomplished by pressing the control and delete keys to cut, and then the control and insert keys for paste. This means that users can cut and paste in a spreadsheet the same way they do in their word processors, and, hopefully, the same way they would do it in your application.

Many software producers fail to capitalize on this great cost-savings potential and instead choose to write a "new and improved" user interface. As a user of such programs, I can testify that such user interfaces tend to be neither new nor improved but rather very frustrating. Users of exotic interfaces have to refer to the manual each time they want to use a new feature or perform a task they had not done recently. In the final analysis, therefore, productivity is lost, time is wasted, and discontent levels are high—all because some developer either did not know or did not care for Windows interface standards.

I will revisit this issue again in the chapter about user interface standards. However, for the purposes of this chapter, you can produce applications that conform to the Windows standards by hiring people who are familiar with the Windows operating system.

DO HIRE PROGRAMMERS WHO HAVE RELATIONAL DATABASE DESIGN MODELING EXPERIENCE. Unfortunately, at the moment, relational database design is still an art and so you need to hire people with specialized database skills. These people should know how to design a normalized database, insert the hooks that prevent multiple-user access of the same record, or prevent the insertion of records whose information has been changed since they were first accessed.

You can determine a candidate's database experience by asking her to quickly draw an entity relationship diagram for, say, an employee database distinguishing between part- and full-time employees. A resulting diagram may look like the one shown in Figure 9.1.

DO HIRE PEOPLE WITH SQL (STRUCTURED QUERY LANGUAGE) EXPERIENCE. But, again, downplay the importance of this requirement when you encounter an otherwise superb candidate. He or she will pick up this skill rather quickly.

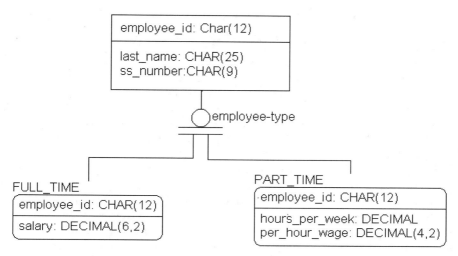

Figure 9.1 *Example of database schema*

A good way to find out what SQL experience a candidate possesses is by asking him to write an example of a stored procedure in SQL to modify an employee name in the employee table. The result could be:

```
CREATE PROCEDURE usp_insert_employee
       @new_name VARCHAR(50), @employee_id int

       AS

       UPDATE employee_table
       SET employee_name = @new_name
       WHERE employee_id = @employee_id
 GO
```

Do hire people that have experience with spreadsheet, database, and word processing applications. These can become components of your system and, thus, save your team from having to develop such functions from scratch.

A simple question about what spreadsheets, databases, and word processors the candidate uses on a day-to-day basis can reveal if the person lives in the real world. You may also want to ask what she likes about each of these applications and why she chose those particular tools. A person who knows nothing about these applications will hang herself by giving you answers that do not make sense.

Do try to hire at least some team members who have network—any network—background. (But don't make this an absolute must.) The reason for this requirement is not because such expertise is needed to develop applications. In fact, from a business application design point of view, the network is just another "disk drive" or network address and is completely transparent otherwise. Rather, network experience comes into play in the debugging process because running software, and especially client-server software, over the network creates some unique problems by virtue of adding a level of complexity to the system. When a problem is encountered, it could have originated with the client application, the network, the server, or could be due to the interaction of all three. This represents a four-dimensional world compared with the one-dimensional aspect of a stand-alone application (ignoring, for the moment, the hardware and the operating system which are common elements in both paradigms).

Subsequently, network background is important. It is not crucial, however, because you may only need one person on your team who knows anything about a network to be able to solve many of the problems you will encounter. Sometimes your organization already provides such network expertise and so it may be outside of the scope of your team. Either way, do not let lack of network expertise stand in the way of hiring an otherwise qualified candidate. And remember that the nature of network technology is such that even your best network expert may not be able to untangle a bug in the system and you will need to call the vendor for help.

If you follow many of the suggestions of this chapter, you will be able to bring on board a smart, willing, and able team of programmers, testers, and technical writers. Of course, the next obvious question is: How many people should you hire? This subject is covered in the next chapter.

_____ CHAPTER 10 _____

How Many People to Hire

Next to whom you hire, how many people you hire is the most important people management issue you face. If you enlist too few people, you may not only miss your deadline but you will likely frustrate and demotivate the poor souls who will work 80 hours a week to meet an unrealistic schedule. On the other hand, if you hire too many people, you risk encountering what economists call diminishing returns. That is, employees will step on each other's work and you will be spending all of your time either refereeing their fights or scrambling to meet their needs.

Imagine an analogous situation whereby instead of developing a software project you are cultivating a corn field. If you try to grow corn without hiring enough farm hands, the workers are not able to plant, weed, remove pests, or harvest fast enough. Most of your corn will either wither prior to harvest or will be left to rot in the field. On the other hand, if you hire too many farm hands they have little room to maneuver and end up trampling the sprouting plants in their attempt to accomplish their task. Naturally, you want to hire just the right amount.

Generally, when it comes to software development, the fewer people involved the better. This is because application development is a brain-intensive activity that does not lend itself very well to teamwork. When more than one developer is involved, many hours are wasted on having to communicate the most minute details using imperfect and slow technologies such as verbal communication, e-mail, meetings, meetings, and more meetings. This can be easily observed in the productivity curve in Figure 10.1 if you note that the slope of the curve is reduced as you approach the optimal point (the

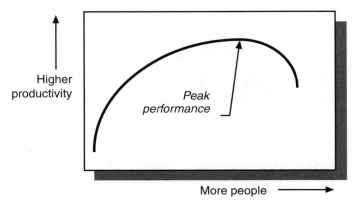

Figure 10.1   *The productivity curve*

top of the parabola). In other words, the marginal productivity gained from an additional hire (prior to optimal staffing) is slightly less than that achieved with the prior hire.

That is not to say that team development is unachievable. In fact, schedules and delivery dates require us to regularly work in teams. It just means that not only must you hire no more than the minimum number of people you can get away with, but you must also break up the project in such a way that each person's tasks can be accomplished as if he were working on his own complete project.

For example, suppose you hire five programmers who, when working on their own, can write a hundred lines of code a day. Much to your surprise, however, if you put them all in a room and tell them to develop a 500-line application—a simple compiler, for example—you will not be done in a day. Each programmer will likely immerse in every aspect of the program requiring endless communication and planning sessions to decide who writes what and how. In fact, you will be lucky to be done in several weeks. But if you took the five programmers and put them on five different locations telling each to write a different function of the compiler—syntax checker, translator, linker, and so on—you may very well be done in close to a day (provided, of course, that the inputs and outputs of each module are well defined; but more about that later). Evidently, the same work can be done much faster by the same five programmers if each is given a distinct section of the project that seems to the programmer as if it were a stand-alone application. The project, thus, becomes a collection of mini-projects.

One way to accomplish this with Visual Basic is to divide the project along user functionality—vertical lines in the following example.

EXAMPLE OF VERTICAL AND HORIZONTAL PROJECT TASKS

PROJECT X	Customer Information Entry	Security Information Entry	Transaction Entry
Display Manager			
Edit and Validation			
Database Interface			
Report Generator			

In the past, it was next to impossible to allocate a project along end user functionality. That is because third-generation languages were very difficult to manage and develop in a piecemeal fashion. For example, a manager who wanted to ensure standard user interface among all the mini-projects would not only have to specify the look and feel of each text box and combo box but would also have to work hard on standard implementation. She would then be left with the huge task of having to maintain several pieces of code each doing largely the same thing. Not surprisingly, therefore, mini-project implementation was viewed as not a very smart way of developing software. Instead, work was broken up along technically functional lines (horizontal tasks in the foregoing table). Under such a scheme, all combo boxes, text boxes, and other screen controls were developed by a single person who would maintain the code in a central location. Programmers' responsibilities were encapsulated in such task names as display manager, file manager, database engine, operating system interface, and so on.

By contrast, object-based languages such as Visual Basic, by definition, standardize the horizontal components. VB, therefore, permits us to capture additional efficiency from the productivity curve by better managing diminishing returns. Yet, this great feature is often underutilized because many managers still ignore the diminishing returns curve and make the mistake of dividing the work horizontally along the technical function hierarchy rather than vertically along end user function lines. That is, they hire one person to design the screens, another to write the database interface, another to develop the edit and validation routines, another to do serial communication, and so on. These managers could do much better if they divided the tasks so each programmer writes *all* the tasks—screen display, edit and validation, database interface, and serial communication—of a small part of the project. These mini-projects can then be combined together as a loose collection of applications, each launching the other.

Visual Basic, as well as other object-oriented languages, makes this vertical division very easy to accomplish. In fact, one would have a hard time building a system in Visual Basic that was not divided, at least to some extent, in such a fashion. That is because programming in VB consists of assembling building blocks. Projects contain forms and modules. Form objects, in turn, contain control objects, and each of these objects is encapsulated to a very high degree. To break the project horizontally means that these self-encapsulating objects have to be broken up, which is not easily done.

Subsequently, one of VB's *secret* side effects is higher productivity by virtue of correct labor division. Another side effect is that it is somewhat easier to determine staffing levels when using VB. A project broken up into mini-projects, each attainable by a single programmer, is easily planned for. This simply means that a manager need only count the number of these mini-applications and that is the number of programmers he needs to hire.

Take, for example, a data entry application. Suppose such an application consists of 12 data entry screens, each having an edit and validation function. Information is obtained from the database, displayed on the screen, and then written back to the database after editing. Since the functionality is often similar between screens, it is easy to break the project by data entry screens.

As discussed in the scheduling chapter, an average programmer can program all the functions mentioned previously associated with a single screen in 1 to 2 days. We then add a day for requirement gathering and a day for unit testing and integration for a total of 3 to 4 days per screen. It should therefore take, at most, 48 person-days to finish the project (12 data entry screens multiplied by 4 days each). To staff for this project, therefore, we take the promised delivery date, say a month from today, or 24 working days, and use it to divide the person-day estimate to arrive at the figure of two programmers.

This is a simplistic example, of course. We have assumed that the users know exactly what they want; that the database server is set up and ready to go; that the programmers write perfect code and that no system testing and no quality control are needed; that no beta testing phase is required; and, finally, that documentation and training are not necessary. But even in this dream world, the example serves to illustrate that if you stick to the mini-project methodology of planning, you will soon be able to accurately predict productivity within the construct of your environment. You can then apply the methodology to take into account even these tasks I purposely ignored previously.

THE LEARNING CURVE

One observation I had resisted mentioning until this point is the small impact the learning curve has on this planning methodology.[1] By contrast, in any language other than VB the learning curve plays an enormous role. That is to say, the lessons learned by the programmers in developing the initial database application make the next database application a little easier to develop and, therefore, takes less time to develop.

---

[1] I reserved the learning curve analysis to this chapter rather than include it in the scheduling discussion since it relates more closely to people than to the mechanics of scheduling.

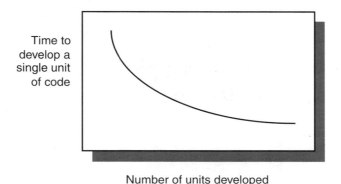

Figure 10.2   *Illustration of a typical learning curve*

A learning curve certainly exists in Visual Basic and we will discuss it further in the section on measuring productivity. However, for planning purposes the VB learning curve can be ignored because it is not very steep. (See Figure 10.2.) In other words, since most of the code is encapsulated, the knowledge base that must be learned and transferred to the next project is a fraction of that in the traditional development methods. Surely it may take a good VB programmer an extra day or so to familiarize himself with the application of the first screen he develops, but this extra time is lost in the built-in margin of error. So when we estimate that it will take 3 to 4 days to develop an average screen, we are safe to assume that this figure holds for the last as well as the first screen developed.

WHAT ABOUT THE PARAMETERS?

Earlier in this chapter, we had touched briefly on the importance of correctly specifying the inputs and outputs of each mini-project. This is perhaps the key to the success of the methodology when it comes to integrating all the mini projects into a single application.

Alas, it is not as important as it seems at first glance. If you are careful in how you break up the project into mini-projects so the input/output problem is minimized, you will be able to trivialize the importance of this issue. Much in the same way a diamond cutter splits a diamond along the lines in the stone that have the weakest bonds, you must divide the project where the communication needs between the modules are at the lowest level.

For example, a project may consist of two data entry screens, one for client name and another for address, and two similar report-generating screens. If you give one programmer the name functionality and another the address functionality, you must spend a lot of resources specifying how one programmer's module is to tell the other's module which client record it is working on. But if you assign one programmer both data entry screens and the other both reports, there is very little communication needed between the two modules and integration is, thus, much simpler.

CHAPTER 11

How Best to Organize
the Development Team

Having hired the right people in the right number, you are faced with the decision of how to organize the group for optimal performance. How you shape the organization will have a distinct effect on the success of the project. If you create too few levels of management, you may be bogged down in tasks that may have been better delegated. On the other hand, if you build a rigid, multilayer organization, you might be stifling upward communication and risking the possibility that your direct reports will hide from you important problems. A careful balance must, therefore, be struck between these two extremes.

The organization's structure invariably depends on the number of people on the team. From a narrow perspective this number is derived from the size of the project and its delivery schedule. The larger the project and the less time allocated, the larger the staff necessary to meet the goal. Since organizational behaviorists inform us that the optimal team size a manager can comfortably handle is eight to ten subordinates, it is possible to estimate the number of managers and levels of management needed. Anytime the number of direct reports increases beyond the optimal eight to ten subordinates, you will be well advised to hire or promote some additional managers and break up the team accordingly.

From a broader perspective, however, there are factors other than the size and scope of the project that are likely to influence the size and structure of your organization. For example, your company's talent development committee may decide to create positions reporting to you that serve little purpose other than to train up-and-coming managers. This superimposed organization has limited positive effect on the project, yet you may often have no control over its implementation.

But regardless of the size of the project, the number of subordinates, and external issues, there are several universal rules to follow when deciding how to organize the team.

ACCOUNTABILITY

The best way to ensure that a project succeeds and meets the deadline is to make individual players accountable for each and every aspect of the project. That is, you as well as all the other team members must know and understand what is expected of each player at any given juncture. Team members must also be assured in no uncertain terms that should they fail to meet their assigned goal, they, and no one else, will have to answer to you about their deficiency. Likewise, they should also be convinced that if they succeed or exceed expectations, they, and no one else, will receive the recognition, credit, and rewards.

As sensible as this idea sounds, accountability is rarely evident in corporate America. A universal truth—so common it has become a cliché—is that when things go wrong it is the troops in the trenches who suffer the brunt of the blame; but when things go right, management takes the credit. This situation is aggravated by the fact that, from the beginning, few teams are organized to encourage and facilitate individual responsibility. For example, software development teams are often arranged so that they are led by a technical lead *and* a business analyst. The two are supposed to work together to move the project forward. At first, this arrangement sounds reasonable enough. The technical lead should concentrate on technical issues while the business analyst is supposed to gather user requirements and manage the nontechnical aspects of the project. Yet, on closer examination, it becomes clear that no one person is accountable for the project's success and on-time delivery. When the schedule slips, therefore, inquiries as to the cause will most likely be answered with "it is not my fault; the specifications were not done on time," or "it is not my fault; the programmers did not work hard enough."

This situation could have easily been avoided if either the business analyst or the technical managers were organized so one worked for the other, with the senior position made accountable for the entire project. The subordinate position is, then, accountable to the senior position to accomplish a very specific task. Alternately, the two positions could have been organized to operate independently of each other, with each having a very specific set of goals. Such goals may be: finish the specifications by June 1, or finish coding three months after receiving the specifications. Under such arrangements, the manager as well as all team members know exactly who is to be blamed for failure or recognized for success.

Accountability ensures responsibility, and responsibility makes the project succeed. To instill accountability in your team members, organize the group in such a way that no team member can hide behind, or be hidden by, someone else.

EMPOWERMENT

It makes no sense to hold people responsible for the success or failure of their individual tasks if they are not empowered to obtain the resources necessary for success. Doing one without the other is not only hopelessly unworkable, it is also extremely frustrating and stressful to the employees. Team members who could otherwise easily accomplish their assigned tasks can often be stymied in their tracks waiting for the organizational bureaucracy to provide them with a much needed tool. At times, the bureaucracy is not only slow but rather unyielding. Who among us, for example, has not been asked at least once over the course of our careers to *justify* the need for a certain requisitioned computer, or a printer, or other such items? In some organization, such a request is as good as the kiss of death to the said requisition. Yet the poor soul who depends on this computer or printer to be able to meet a deadline is often left powerless to change or even speed up the bureaucratic wheels.

It is, therefore, imperative that you give your team a free hand in obtaining the resources they deem necessary. This means the ability to obtain whatever hardware or software they need, the authorization to sign up for and attend training classes and conferences, and the means to set up their working environment any way they see fit. Likewise, team members should be trusted to work flexible hours or even telecommute from time to time so they can meet their family needs without sacrificing their commitment to the project. Finally, team members should be allowed to communicate directly with the users without having to go through *proper channels*.

The implication of empowerment on the structure of the organization is that the management control must be kept very loose, if such management exists at all. In fact, any *management* you install under you should be put in place for external purposes only and not to create an internal bureaucracy. Traditional management responsibilities such as approving purchase requisitions and work orders should be replaced with a facilitating function whereby the *manager* uses her title to slice through red tape and arrange for fast and efficient purchases or implementation needed by team members.

Incidentally, another perfectly good use for such a manager or lead position is to provide cover for embattled team members. As mentioned earlier, a programmer should be able to approach the end user directly to ask pertinent questions and clear up misunderstandings. By the same token, however, the programmer should be able to direct the end user to a *manager* if the user exploits the opportunity and requests additional features or modifications of existing design.

SHALLOW ORGANIZATION

It is an often denied, yet always a true fact of life, that middle management is to free communication what superglue is to lubrication. The reason for this communication impediment is natural and understandable, albeit regrettable. Middle managers have been conditioned by past experiences to avoid bringing their boss bad news lest they are blamed, correctly or incorrectly, for the failure. Likewise, these managers often fail to carry the boss's message to their subordinates because information is power. The more they tell, the less power they pack. Therefore, any layers of management you install between your front-line soldiers and yourself impedes your message from reaching the troops and obstructs you from finding out what is really going on. The more layers, the more obstructions.

This propensity to impede communication is somewhat perplexing if one stops to question the need of *traditional* middle management in the first place. Indeed, if you had hired the best and the brightest technical staff, as suggested in this book, and empowered them to do their job, the role of a middle manager is, arguably, minimal. Most professional programmers are self-motivated and self-managed. Many also despise being *managed* anyway.

Clearly, therefore, your organization must have as few layers of management as possible and preferably none at all. Unfortunately, if your project is very large or if you manage several projects at one time, you will find middle management a necessary evil. As mentioned earlier in this chapter, research has shown that a manager simply cannot manage any more than eight to ten direct reports at one time without slipping important responsibilities. However, you will be ill advised if you let this fact cause you to build a deep organization. There are plenty of alternative ways with which one can delegate management responsibilities to quasi-managers without relinquishing control of the communication infrastructure of the team. Such *management avoidance* methods will be discussed more broadly in the chapter on management style, but the correct organization design is instrumental in achieving such a goal.

Practically speaking, one management avoidance technique is to rely on office assistance. This means that if you find yourself managing a large project and need help, hire an administrative assistant instead of a manager. Delegate all administrative tasks to this assistant who can handle the routine tasks of obtaining resources and arranging the development environment. Note that I did not say secretary, since I hardly think anyone needs to employ a person who does nothing more than type memos, take messages, or open mail. In fact, it is beyond me why in today's voice-mail-e-mail-word-processor-beeper-cellular-phone world how secretaries exist in the first place. Administrative assistants differ from secretaries in that they do not attempt to do anything that a computer can do better and faster. Instead, they spend their time keeping office supply closets stacked, copying manuals, arranging sitting assignments, planning for delivery date celebrations, and all other such administrative tasks.

Another management avoidance technique is to delegate some of your own management duties to the existing team members. A chunk of your duties that is best delegated is the monitoring and reporting of the project status and the technical issues. Chances are that you are ill prepared to accomplish this task in the first place since the more you are responsible for the harder it is to find the time to be involved in day-to-day development. If, indeed, this is the case, resist the urge to hire a manager between you and the development team and, instead, choose one of your programmers as a lead developer to whom you can delegate the monitoring duties: This person can answer questions such as: How is the project going? Are we going to meet the deadline? Who is holding us back? Who is a hero today? And so on.

The advantage of a *lead developer* over a *manager* is that she can accomplish the monitoring tasks without becoming an obstacle between you and your team members. She is not responsible for the project status (other than her own duties) and so she would not be afraid to convey to you when things are not going well. Thus, communication is not inhibited and problems are not shoved under the carpet. But remember the accountability rule. Hold the lead developer accountable for passing this information up to you just as you would hold her accountable for completing any of her other assigned tasks.

Finally, *management avoidance* means keeping task division to a minimum especially in small projects. This is perhaps a somewhat difficult thing to do since the temptation to divide tasks between team members along functional lines is so strong. The typical manager finds it crucial to have testing, documentation, specification, and support functions all separate from each other and from the development function. However, for small project teams and with the possible exception of the documentation function, it is not at all desirable to divide your project this way. Rather, it is much better to entrust the entire task—designing, programming, testing, and implementation—to each team member.

Documentation, should, at least in theory, be no different. The people who develop the code could conceivably be entrusted with documenting its features. Unfortunately, two factors come into play, which together make this situation unrealizable. First, programmers write horrible documents and, second, they hate doing it. Subsequently, any attempt to force programmers to write documentation is not worth the effort.

So, how do we apply all this to designing an organization? Some examples follow.

SMALL PROJECT: Up to four programmers (see Figure 11.1).

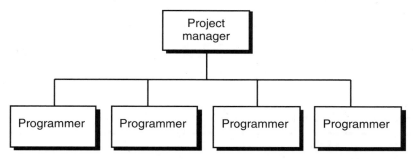

Figure 11.1 *Each programmer is responsible for specifying, testing, and documenting his or her part*

MEDIUM-SIZE PROJECT: Four to six programmers, testing and documentation functions (see Figure 11.2).

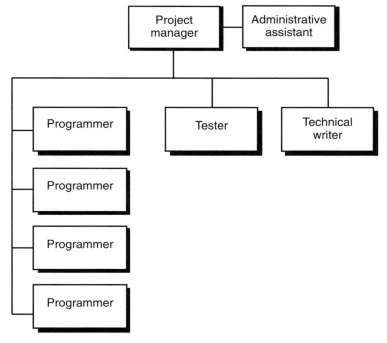

Figure 11.2 *Organization for a medium-size project*

LARGE PROJECT: More than 6 programmers, testing, business analysis, and documentation (see Figure 11.3).

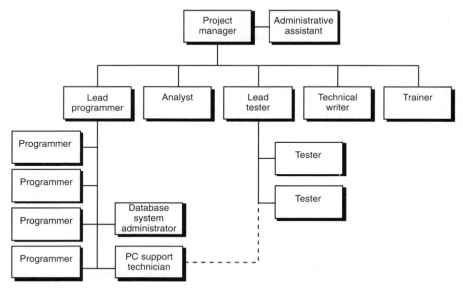

Figure 11.3   *Large project organization*

The role of the technician in the foregoing organization is to support the programmers with installations, backup, and upkeep of the workstations. At low activity periods, the technician can be assigned to the testing team both as an extra tester and as someone who can install the latest system built on the tester's workstations, hence the dotted line. These responsibilities provide an excellent learning environment for the technician to be able, later on, to implement the system in the field.

Trainers are optional depending on the scope of the project. They usually join the team late in the project.

_____ CHAPTER 12 _____

How Management Style Affects the Development Process

Management style is defined as the manner by which a manager carries out the set of tactics needed to achieve a specified objective. For example, a typical project manager's objective is to design, develop, and implement a new system to replace an aging legacy system. Tactically, this objective translates to planning, hiring, motivating, monitoring progress, and obtaining resources. The manner by which the manager chooses to carry out these activities is his or her management style.

Let's take, as an example, a schedule slip-up in the project in order to demonstrate differences in management style. One manager, for instance, may choose to deal with such a delay by assembling his team together and throwing the proverbial fit. Another manager may ignore the whole issue and pray that no one will notice. Yet a third may actually sit down with each team member and try to figure out what caused the delay.

Obviously, management styles vary widely across the spectrum of managers. Some managers are very effective because their style meshes well with that of their subordinates and supervisors. Others fail miserably because they attempt to manage a certain situation using the wrong paradigm.

Moreover, style is a curious thing. It turns out that management style matters much more to subordinates than it does to superiors. When employees are asked their opinion of their manager they often site what is really the manager's style as evidence of desirable or despised attributes. This is because to most employees it is not readily apparent how effective a manager may be in obtaining resources or shielding them from the bureaucracy. Rather, employees tend to notice how the manager communicates with them or how she lets them know she approves or disapproves of their actions. Upper management, on the other hand, tends to pay much more attention to its subordinates' substance than to style (as evidenced by the fact that the biggest jerks on the face of this earth are often promoted while nice people are rationalized). So the moral of the story is:

> Because employees are affected by style, the wrong management approach can hurt a manager's ability to get things done. But because management values substance, the right style hardly guarantees success.

Yet, despite the fact that upper management often ignores one's management style, I still believe that the issue is highly relevant in some specific situations. This is especially true anywhere a manager depends heavily on his subordinates' know-how, initiative, and professionalism such as in software development. After all, a programmer who hates the way her manager treats her may spread discontent among her colleagues, set the manager up for an embarrassing fall, or simply leave for a better situation. But even in industries that have traditionally paid no attention to management styles, the topic is fast becoming pertinent. Clearly, postal supervisors are much nicer to their subordinates these days than they were before postal workers learned how to use automatic firearms.

Alas, management style is not a highly covered topic. Rarely is the subject discussed in management textbooks or in academic circles. True, there are some management consultants who touch on style issues during their broader analysis and, occasionally, a book such as *Zapp, The Lightning of Empowerment*[1] becomes popular, but, generally, style is ignored. The reason for this void, at least in part, is because it is not easy to make general observations about which style does or does not work across all scenarios. The methods successfully used by one manager in a particular situation may fall short if tried by a different manager under different circumstances. For example, President Ronald Reagan's approach of concentrating on the forest rather than the trees in his administration's decision-making process served him well. Yet such a management style failed President Lyndon Johnson who did not receive enough information about the Vietnam War to make the correct decisions.

Fortunately, the audience of this book is fairly homogenous with regard to industry, nature of subordinates, and mission. There are several issues, therefore, that can be reasonably generalized in order to closely examine project management style. Keep in mind, however, that the ideas covered in this chapter may not serve you well outside the world of system development.

SET CLEAR GOALS

By far, the most important attribute of a manager with superior style is the habit of stating publicly the goal of the project. This is because a manager

---

[1] William C. Byham, Ph.D. and Jeff Cox, *Zapp, The Lightning of Empowerment* (New York: Fawcett Columbine, 1988).

should never assume the team knows what its purpose in life is just because the specifications are complete. Yes, complete specifications are nice but even the best specs are silent on issues such as priorities and scheduling. A void is thus left that is often not noticed until the project is late and out of scope. All of a sudden, the surprised manager finds out that the reason the project is late is because Mike has been working to improve performance of the system while Diane was trying to improve maintainability. Oh, and also neither one knew exactly when the application was expected for delivery.

It may seem like a cliché but for the project to be successful, each and every member of the team needs to be on the same page, devoting every available ounce of energy toward a common goal. The only way to achieve such an outcome is to state the project's goal and ensure that team members understand it. In the words of Steve Maguire in his book, *Debugging the Development Process*: "Establish detailed project goals to prevent wasting time on inappropriate tasks."[2]

Advertising the goal can simply be accomplished by writing it down on a single sheet of paper and then distributing copies to be hung in every cube, preferably, right above the computer monitor. Some managers may choose to be more elaborate and also order T-shirts, wallet cards, and buttons proclaiming the project's mission statement. Either way, the goal should be stated briefly and simply so that every member of the group can recite it by heart upon prompting.

A sample goal statement may look like this:

DESIGN, DEVELOP, AND IMPLEMENT AN ENTERPRISEWIDE PAYROLL SYSTEM THAT

⇒ Is Bug Free
⇒ Matches The Final User Specifications
⇒ Is Delivered To The User's Desk On July 15, 1997
⇒ Is Fully Documented
⇒ With A Primary Emphasis On Maintainability
⇒ And A Secondary Emphasis On Performance.

To some readers, this may seem like a totally useless exercise. Trust me—it is far from being one. This particular goal statement tells the programmers that no defect will be tolerated; it specifies the delivery date; and it tells them that the highest emphasis should be placed on code maintainability rather than on performance, storage space, or cost. As such, it ensures that when it comes time for team members to interact on a technical level, they at

---

[2] Steve Maguire, *Debugging the Development Process* (Redmond, WA: Microsoft Press, 1994), p. 15.

least know the direction the team is marching toward. They will, thus, be able to make intelligent decisions concerning allocation of their own resources and their requirements from other team members even without a manager's intervention.

Incidentally, be careful not to make the goal unachievable. Note, for example, that in this case *delivered within budget* is not a team goal. It may very well be a management goal but specifying both a timetable and a budget can overconstrain the project into an unrealistic goal. For example, finishing a system by next month may be doable given enough resources. Likewise, expending only half a million dollars in development of the project may be feasible given enough time. Doing both at the same time, however, may be impossible. It is, therefore, your responsibility and not your team's responsibility to ensure enough money is provided to meet this goal.

But the mission statement serves a much wider audience than merely your team. For one, getting your boss to sign off on the goal statement is just as important as selling it to your subordinates. So before presenting the goal to your team, you may want to, first, sell it to your management. Doing so will confirm that the stated goal is in line with your management's own mission and that you are in sync with organizational goals. As an added benefit, you may be able to use an approved goal to shield your project from interference later on.

Finally, the users should approve the goal statement as well. Even though users rarely wish to get technically involved beyond the functional specifications, they still need to know your team's stated mission. Such understanding may improve the process of communication between the development team and the user community. A user who knows that a developer is rushing to meet a mutually agreed upon delivery date is likely to be more cooperative than one who does not.

CALL FEW LARGE MEETINGS

Generally speaking, meetings that involve more than two people are an enormous waste of time since rarely is anything constructive said or done in such meetings. Instead, large meetings and conferences take up valuable development time and encourage busy-work by creating an artificial need for information. True, sometimes, meetings are a necessary evil. For example, resolving several conflicting sets of requirements submitted by different users is often not easily accomplished unless all the players can be assembled together in one room. But most other times, large meetings can be avoided and other means can be used to reach satisfactory resolution to whatever issue is at hand.

Large meetings are not very productive mainly due to two fundamental reasons combined with the usual evils of corporate mismanagement. The two basic reasons are simple: First, by collecting several people in one place you convert an otherwise parallel (synchronous) process into a serial (asynchronous) process. In other words, the attendees could have been doing work at their desks during the time of the meeting but instead they are forced to mostly sit quietly and observe the work done by other attendees, one at a time. Compare this situation with the much preferred exchange of e-mail or voice mail and you find that once a message is sent, the author can proceed to do other work while his query is being answered by others.

The second fundamental reason meetings fall short is because they are a distraction. A person invited to a meeting has to drop whatever he or she is doing in order to attend. When the meeting is over, the attendees want to resume their previous task only they may have forgotten their trend of thoughts or their intended goal. I doubt very much Einstein would have been able to develop the theory of relativity were he to belong to an organization that called frequent meetings.

Combined with these two very basic notions is the fact that meetings are often poorly run. In essence, some managers terribly misuse the meeting—not a very productive tool to begin with—so that any inherent loss of productivity is greatly multiplied. One such type, for example, approaches meetings much in the same way one goes fishing—no plan, just a vague notion of what it is he or she wants to catch. Of course, even if the person catches no fish, he or she still has a good time. You can usually spot such managers right away when they start a meeting by saying something like: "I have nothing new to report but why don't we go around the table and see what everyone is doing?"

We can do very little about the inherent shortcomings of large meetings. But there are certain principles we can follow to help prevent any additional productivity losses:

CALL A LARGE MEETING ONLY WHEN ABSOLUTELY NECESSARY. Before calling any meeting, ask yourself whether whatever it is you are trying to accomplish cannot be achieved more effectively by other means. For example, if you need to dispense information to your troops, could you do so by e-mail rather than by a gathering? Resort to meetings only if there is no other alternative.

NEVER HOLD A STATUS MEETING. Of all the different types of meetings, the status meeting is perhaps the most wasteful and least productive. Worse yet, many managers also require their subordinates to write a formal status report as a pretext or a follow-up to this meeting so the productivity decrease is multiplied. Yet, if one examines the issue closely, one discovers that status meetings are not necessary in the first place. Whatever information it is the manager is asking for can easily be gathered through e-mail or in a one-on-one conversation with each team member.

Many people would argue that the purpose of a status meeting is not only to gather information but also to ensure team members are aware of what the rest of the team is doing. These people claim that e-mail or personal discussions fail to achieve this outcome. I strongly disagree. A written compilation of all the submitted status reports, sent by e-mail, can be read by all team members at leisure, thereby reducing the distraction aspect of a meeting. In fact, most managers already compile such reports to submit to their own managers and so it should not be a problem to make some additional copies for the rest of the team. If a member of the group reads about something interesting in this report, she can approach the appropriate party on her own. She certainly does not need a formal setting for such interaction to occur.

Status meetings are a bad habit. Give them up and live much healthier lives.

HAVE AN AGENDA. If you absolutely, positively need to get more than two people in one room (or in one telephone conversation) plan, plan, plan. Steve Maguire suggests that ". . . before calling any meeting, be sure you know exactly what you want to achieve and when you need to achieve it. Then make sure you do achieve it."[3] Have an agenda of what you are going to discuss and a very good notion of what you expect to get out of the meeting. Put time limits on each item of the agenda. Distribute the agenda as well as any hand-outs to every invitee well in advance of the meeting. And, most importantly, follow the plan. Start on time, proceed with each agenda item on time, and finish as promised. Those participants who are late or unprepared should not be allowed to penalize the rest of the attendees.

If you get bogged down on one item beyond the allocated time, offer to meet again about this one issue at a different time. Suggest that a member of the team take it upon himself to explore this subject further and present a solution within a week or so. Then move on to the next subject.

Finally, make sure that you accomplish what you set out to do or the whole thing was a waste of your time. If you cannot get the meeting attendees to reach a resolution one way, conclude the meeting in the opposite direction. Remember that a negative result may not be as desirable as a positive result, but it is much better than no result at all. For example, if you called a meeting to ask for more money to finish your project and both your boss and the controller express reluctance to allocate additional resources, it is much better for you to conclude that no additional resources will be allocated than to leave the meeting without reaching a consensus. This way, you have not wasted your time and, therefore, you can go on to make the appropriate decisions. Sometimes you may even find that by stating publicly what no one is willing to say outright you will have forced a positive decision. Don't be surprised, therefore, to hear some attendees change their minds once you state your conclusion.

Incidentally, in the absence of a concrete outcome, it is fine to conclude the meeting with a plan of action. In the foregoing example, the controller may offer to have one of her analysts review your request before she approves.

[3] Ibid., p. 85.

That is a perfectly good outcome as long as there is a timetable and an agreement to meet again at the conclusion of the analysis.

Keep the Meeting Short. As meetings are a drain on productivity, the less time spent in them the better. Try not to digress to other subjects or to concentrate on items that apply to only a few of the attendees. One way to ensure meetings take no longer than needed is to avoid bringing in snacks or arranging for refreshments. This way, at least, you have to end the meeting before lunch or dinner to prevent some attendees from keeling over in hunger.

Start on Time. Surely you have heard this piece of advice at least a hundred times: Don't penalize the people who show up to the meeting on time by waiting for those who are late. Well, like many other clichés, this one is also true. But it is true not only because starting on time ensures a shorter meeting; by always being prompt you also prevent a situation whereby your subordinates and colleagues know that your meetings always start late and, thus, never show up on time.

Hold Meetings at the End or Start of a Day. In Steve Maguire's words: "If you must hold a meeting, minimize the amount of interruption it will cause. Schedule the meeting so that it won't break up an otherwise large block of time."[4] That is, schedule meetings at times during which the attendees have not yet started anything—as in, early morning—or are about to finish whatever they are doing—late afternoon.

Avoid Follow-Up Report. Don't duplicate work and especially don't repeat unproductive work. Avoid the inclination to ask team members attending the meeting to write reports that describe what they have said in the meeting. If you need to document an agreement or to note something noteworthy, do it yourself.

MAINTAIN HIGH TEAM SPIRIT

Organizational behaviorists swear that there is little correlation between high team spirit and high productivity. In other words, high team morale does not necessarily translate into increased output. Sad, but evidently true. As it turns out, sweatshops are just as productive as workplaces thought of as *fun*. In fact, studies have actually suggested that in some industries, a rigid, no-fun work environment actually results in better productivity than a fun-filled, relaxed atmosphere.

But, arguably, there is more to this story than just productivity. Concentrating on the low correlation between productivity and morale fails to distinguish some very important side effects of low morale. Yet, these side effects can have several disastrous implications to the software development process:

[4] Ibid., p. 89.

First, low morale inevitably leads to high turnover. Remember that in the high demand, low supply world of application development, programmers are not tied to any specific job. If the guy down the street pays just as well but has a video game in the basement, than "Ba-Bye." Consequently, the environment you provide your programmers becomes very important. Second, it is hardly a secret that low morale causes absenteeism. A person who does not look forward to going to work every morning because he hates the environment in which he works is going to be easily swayed to stay at home: "Johnny can't come to work today because he developed a severe case of beach fever. Or is it golf syndrome?" And, as we all know, high absenteeism causes schedules to slip and deadlines to be missed. Finally, low morale saps energy and inhibits motivation. Ask a team member whose spirit is lacking to stay late and help debug a pressing problem and you are likely to be turned down. After all, the programmer enjoys activities such as playing softball, watching television, or going out with friends much more. She would do just about anything rather than hang around a demoralizing workplace.

Because of these and other potential side effects, it is always in your best interest to try to keep the team spirit up. Luckily, if you are a Visual Basic shop, this task is easier than in more traditional development environments. With few really tough obstacles to conquer and many visible quick successes, chances are that your VB team is already well on its way to being a happy team. Contrast this with a traditional C shop and you will find that the situation is different: The C development team usually works long hours to meet aggressive schedules. Their VB counterpart can go home at reasonable hours and still meet its schedule. The C team stays at the office well into the night to try to debug memory allocation problems. The VB team goes out after work for a drink and that always important bonding session. The C team regularly huddles in groups of three to four programmers analyzing what the computer is really doing with their program. The VB team members work individually in their cubes listening to their CD Walkmen. And so on. And so on.

But Visual Basic, by itself, is not a morale builder. A good manager, on the other hand, can be. There are many, many ways to build up and improve team sprit and programmers' morale. More, in fact, than we can ever cover in this book. However, all such suggestions can be summed up in one phrase, various versions of which are as old as dirt:

> **Treat your team
> the way *you* would
> like to be treated.**

Some examples of this include:

Do . . .	Don't . . .
• Praise the group and individuals often.	• Yell and scream at group members.
• Buy the team lunch every so often.	• Humiliate members in public.
• Communicate on an individual basis.	• Call frequent long meetings.
• Set achievable goals.	• Set unrealistic or sadistic goals.
• Organize off-site outings to discuss problems.	• Avoid dealing with problems.
	• Stifle personal growth.
• Send members for training.	• Insist on 80-hour weeks.
• Encourage members to have a life outside of work.	• Browbeat members to forsake family responsibilities.
• Allow flexible hours and telecommuting.	• Hide in your office and be unapproachable.
• Keep your door open and talk to each team member at least once a day.	• Ignore successes.
• Reward accomplishments.	• Institute rules against computer game playing.
• Provide ample toys for the kids to play with (as long as they do their homework).	• Institute or enforce silly rules.
• Cut through red tape to get resources.	

A couple of these suggestions deserve to be elaborated upon because their implications reach far beyond simply improving team morale.

ENCOURAGE EMPLOYEE GROWTH

Clearly, hiring people whose skill level and expertise fit the task at hand is just the beginning. Since the computer field is never at rest and new products and technologies always come up, you must constantly allow your team members to *catch up*, so to speak. For example, such catching up can be accomplished by setting some time aside each month to evaluate new products or by sending the programmer to a formal training class. Alternatively, it can be done by sending the group member on a *sabbatical* to another group in the company that is employing new technology. It can also mean allowing the programmer to assume responsibilities away from your project. Steve Maguire puts it this way: "Don't jealously hold onto your best programmers if they've stopped growing. For the good of the programmers, their replacements, and the company, transfer stalled programmers to new projects where growth can continue.[5] Make sure each team member learns one new significant skill at least every two months."[6]

---

[5] Ibid., p. 115.
[6] Ibid., p. 118.

GIVE FREQUENT FEEDBACK

How to provide positive or negative feedback heavily depends on the type of programmer you are dealing with and the motivational issues involved. A discussion of this subject will, thus, follow in the motivational chapter. However, how often you provide feedback is more of a management style issue.

Organizational behavior research shows that providing feedback is perhaps the most important motivational tool a manager possesses in her tool box. But I hate to view feedback as just a way to motivate the team. I would much rather view it as a way to steer the project toward the goal. Just as a cattle rancher drives huge herds by encouraging progress and correcting wayward behavior, you can lead a team of programmers, who would otherwise stray off course, toward a desired conclusion.

A good manager should, thus, regularly inform her team members on how they are doing. Praise programmers immediately when they have done something right. Admonish them if and when they do something wrong. But whatever you do, do not wait to provide feedback. And especially, do not wait until the annual review.

ELIMINATE RED TAPE

Bureaucracy has the same effect on team sprit that a herd of stampeding elephants has on a wheat field in its way. Surely, we have all witnessed a situation where an enthusiastic, somewhat naive, rookie programmer approaches his manager with a great suggestion for improvement only to be told that to implement his ideas he needs to provide written justification to be approved by at least six levels of management. Most likely, the programmer will not only forget about his suggestion but, unless he is a certified lunatic, never bring up another idea again. And because he no longer feels empowered to improve his environment, he is likely to lose much of his enthusiasm. Maybe he will even become cynical and destroy the rest of the team's morale.

Despite what you might have been told, bureaucracy and red tape are not a fact of life in a corporation. They are merely self-perpetuating monsters that enforce their own existence. *Of course*, the rules say that in order to start a new project you need six signatures from various people whose combined intelligence approaches that of an earthworm. But who says that a project has to be classified as new when it can be tagged as a maintenance effort? Maintenance, in most companies, is an expected expenditure and, so, requires no approval. Believe it or not, as a manager you have a tremendous amount of latitude in how you classify efforts and obtain resources. Subsequently, you must use this freedom to eliminate as much red tape from the path of your team as possible. If a programmer's efforts are stymied by red tape, it is you who has failed and not your company. If a programmer wants you to buy her a new CD-ROM drive, make sure it is you and not your programmer who fights the war to convince the nincompoops that a new CD-ROM is not "just another toy" for the developers. If your team needs office supplies but is told that the company no longer buys office supplies (as many companies have done recently), you get them the supplies even if you have to classify them as memory chips. And if a programmer has a good idea to improve a small part of the world, give him the freedom to go ahead and do whatever he thinks necessary.

BUFFER YOUR TEAM FROM UPPER MANAGEMENT AND THE USER COMMUNITY

Even though you may want to encourage free and open communication between the user community and your team, it is not a good idea to condone a situation where the users can directly pressure a developer to add or enhance features. Under such a demand, programmers experience tremendous frustration trying to complete both the features that are on the team's priority list *and* those the users want outside of the specifications. And so, this scenario is a morale buster of the first degree. Note that a similar situation may also evolve if upper management regularly approaches team members directly with specific requests.

Both of these are touchy situations, to say the least. Many of us (yours truly included) feel very uncomfortable when we have to tell our boss that he is doing something very stupid. Likewise, the users are our customers and so we try to avoid having to turn their requests down. Nonetheless, managers who wish to maintain high morale must shield their team from such outside interference.

Personally, I found that the best way to approach this problem without angering the offenders is to point out the cost associated with the request: "Hey, boss. You know that report you wanted Mark to prepare for you? You know, the one detailing the effects of Windows NT on solar dark spots? Well, if you still want him to write it, the HotShot project may be delayed by two to three days. Is that OK with you?" Usually the answer is, "Oh, I didn't realize this is the case. Why didn't Mark say something? Please ask him to write the report only after he finishes his current tasks."

But sometimes you encounter a real moron who does not really wish to deal with the whole issue. If you are lucky, the offender may say something like, "The report is very important. I promised it to my boss by 3:00 P.M. sharp and I don't want to show up without it." If you are not so lucky, the response will be an angry, "I don't really care. Mark can stay late the next three months to catch up." But no matter what type of response you get, it is important to stand your ground. Veto the request if you can. Otherwise, if you get no cooperation, follow up the exchange with written e-mail stating matter-of-factly your understanding of the situation. This memo should describe the request and explain the consequences. Send it to your boss and copy the requester (if the two are the same, no need to copy, of course). This way, when the time comes, and you are called on the carpet to explain why the project is late, you will be able to pull out a stack of memos detailing each and every cause. (Don't get me wrong. You may still get fired, but the likelihood is much lower than if you have no concrete proof.)

If you consistently handle every request in this manner and you let it be known that only you set the schedule and the priorities, both your boss and the users will begin to submit their requests to you first. This will enable you to become a buffer for your team, allowing them to concentrate on their assigned, and presumably, achievable tasks. Morale will, thus, not be damaged by the corrosive effects of frustration.

LET YOUR TEAM MEMBERS TAKE THE CREDIT

Being a buffer between the team and the outside world, however, does not mean shielding your team from exposure. Few actions anger people more than a manager who takes their work, whether it is a report, a presentation, or a segment of code, replaces the author's name with his own, and then submits it to the requester. Yet this shameful practice is prevalent among all ranks of management. A team led by such a manager is usually demoralized and disgusted.

Insecure managers who feel that they must take credit for each and every fragment of work done by their team eventually get no credit at all. In the final analysis, their management gets the impression that they do not know how to delegate. Also demoralized employees tend to resign more frequently than their highly spirited peers. When they leave, these employees often go through exit interviews, leaving no truths untold. The transcript of exit interviews are then circulated around upper management. It is not clear how many resignations it takes to dislodge a bad manager but rest assured that no one is ever fooled by these managers' *credit theft*.

In fact, the only way a manager can get recognition is if the team shines. Since we know managers cannot be credited with doing their team's work, they must strive to gain recognition for leadership and management ability instead. From such a perspective, a manager can show merit by advertising work done by her subordinates and pointing out great achievements. For example, a developer who is allowed to present to upper management her latest and greatest widget analyzer routine will cause the audience to notice how good a job her manager is doing. After all, who set the priorities that caused this project to succeed? Who got the resources? Who hired and motivated the developer?

So since shielding a team from deserved credit is demoralizing and self-destructive, it makes no sense whatsoever to do it. Let your people shine in public as often as possible, and you will be cultivating a proud and spirited team.

DON'T WORK 80-HOUR WEEKS

In his book, *Debugging the Development Process*, Steve Maguire points out that "[t]he need to work long hours is a clear indication that something is wrong in the development process, whether it's because the team is doing non-strategic work or because the team is being bullied by a misguided manager . . . managers must never confuse 'productivity' with 'time at the office.' One person might work far fewer hours and produce more than somebody who works twice as long."[7]

I could not agree with this analysis more. Having to work continuous 80-hour weeks is a demoralizing and wasteful practice. It is also unfair. A developer who has to put in every waking hour at the office is missing the experience of his children growing up, is prevented from enjoying what life has to offer, and is putting incredible strains on his marriage and other relationships. Nothing, not even a job, should do this to anyone.

Long hours are almost never necessary. More importantly, as Maguire points out, working a lot of hours does not improve productivity. This is a very important point so let me make it again: There is absolutely no correlation between the number of hours worked and the amount of work done. Aside from the difference in work rates between team members that Maguire cleverly observes, there is also the issue of what is really being accomplished in those extra hours the developers are forced to put in. Chances are that since they are prevented from taking care of personal business after work, the team members accomplish private chores during work. Throughout the day, they may write checks, pick up dry cleaning, write letters, or make private phone calls, all tasks they used to perform in their free time. They may also be eating dinner at work since they are asked to stay late into the night. And so, if one were to closely scrutinize the amount of work done during a 12-hour day, for example, one is sure to discover that it is hardly any more than the amount accomplished in an eight-hour day. Only the 12-hour days produce side effects of continuous exhaustion, frustration, and low morale.

Developers are usually forced to put in long hours because of one of three reasons:

1. The due date is unreasonable or the schedule is poorly planned.
2. Management believes in working long hours "to get the most out of every dollar."
3. Problems encountered during development are being addressed with sheer force rather than by analysis.

All three of these possible causes are undesirable and avoidable. A poorly devised schedule or an aggressive due date is a management mistake, the consequences of which should never be inflicted on the development team.

---

[7] Ibid., p. 169.

We had already talked about the fact that working long hours never produces higher productivity. And, working 80-hour weeks does not solve any implicit problems in the development process.

Maguire uses an illustration of a sinking boat, taking on water fast, to point out the fallacy of the long workday argument. The captain of the boat can employ every sailor on board to bail out the water and force them to work every hour of the day until they keel over in exhaustion. Yet, the boat will still sink unless the hole is plugged. You see, the real problem is the hole, not the fact that the sailors are not bailing out enough water. Unless this problem is solved, no amount of work will remedy the situation. Clearly, long hours do not solve problems.

Follow these suggestion to avoid the trap of long work hours:

- If your project is slipping, something is wrong. Don't ignore the causes and demand long hours of the team members. Find and fix the problems[8].
- Beware of the misguided belief that long hours result in greater productivity. If anything, long hours only hurt productivity.[9]
- Weekends belong to the team members, not to the company. Teams don't need to work weekends in order to beat the competition.[10]
- Train the development team to work effectively during a normal workday. Don't allow them to work long hours, which only serves to mask time-wasting activity.[11]
- Fight any upper-management pressure to have your team work an unreasonable schedule.

More about management issues in coming chapters.

---

[8] Ibid., p. 154.
[9] Ibid., p. 158.
[10] Ibid., p. 160.
[11] Ibid., p. 164.

CHAPTER 13

How to Measure Productivity and Other Aspects of Development

As a manager, you have an obligation to measure analytically your team's output. There are several reasons for such due diligence. First, it is a good idea to review on a regular basis one's own assumptions about how fast certain tasks can be reasonably accomplished. Say you estimated that a data entry screen would take three days to complete, and it is now the fifth day and the programmer is nowhere near done. Maybe you were a little too aggressive in scheduling and so the next time you estimate the schedule for such a screen you should allocate more time. Maybe the programmer is just slacking off. Without continuous monitoring, you may never figure out which of these is true.

Second, you must measure your team members' performance to be able to answer a number of questions such as: Are they working as hard as expected? Are you paying them enough? Are you paying them too much? Have they encountered a problem you may be able to help with? Are you giving them enough to do? And so on.

Third, measuring productivity increases your ability to be fair by leveling the playing field for individual members of the teams. By comparing team members' performance to one another, you know whom to reward and how to best compose future teams for optimal performance.

Finally, perhaps the most important reason to employ productivity measurements is to provide you, the manager, with a feedback mechanism that measures your own effectiveness. In the absence of productivity measurements, your job may be likened to bowling in the dark. Imagine you are in a pitch-dark bowling alley and you are given ten balls to throw at some presumed set of pins. At the end of the session the lights are turned on and you are told that you had struck down 75 pins. Clearly, this information is useless. What did you do right to knock down these pins? What did you do wrong to miss some of the pins? Since visual feedback was not available during the match, you failed to learn from your mistakes and could not improve your aim.

Managing without measurements is likewise silly. The only indication of success or failure available to you without such tools is at the end of the project when it is already too late to do anything about it. Productivity measurements permit you to obtain immediate feedback while the project is going on, thus, turning on the lights in the bowling alley.

Yet, this business of productivity measurement is not at all obvious. I recall a conversation I had with a consultant at a nationally renown consulting firm. He was completely puzzled by my suggestion that performance measurement in software development is important. "Don't programmers all work as hard as they can?" he asked. Then he pondered: "Even if you were to determine that performance varies, what can you do about it?"

Well, anyone who develops software in a team setting knows that programmers do not always work as hard as they can. Even those who toil exhaustingly may actually produce more if they were to work a bit differently. In fact, programmers have as wide a set of working habits as any other profession. Some like to finish everything early and rest for the remainder of the project. Others like to procrastinate until a deadline is looming and then work around the clock to finish their assignments. Still others work very hard all the time but when you look closer, you find out that they are mostly spinning their wheels. And, then, of course, there are those programmers who do not work so hard but still manage to finish on time.

And, yes, there are things you can do about low productivity even in a professional setting. But these will be covered in the chapter on motivation.

MEASURING PRODUCTIVITY VERSUS GOOD MANAGEMENT

Before we proceed to discuss in details the methodology by which one can measure and monitor productivity, a word of caution is in order. Productivity measurements and ratio analysis do not, in and of themselves, make for good management. Rather they are merely one arrow in the manager's quiver that can, if used correctly, aid in the tasks of management.

The analogy can be drawn between productivity measurements and a car's dashboard instruments. These instruments help little in navigating the automobile or in steering it toward the desired destination. Rather, the driver must rely on other means, namely sight and sound for guidance and collision avoidance. In fact, the instruments are not at all necessary for the driver to be able to drive from point A to point B. But without instrumentation it is rather difficult to control other factors of the trip, such as the length of time it takes to complete the trip, or to ensure the car arrives at point B in good condition. Only with the aid of instruments can these other factors be achieved. In other words, the instruments provide vital but nonsufficient feedback to the driver.

Productivity measurements are like these automobile instruments. They provide crucial feedback so that correctly monitoring these measurements can ensure timely and problem-free delivery. Yet one should never make the mistake of trying to manage the project simply by virtue of productivity ratios. This, in essence, would be as foolish as trying to drive an automobile by instruments alone. An infamous example of such a management failure was the practice of measuring success in the Vietnam War by counting dead enemy soldiers. History tells us that this closely watched body count was perpetually increasing as we were progressively losing the war. In essence, no one in Vietnam bothered to look up from the dashboard to determine that the car was going backward.

As a manager, never make the mistake of substituting good management practices with the ratios and productivity measurements described in this chapter. Rather, use this material to complement the other tools you have in your possession.

WHAT IS PRODUCTIVITY?

Productivity is classically defined as output compared to input. In manufacturing, productivity is easily measured. One needs only to take the hours spent on manufacturing and divide it by the number of units produced to arrive at a versatile productivity figure. Financial types replace hours with labor cost to determine a dollar-per-unit-produced ratio but the idea is basically the same.

In software development measuring productivity is a bit more difficult because what constitutes output is not easily defined and, therefore, is hard to measure. Programmer productivity is not merely the amount of program produced but also the quality of the code and the satisfaction of the end user. Furthermore, it is not at all clear what it is that makes up a unit of software. Is it the number of lines written? The number of function points coded? The number of routines produced?

This is, by no means, a trivial problem. One should exercise extreme care in how one measures productivity since the outcome produced by the measured entity directly depends on how one measures this outcome. For example, if you were to measure the number of lines written, your programmers would soon realize that they can improve their standing by writing more lines of code. Therefore, routines that could be written in two or three lines are going to sprout additional lines. Likewise, lines that could be combined to save space may be intentionally broken up into their verbose components. On the other hand, if you were to measure function points instead of lines of code, you risk punishing those programmers who take on more complex functions. This, in turn, can drive team members to seek the less complicated work so as to improve their "productivity."

Visual Basic makes these problems a little less difficult since so much of the program is already *written* by the time the programmer sits down to work. Most of the hard work is already done and many of the remaining tasks are homogenous. Subsequently, a unit of output is more easily defined than in more traditional languages.

Nonetheless, Visual Basic productivity is still not as easily measured as manufacturing productivity. It is easy enough to measure input, say, hours worked, or, better yet, dollars paid. But there is no one factor for us to use that fully describes the entire range of a programmer's output. Instead we must consider a combination of outputs that, in turn, produce several productivity figures. These include:

Output: Source Code

- Lines of Visual Basic and/or SQL written[1]
- Lines of in-code documentation (comments) written
- Visual Basic routines and/or SQL stored procedures, triggers, and views written
- Data entry screens/reports fully developed
- Bugs discovered and fixed

Output: Quality

- Bugs discovered after release to the next phase
- Design changes requested by the user after release

Inputs

- Hours worked during the period of output
- Money paid for the period of output

These measurements are used to develop not one but a series of productivity indicators such that the various ratios correct for each other's shortcomings. What is hidden by one ratio is discovered by another and whatever undesirable effect one ratio has is discouraged by the other. This situation is analogous to the ratios financial analysts examine when they analyze a company. They have a variety of indicators such as price-earnings ratio, current account ratio, debt ratio, and so on, to determine how the company is doing. Likewise, we use the following ratios to determine programmers' productivity:

---

[1] SQL lines are used in this chapter to denote lines of code written on the database side of a three- or two-tier system. These include stored procedures, triggers, views, and other server-side code. If non-SQL databases are used, substitute the appropriate language name instead of SQL.

COST PER DISPLAY ENTITY (CPD)

$$CPD = \frac{Cost}{OutputEntities}$$

Where Cost = Money paid the team member for the period
OutputEntities = Data entry screens or reports fully developed

Measures:

- Productivity adjusted for level of expertise.

Advantages:

- Easy to compare output of different programmers since it is self-correcting for expectation levels (crack programmers are presumably paid better than junior programmers).
- Simple to measure.
- Corrects for *verbose* writing in the lines per hour (LPH) ratio (programmers who write a lot to increase their LPH ratio will suffer in this ratio).

Drawbacks:

- No indications of how well the screen was developed.
- Not very suitable for analytical functions that are screen poor.
- Not easily transferable between different locations due to different pay rates.

Typical Value:

- Between $2,000 and $5,000 per display/report (New York area rates).

LINES PER HOUR (LPH)

$$LPH = \frac{(VBLines + SQLLines + CommentLines)}{Hours}$$

Where VBLines = Lines of Visual Basic
SQLLines = SQL Lines in stored procedures, views, and triggers
CommentLines = Lines of in-code documentation written
Hours = Hours worked during the period of output

Measures:

- Sheer coding productivity.

Advantages:

- A simple ratio that everyone understands.
- Better suited to analytical code than the screen cost ratio.

Drawbacks:

- Requires incremental accounting (lines written and hours worked since the last measurement) and a good tool to count lines.[2]
- No indications of how well the application was developed.
- May encourage verbose writing and discourage use of ready-made objects.
- Does not correct for differences in output expectation. (That is, more is expected of high-paid programmers, yet this ratio ignores pay.)

Typical VB Values:

- Between 40 and 50 lines per hour.

COST PER ROUTINE (CPR)

$$CPR = \frac{Cost}{(VBRoutines + SPs + Views + Triggers + Views)}$$

Where Cost = Money paid for the work during the period
VBRoutines = Visual Basic routines
SPs = SQL stored procedures written
Triggers = SQL triggers written
Views = SQL views written

Measures:

- Productivity adjusted for level of expertise.

Advantages:

- Easy to compare output of different programmers, since it is self-correcting for expectation levels (crack programmers are presumably paid better than junior programmers).
- Encourages writing small routines and thus better maintainability.
- Encourages use of library routines as programmers get credit for a routine whether they write it or *borrow* it.
- Better suited for analytical code that is screen poor than the display cost ratio.
- Tells us if the programmer is correcting bugs as he goes. Otherwise routine productivity will drop as the project nears completion.

Drawbacks:

- No indications of how well the routine was developed.

---

[2] Visual Basic permits, in fact, encourages, saving program files as text files. This makes it easy to develop simple tools to count lines and tally them by type. However, there are no such tools on the market today.

- Not easily transferable between different locations due to differences in pay rates.
- Not easily measured. Need a program to extract the information.

Typical Values:

- Between $60 and $100 per routine (New York area rates).

CODE TO COMMENT RATIO (CCR)

$$CCR = \frac{CommentLines}{(VBLines + SQLLines)}$$

Where CommentLines = Comment lines written within the code
VBLines = Visual Basic lines of code written
SQLLines = SQL lines of code written

Measures:

- The level with which the programmer is documenting the code.

Advantages:

- Simple ratio that everyone understands.
- Encourages writing lots of comments.
- Normalizes comments output to code output so meticulous programmers are not penalized.
- A cumulative ratio. No need for incremental measurement to track progress.

Drawbacks:

- No indications of how well the comments are written. May some comments really be blank lines?
- No credit is given to people who go in to correct or enhance other people's code.
- Not easily measured. Need a program to extract the information.

Typical Values:

- Between 1/4 to 1/3 comment lines per code lines.

BUGS FIXED PER LINES WRITTEN (BPL$_{BR}$)

$$BPL_{BR} = \frac{BugsFixed}{(VBLines + SQLLines)}$$

Where BugsFixed = Bugs fixed during the time period
VBLines = Visual Basic lines of code written
SQLLines = SQL lines of code written

Measures:

- The programmer's diligence in fixing bugs as soon as they are found.

Advantage:

- Encourages fixing bugs as soon as they are found.

Drawbacks:

- Depend on the programmer to report the correct number of bugs fixed. You may have to create a little *bureaucracy* to accurately account for this number.
- Generates inaccurate results for non-steady-state situations. (Since the less code is written the larger this number, someone fixing another programmer's code without writing any new code will generate a huge number.)

Typical Values:

- Between 1/20 to 1/40 bugs fixed per code lines.

BUGS FOUND (AFTER RELEASE) PER LINES (BPL$_{AR}$)

$$BPL_{AR} = \frac{BugsFound}{(VBLines + SQLLines)}$$

Where BugsFound = Bugs found after release
    VBLines = Visual Basic lines of code written
    SQLLines = SQL lines of code written

Measures:

- The programmer's diligence in testing and fixing bugs.

Advantages:

- Encourages fixing bugs as soon as they are found and discourages release of untested code.
- Cumulative ratio. One number tells the whole story for the entire assignment.

Drawbacks:

- Depends on accurate reporting of bugs and correct fault assignment. May require a little bureaucracy to account for this correctly.
- Will cause tendency to hide bugs or to blame bugs on other people. Team cooperation destroyer.

Typical Values:

- No bugs after release should be acceptable.

COMPLAINTS REGISTERED PER COST (ECPC)

$$ECPC = \frac{Complaints}{CostOfModule}$$

Where Complaints = Complaints registered by the user
CostOfModule = The cost expended on developing the item about which the users complain.

Measures:

- Customer satisfaction.

Advantages:

- The only quantitative way to measure customer satisfaction.
- Self-correcting for caliber of programming talent.

Drawbacks:

- Subjective. Different users have different opinions and expectations.

Typical Values:

- No complaints are acceptable.

AN EXAMPLE OF HOW TO USE PROJECT RATIOS

	Routines	Total Lines	Code Lines	Comments	Screens	Code to Comment Ratio (CCR)
Module 1						
VB Code	777	24,835	20,775	4,060	23	0.20
Sybase Code	151	4,451	4,179	272		0.07
Help File		989		989		
Module 2						
VB Code	72	2,383	1,939	444	3	0.23
Sybase Code	22	790	724	66		0.09
Common Module						
VB Code	85	5,808	3,626	2,182		0.60
Total	1,107	39,256	31,243	8,013	26	0

Statistics

Project Start Date	22-Jul-94
Project End Date	5-Nov-94
Holidays	3
Workdays	73
Cost of Programmer	$54,750

Ratios

Cost per Display Element (CPD)	2,106
Lines per Hour (LPH)	67.2
Cost per Routine (CPR)	49

SHOULD THE RATIOS BE PUBLISHED?

A natural question to ask at this point is whether or not the productivity ratios should be revealed to the team on a regular basis. The answer is an unequivocal: It depends. Certainly the fact that you are collecting this information as well as what factors go into each measurement should be made public. First, it is only right and proper to tell each and every member of the team how he or she is being measured. Second, failing to tell team members that they are being monitored sows seeds of future discontent when they discover this fact for themselves.

I also believe very strongly that individual team members should be told their own ratio results on a regular basis. How else will they improve their performance if their productivity measurements are hidden from them?

But the question of whether or not members should be told of their colleagues' scores is not that simple. Human resources professionals would surely object to any such publication on the grounds that it would affect the expectation for reward distribution. That is, the guy with the highest overall score would expect the largest raise. Yet we have already discussed the fact that productivity measurement is but one aspect of overall performance and should not be the sole basis for reward distribution.

Furthermore, the impact of such *score keeping* on team spirit and cooperation is not exactly clear. Some would argue that score cards, public or private, could destroy cooperation. This is especially true if team members believe that by helping other members they risk improving the others' scores. After all, no one helps their friends cheat on, say, the SAT college entrance exams because another's success may turn out to be detrimental to one's own.

Then, again, others claim that the right type of productivity measurement actually induces cooperation since credit is given to team members whether or not they actually write the code by which they are being measured. From that perspective, team members may engage in a little I'll-scratch-your-back-if-you-scratch-mine type of cooperation. Code sharing is thus encouraged.

Moreover, if you are willing to set aside some of the risks discussed earlier, publishing the scores regularly can create a level of competitiveness among the staff that, on the whole, is rather healthy. If everyone strives to do the best in every category, the overall performance of the team would surely improve. Besides, the mere existence of a fiercely competitive environment may also improve morale and produce a fire-in-the-belly brand of excitement—aspects that are often missing from the mundane and boring setting of the average programmer.

I therefore must side with those who advocate publishing the scores of the entire team. What the heck? Make a big deal out of it. Promise prizes at the end of the project and such titles as the fastest programmer, the most efficient documenter, and so on. I suspect you will find that it will be much easier to motivate the team late in the project if they set their goal on such secondary objectives than without such competition. Just make sure team members understand that their compensation and promotions do not depend solely on productivity ratios.

CHAPTER 14

How to Motivate
the Development Team

Programmers are, for the most part, highly paid professionals who are often self-motivated. They, therefore, rarely present management with the type of motivational problems that are sometimes prevalent in other situations. In fact, many programmers regard the heavy-handed management associated with traditional motivational tactics as energy sapping. They much rather prefer to be left alone with broad guidelines and a well-planned schedule than to be micromanaged by others. Nonetheless, as a manager you will occasionally encounter some bad attitudes or undesirable work habits that you will have to confront. Hopefully, this chapter will help you do so effectively.

The practice of good people management is a goal that, typically, all managers strive to achieve regardless of the development environment. However, the rapid pace at which Visual Basic projects move makes people management more critical than it may be in more traditional development cycles. Just as a flat tire on a race car during the Indianapolis 500 is dealt with differently than a similar mishap on the family day trip, so must the resolution of motivational problems be diagnosed and solved differently in the rapid application development cycle.

Let us contrast the two environments to make this point clear. In the traditional, long-term, development environment, a manager usually tries to build team spirit at the onset of the project. This is often done in a variety of ways. In some teams everyone socializes together after work, or participates in extracurricular activities such as a softball team, or a hiking club. Other teams develop a coherent structure by nurturing an *us-versus-the-users* attitude whereby team members, encouraged by their manager, circle the wagons and help each other fight off the user onslaught of requests for features. This team spirit is commonly developed over weeks and months and aids in motivating the programmers to do what is right for the team.

Also, since the pace of traditional projects is somewhat slow, there is generally little, if any, attempt to measure real-time performance. Rather, the performance measurement tool of choice is always the project schedule as indicated by the Gantt or PERT charts. And since project progress is measured in weeks and months as opposed to days, any slip-up is easily detected in time to handle it, albeit not always in the correct way. (Note the horrific on-time delivery record of major retail software in the past five years. But that is another story.)

The bottom line is that when a motivational or performance problem springs up in this third-generation language (3GL) environment, there is often plenty of time to solve it. Most often, the method of choice is by either letting other programmers pick up the slack or by *reassigning* the problematic team member to lesser duties.

That is not to say that third-generation language projects are developed at a leisurely pace. On the contrary, these projects are often brutally hectic and require much management intervention to keep progress moving forward. Rather, the extra time afforded a manager to deal with performance problems comes from the inherent longer development cycle, not from any relaxed schedules.

Few of these third-generation management techniques apply to a Visual Basic project. A short project life cycle means that there is rarely an opportunity to develop team spirit. Progress must be measured in days and hours, rather than in weeks and months. Subsequently, it is harder to detect slip-ups. And the lean and flat structure of a VB project team means that a slacking team member cannot be easily reassigned. There are simply no other jobs to which this person may be assigned. Consequently, motivating individual team members right from the start of the project and monitoring their and the project's progress become critical issues in a typical VB project.

The monitoring task is perhaps the easiest of the two. We have already talked about how to measure individual performance in the chapter on performance ratios. Implemented correctly, these ratios can and will detect performance problems nearly instantaneously. To complete the picture, you must combine these ratios with a well-thought-out project plan that is graduated in increments of days and fractions of days. Identify and include in this chart a sufficient number of milestones so that you can flag a schedule slip as soon as possible. If you define your tasks by data entry screens, for example, mark a milestone for each screen to be designed, developed, and unit tested. Do not wait for an entire module to be completed before you detect a problem.

Motivating individual team members, on the other hand, is a much more challenging task. Getting other people to do what you want, especially when they do not agree with you, is difficult and time consuming. However, if you succeed, the accomplishment is extremely rewarding.

There have been many books written on motivational theory. A large portion of management training, whether in business school or in management training seminars, is dedicated to this subject. It is, perhaps, the most studied of all management disciplines since it is such a fascinating subject. After all, if we could devise a magic formula that could guide us on what we must do to make employees adequately perform their jobs we would have very little else to do. Unfortunately, to date, no such formula has been devised. The problem is not that organization psychologists cannot persuade mice to learn a maze by sprinkling some mice food at the desired goal. Nor is it that they cannot accurately document cause-and-effect scenarios in the workplace. The problem is that human beings are a diverse and complex bunch of animals that just refuse to fit themselves neatly into any single motivational theory.

I can spend the rest of this chapter discussing traditional motivational theory. Heaven knows, I have taken enough courses on the subject to make me a minor expert. I can talk about Maslow's pyramid,[1] theory X, Freud, and so on, but in my opinion, doing so will really be wasting your time. My experience tells me that very little of this material applies to the development cycle of a Visual Basic project. Sure, people need to fulfill their need to eat before they can sit to program, as Maslow's research suggests, but how many starving programmers do *you* know? That is not to say that motivational theory is not important. It is just that a typical crack programmer is so far removed from the average laboratory mouse along the evolutionary chain that conventional motivational theories fail to adequately address the complex set of issues he or she presents.

For example, it is hardly a secret that the average professional's passion for financial rewards is just as strong as anyone else's. So motivational theory may point to this money *carrot* as one of several incentives a manager might want to use to motivate a slacking programmer. Yet, in an environment where there is no shortage of work, little employer loyalty, and certainly no shortage of money, this incentive loses its motivational power. Likewise, the risk of dismissal is a lame threat for many of the same reasons.

I am trivializing motivational theory, of course, to demonstrate that what may be perfectly adequate techniques in other professions and industries do not fit very well the software industry and certainly not the VB development environment. So instead of reciting conventional wisdom, I will concentrate on passing to you some techniques that I have found, in the past, to be helpful in motivating programmers. Yes, I know, this is known as anecdotal evidence, and as any scientist would say: More than one anecdote

---

[1] Abraham Maslow (1908–1970) was an American psychologist and a founder of humanistic psychology who developed a hierarchical model of human motivation, in which a higher-level need, ultimately that for self-actualization, is expressed only after lower-level needs are fulfilled.

does not constitute data. But, then again, I do not claim to be a behavioral scientist, just a good manager.

A basic assumption I make in writing the rest of this chapter is that you have hired the best and the brightest programmers you could find and that you are paying them well. As we discussed earlier, the reason to hire the smartest programmers is to ensure project success. Naturally, you want to pay these programmers well so you will not lose them to a competitor. Well, as it turns out, by following these two rules you also reduce the number of motivational problems you are likely to experience. That is because highly paid professionals are often, but not always, self-motivated. They take great pride in their work and welcome any challenges their daily journey presents them.

Then, again, highly paid geniuses are hardly a day in the park to manage. Most have strong opinions about just about everything and nearly unchangeable work habits. You will more easily balance the U.S. budget than succeed in changing the mind of a crack programmer. There are ways, of course. To describe what these ways are, we must divide them according to several commonly occurring characteristics.

But before we begin, allow me to reiterate a very important point: Motivating programmers does not mean micromanaging them. On the contrary, attempting to cajole and manipulate an employee who is already well motivated is likely to have the opposite effect. Subsequently, if a team member completes her assigned tasks on time and with few problems, leave her alone. The suggestions I list here apply only when a team member fails to deliver on a consistent basis.

THE PRIMA DONNA (*LARGOS EGOS*)

This species of programmers is perhaps the most numerous among the well-paid developers. In fact, there are various degrees of prima donna characteristics in just about every programmer, with the best displaying the most obvious traits. You can spot a prima donna by looking around a suspect's work environment. Often you may find a poster saying something like "Damn, I am good" or "I am never wrong. I thought I was wrong once, but I was mistaken." When you ask a prima donna a question, the answer is often preceded by a barrage of insults to your intelligence such as: "Well, any low life, beginner programmer, elementary school graduate would know the answer to this question."

The prima donna's worst aspect, from a managerial perspective, is that he is good and he knows it. He suffers from an ego the size of the state of Texas. Consequently, he cannot be motivated with the promise of money or material goods. If you give him a raise or a paid vacation day for a job well done, he will not appreciate it because he believes he is entitled to it. If he refuses to implement one of your direct orders, he knows there is little you can do about it. He knows that people like him are hard to find and so you would not dare fire him for insubordination. He may even face you in meetings, directly contradicting your or another team member's opinion in the hope of showing how smart he is.

The prima donna also has a very low opinion of those programmers who have not proven to be as good as he is. He may, indeed, refuse to work with people whom he believes to be inferior to him in their mental abilities, which include just about everyone. For that matter, God help those whom the prima donna has decided are not worthy of being on his team. They will be ridiculed and embarrassed in public until they are either transferred or quit.

So how do you motivate the prima donna? How do you make him do something he does not agree with? How do you convince him to work harder, for example? The trick lies in understanding the prima donna's psyche. You should realize that he draws his arrogant tendencies from the fact that the rest of the world recognizes his special talents. If, from the first day you meet him, you refuse to acknowledge that you think any more highly of him than any programmer of average abilities, you will present him with the challenge of having to prove his ability to you. As such you will have him where you want him.

During the late 80s and early 90s Bill Parcell was the coach of the New York Giants professional football team. He successfully turned around a losing franchise and even won two Super Bowls. The team relied heavily on Lawrence Taylor, perhaps, the greatest linebacker to ever play the game. The problem with Taylor was that he was a prima donna. He was so good and faced so little competition matching his talents that he began to slack off in practice and risked not being prepared for games. Naturally, Coach Parcell could not get Taylor to prepare better, emotionally or physically, by withholding pay or by threatening to bench him for a game or two. Taylor was just too valuable to bench or lose to another team.

Instead, Parcell spent the week before big games talking to the press. He would say to reporters something like, "Taylor is getting old. He just doesn't have it in him any more." Or "running back so and so is going to make mince meat out of Taylor. He is no good any more." Or "Dallas is too tough for us. We do not have the talent to beat them." When Lawrence Taylor read these statements in the paper, he would become furious. He would get so mad that for weeks he refused to speak to Parcell. Yet the strategy worked. The more Parcell downgraded his talents in public, the better Taylor played. He just could not stand having the public think that he was not the greatest football player that ever lived.

You can motivate your prima donnas much in the same way. Depending on the degree of arrogance you experience, you can undertake various strategies. For example, if your developer answers your request with something like "a good manager would not make me do this," reply that "a good programmer would be able to accomplish this request in no time. He must not want to do it because he does not know how to do it." If he persists in his resistance, offer to send him to a training class on the subject. Nothing infuriates the prima donna more than the notion that someone else may know more than he does. If he slacks off in his work, point out how another team member finished the same amount of work in half the time (never mind that it was not the same amount of work).

But, whatever you do, never, never, never, acknowledge in public, while the project is under way, that you know the prima donna is good. And never reward him individually while the project is under way. Never praise him if he is present. Never say to his face anything other than how average you think he is. Instead, stick to team rewards. There will be plenty of time for reward and praise once the project is over.

Surely, this is very controversial advice as many people believe, and I am one of them, that praise and rewards are very important motivational tools. You can never praise someone enough. Indeed, praise and rewards are crucial when you deal with normal egos, but in the case of the prima donna they are useless. Remember, the prima donna knows he is good. When you praise or reward him, he does not see your actions as the results of his good work but rather as a deserved entitlement. These actions do nothing but swell his ego and compound the problem.

THE INSECURE PROGRAMMER (*CODUS INSECURUS*)

This character is the direct opposite of the prima donna in that her ego is smaller than the average programmer's and thus she does not believe in her own abilities. As a result she may shy away from taking on responsibility. An insecure programmer may give you a thousand reasons why she cannot accomplish what it is you are asking her to do. When she is finally convinced to take on a problem, she spends hours asking everyone how to do it. She may then procrastinate forever and may miss deadlines still *thinking* about the problem.

This does not mean that the insecure programmer does not have what it takes. She may, in fact, be an excellent programmer. Only she does not believe so, and so she lacks the confidence to move ahead with her assigned tasks. The first thing you should do, therefore, is determine the source of the insecurity. If you find out that the programmer is insecure because she truly does not know what to do, and that this fact surfaces over a number of different assignments, you must decide whether she belongs on your team.

A rapid application development effort is not the ideal training ground for someone on whom you depend to meet an aggressive schedule. It is perfectly acceptable to take on a new hire for training purposes only, but if the programmer is hired to be a productive member of the team, the apparent lack of skills and ability to learn will only hurt your effort. You do not have the time nor can you afford to spend the resources to train this person. Furthermore, other team members will resent having to *babysit* this individual and cover for her.

If, on the other hand, you determine that the programmer is capable of meeting your expectations, and that her insecurities are rooted in some other causes (perhaps a previous manager), you can remedy the situation, albeit not easily. You should realize that the hesitation the programmer displays in the face of a challenge is probably caused by a past experience where she suffered some adverse effects of failure. This could have been being fired for not meeting a schedule, or being humiliated in front of the rest of the team when an assignment was not completed on time. In other words, her fear of failure is paralyzing her.

The only way to solve this unfortunate situation is to make the programmer fear the consequences of inaction more than she fears the perceived consequences of failure. One way to do so is to clearly state that you *will* tolerate an occasional failure but that you *will not* put up with inaction. Enumerate as plainly as possible what will happen to the employee if she does not proceed on her assignment, and contrast that to what will happen if she does proceed but then fails. It is crucial that you follow up on these promises. If she tries and fail, praise her for trying and coach her toward success. But if she continues to procrastinate, follow up on your threat (whether it is dismissal, demotion, or whatever). By the same token, if the employee makes the effort and succeeds, you should make the experience as pleasant as possible. Praise her efforts to the rest of the team, buy her lunch, and so on.

This may not always work but if it does, it will save you the cost of hiring a replacement. As such, it is worth trying.

THE PROCRASTINATOR (*CODUS MAÑANA*)

This type of programmer is very similar in characteristics to the insecure programmer. Indeed, if the procrastinating tendencies are caused by insecurities, lack of ability, or a desire to avoid failure, you should deal with this character much in the same way you would with an insecure programmer.

However, the procrastinating tendencies may be caused by something completely different: namely, pure laziness. That is, the programmer does not want to work any harder than is absolutely necessary. He knows that if he completed his assigned duties prior to the scheduled date, he will be given other tasks. Subsequently, he paces himself so that his assignment will conclude just in time.

You can easily spot this tendency when you have determined that a team member is an excellent programmer but then you find him spending long hours in the smoking lounge or cafeteria, or taking two- and three-hour lunches. He does this until a day or two before an assignment is due. Then he works as hard as he can, often spending the night at the office, and just barely makes it by the deadline.

This may appear to be a tolerable situation since, after all, this employee does complete his assignment on time. Yet if you examine his performance closely, you will probably find that his work habits have caused him to compromise quality. Programming is a brain-intensive task that requires the developer to coherently think through every possible input and outcome. This is somewhat difficult to do when the developer is under the gun. It is even harder to do at three o'clock in the morning after he hasn't slept for two days.

As with the insecure programmer, the way to motivate this employee to work normally is to increase the pain level of procrastinating above that of having to accept more work. Sit down with the procrastinator and explain to him that his work habits are unacceptable. If he continues to wait until the last minute to finish his assignment you may have no other option but to relieve him of his duties. On the other hand, if he finishes early, offer to give him a paid vacation day or send him to an industry seminar. Use your productivity ratio analysis not only to ensure the developer is coding at an even pace but also to show him that you have a method of monitoring his work habits.

THE PERFECTIONIST (*ANNUS RETENTUS*)

Not that far removed from the procrastinator, the perfectionist has trouble meeting deadlines because she fears the consequences of completing her assignment. The difference is that the procrastinator is lazy while the perfectionist is not. She has trouble finishing her assignment simply because she meticulously spends countless hours ensuring that all the i's are dotted and that all the t's are crossed. She just cannot bring herself to hand in her assignment no matter how well done it is because she is afraid there is something she missed.

This characteristic is not necessarily all bad. Meticulous programmers have their place in the world, and if your project involves some complex algorithm, you will forever count your blessings for having a perfectionist on your team. Surely, you will also try to instill some perfectionist tendencies in all your programmers as you strive to build a bug-free application. The problem presented by the perfectionist arises only when she refuses to sign off on her assignment even though everyone but her believes she is done. Another instance that causes the perfectionist to become an obstacle is when you need a quick and dirty implementation for prototyping purposes and the perfectionist is just not capable of performing this task. The perfectionist is, in fact, a terrible prototyper.

Should you find yourself struggling with a perfectionist, your strategy should be to achieve your goal without destroying the perfectionist tendencies. One way to do so is to have a mutually agreed upon goal that is so specific so that the perfectionist cannot wiggle out of it. For example, get the developer to agree that she will turn over her work when the coding is done and you, acting as a tester, are not able to find a bug after three hours of testing. It is imperative that the developer agrees to this goal, in writing if necessary, because she will have to comply with it later. When the time comes, test the code and if it meets your mutually agreed upon goal, take it away.

Whatever you do, do not give the developer a choice of continuing to develop or test. If the code is not completed or properly packaged to be moved to the next phase, be prepared to deal with the programmer just as you would with any other member of your team who fails to meet his goal. Remember that the developer herself agreed she could meet this goal so you are not being cruel. You are just trying to affect her behavior so she understands that trying to be perfect cannot be rewarded unless she produces a product at the end.

On the other hand, if the perfectionist meets her goal, praise and reward her for her timeliness and not just for her quality code. You want to positively reinforce her newly acquired skill of *letting go* and not her already cultivated tendency to be perfect.

THE ROOKIE (*NUVOUS CODUS*)

Few things in life are more invigorating than watching a kid fresh out of school become acquainted with the corporate world. The enthusiasm for the job and an idealistic, sometimes naive, disposition, combined with a complete and reckless disregard of family, friends, and personal life, makes for a very, very motivated team player. The rookie is the ultimate employee. He will walk through the proverbial wall for you if you just ask. He may often glow for days just because you stopped by his cube to discuss a technical issue, thus, giving the impression that you value his opinion. And he will produce mountains of code for next to nothing in compensation.

Obviously, the rookie displays few motivational problems. However, his inexperience can bring about two potential problems due to the nature of the rapid application development environment. The first potential trouble spot arises from the fact that the rookie is not adept in operating within a political environment. It is easy, therefore, for other, more experienced operators to make minced meat out of him. Second, he is not seasoned enough to be able to identify many technical issues more veteran players tend to take for granted. It is not that the rookie is technically inept. On the contrary, some of today's college graduates know more about computer science than we veterans will ever fathom. It is just that he has not been programming long enough to let certain shortcuts develop in his way of thinking.

Corporate politics is perhaps the bigger of the two problems. Every time you send the rookie to meet with users, present materials to top management, or deal with the bureaucracy, you risk dampening his enthusiasm. And much in the same way the new graduate would work for three nights in a row to finish an assigned task, he may also stay home for three days sulking over something some nincompoop purchasing agent told him while he was trying to requisition a modem. It is crucial, therefore, to shield the rookie from any and all outside influences. Under no circumstances is the new hire to deal with any corporate bureaucrat or users. Assign someone more experienced to get his pencils, requisition his computer equipment, get user sign-off, and so on. Only after a year or so should you let him venture, slowly, into the quagmire we call the corporation.

As far as technical experience, the rookie may know all there is to know about the latest memory management techniques but he may not realize, for instance, that the users are perfectly willing to sacrifice memory capacity for speed. He may, therefore, make the wrong design decisions as a result and spend unnecessary time and effort to improve memory capacity instead of moving on to more important tasks.

To remedy this situation, it is wise to pair the rookie with a seasoned veteran who will act as a mentor. This experienced individual should be given the role of complementing the rookie's enthusiasm with a little sensibility and a notion of historical events. As such, the veteran should review all design decisions the rookie makes and suggest ideas that may not be technically pure but are sound, nonetheless, in view of current reality. By the same token, the rookie can teach the veteran a thing or two about the latest academic research. It is a winning combination. Be careful, though, not to permit the mentor to micromanage the rookie to the point of draining his energy.

Most importantly of all, do not forget to praise the rookie every chance you get (if he deserves it, of course). A good word here and a pat on the back there is as good as a hefty salary raise to a more experienced programmer. As such, it is an excellent motivational tool.

THE ASPIRING MANAGER (*CODUS MCBETHOUS*)

A somewhat difficult character to manage is the person who has decided she wants to be a manager. Normally, this situation is not at all undesirable in a corporate environment since ambition is considered to be a semibeneficial trait. Unfortunately, in the rapid development environment you cannot afford this person the opportunity to get the necessary exposure or to be groomed for a management position. You need total and absolute concentration on the job at hand without any distractions.

The aspiring manager is likely to resent this situation. She starts to think that she would make a better manager than you are. Sooner or later she may even begin to undermine your position, going behind your back to your boss complaining about your management style or decisions.

The best way to defuse this situation is to find out from the start what the personal goals of your team members are. Sit down with each and discuss with them their career plans. If you find a person who tells you that she would like to be promoted to a management position within six months to a year, you found the aspiring manager. To deal with this correctly, you need to be dead honest with both her and your own manager about the situation. If you deem her management material and you believe she is worth keeping, you need to apprise your boss of this situation. Ask to relieve her of some of her technical responsibilities in lieu of assuming a role as your part-time assistant. Explain that the purpose of this move is twofold. First, it allows her to be trained for management while identifying a place for her in the organization. Second, it opens up the position to be filled by a full-time programmer.

If your boss declines this proposal, or if she is not worth the effort, you need to go back to the aspiring manager and tell her that her goal is not achievable within the time period she envisioned. Aside from being the ethical thing to do, you must be honest with her because her next move has direct implications on your project. If she decides to leave, you will be short a programmer. If she decides to stay, she will be demotivated and a drag on productivity. In some situations you may even be able to strike a deal with the employee, although do not advertise it to the company. Tell the aspiring manager that you will assist her in getting another job if she keeps you informed on the status of her job search. Ask her to give you at least a four-week notice, for example, in exchange for a letter of recommendation. Regardless of how you choose to handle it, make sure she knows that slacking performance will not be tolerated and is not part of the deal.

Despite the difficulty of this situation, you are basically making the best of an otherwise hopeless situation. Dealing with the situation in this manner is a win-win proposal not only for you and the aspiring manager but also for the company. After all, you are trying to minimize the damage of losing an employee at a crucial stage in the project. You may actually be pleasantly surprised to find that you had defused the situation since the aspiring manager no longer feels trapped. Her morale will improve and her performance may not suffer. And who knows? You may need her in the future as a contact in another company. At least you have not parted as enemies.

Obviously, there are many more personality types. Actually, most programmers will present a combination of some or all of these types or an entirely different set of characteristics. However, I think you get the gist of my motivational philosophy: Motivate people by finding out what buttons make them tick and then push these buttons appropriately.

CHAPTER 15

What Is the Visual Basic Development Paradigm?

Most managers who follow traditional development models fail to capture much of the time savings that a development environment such as Visual Basic provides. Thus, a new model is needed. This chapter presents a new such development paradigm that better fits the Visual Basic rapid application development cycle.

The rapid application development paradigm that will be presented here is quite a departure from some more traditional models. Take, for example, a typical precomponent model that most development teams follow—the cascading waterfall. This model depicts the development process as a series of cascading waterfalls, each immediately following the other. Analysis and specification represent the first fall, followed by design, followed by development, followed by testing, and finally ending in the implementation, and, presumably, a serene pond.

The cascading waterfall model has two distinct characteristics: First, each stage of the development process—each individual waterfall—must be completed before the next step can begin. Second, there can be no entry in the middle of the process. Modifications to an existing system cannot happen unless the process is started at the top of the waterfall.

The cascading waterfall model actually represents fairly accurately the life cycle of a noncomponent project. By its very nature, such development is a serial process so any other approach could be disastrous. In a world that measures system development in months and years, in which no quick prototyping technique is available, and in which changes to one part of the system can cause irreparable damage to another, it is best to develop software

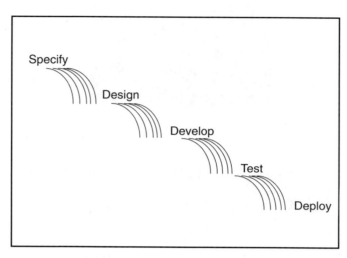

Figure 15.1 *The cascading waterfall model*

the way one builds buildings. That is, the process must have a beginning, a middle, and an end and follow rigid rules in between. The entire set of requirements must first be gathered before any steps are taken toward implementation or the implementation may be wrong. When the specs are all in, all the design decisions have to be made lest the code will not stand its own weight. And, of course, all code must be written before the system can be tested since the system is not really operational until the very last bit of software is custom fitted.

Alas, the cascading waterfall paradigm (see Figure 15.1) is ill suited for component-oriented programming. In fact, any attempt to manage a component-oriented development process using the waterfall paradigm prevents management from reaping many of the benefits provided by rapid application development tools. Why spend months, for instance, writing and rewriting detail specifications when a complete prototype can be developed in days or weeks? Even the most finicky user, who may change his mind numerous times about where exactly the OK button should appear, will not slow down prototyping in Visual Basic enough to justify a complete specification process.

By the same token, why wait until the system is done to test it when major components can be tested and certified much sooner? And why wait until the system is installed to gather feedback from users? Component-oriented programming means that such traditional necessities of development management no longer apply. Specification, design, development, and testing can all be done on a component basis and, thus, much earlier in the process.

That is not to say that total system integration and total system testing are not necessary. They are absolutely essential, and do not let anyone tell you otherwise. However, I am merely suggesting that by the time each component has been built and tested using rapid application development techniques, any other work that still must be accomplished is substantially diminished.

Also, in deriving a new model, I am not seeking the elimination of the traditional steps of software development. I am merely suggesting that the scope of each step has changed, and, more importantly, that the order by which each step is undertaken is no longer crucial. For example, requirement analysis and design specifications are as important in the component-oriented world as they have been in the noncomponent world. The difference is that the specifications no longer have to be written with as much detail and they do not have to cover such items as the user interface. To fully specify a VB system it may suffice to list only the edit and validation rules, the functionality description, and the definitions of any analytics, whereas in days gone by such specification would only scratch the surface. This shrinking of scope is due to the fact that by using VB, the user interface and program flow are much more easily prototyped than specified. And once prototyped, of course, the development process is well under way saving months of writing and *word smithing*.

Similarly, by using VB, the design and development of major components can be started as soon as their individual specifications are completed instead of waiting until the entire system specifications are completed. By contrast, such a *jumping-the-gun* approach would have been very risky in traditional software management since in such environments the entire system is fully integrated so any errors in designing one module can ripple through the whole system. There is no such danger in VB. Components are largely independent and so any minor changes to the specs as a result of other components' design can easily and quickly be incorporated into the already started modules.

In fact, the reason Visual Basic is considered a rapid application development tool is precisely because a project using VB need not follow the cascading waterfall model. By using Visual Basic, a serial development process can be turned into a concurrent or parallel process, significantly shrinking the concept-to-desktop cycle.

To capture the features of component rapid application development (C-RAD), we need a model that better predicts the C-RAD development cycle. The model I propose resembles the Olympic Games symbol of five interlaced rings, and so it is named the Olympic rings model.

The Olympic rings model (Figure 15.2) consists of five interlocking processes: specification, design, development, testing, and implementation.

1. *Specification* means gathering and analyzing user requirements and publishing edit and validation rules, functional needs, and analytic definitions.
2. *Design* involves devising a database schema and a module layout as well as constructing screen and report prototypes.

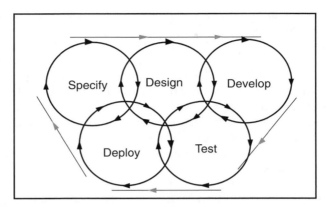

Figure 15.2   *The Olympic rings model*

3. *Development* includes filling in the code behind the prototype and the assembly of different components, off the shelf or home grown, into a cohesive system.
4. *Testing* means the deliberate search for bugs and other problems with either individual components or the entire system, and the process of fixing the bugs.
5. *Deployment* involves installation in the field, training, and documentation.

The Olympic rings model graphically depicts the unique nature of the C-RAD development environment through several distinguishing characteristics. First, the model does not show a series of phases. Rather it models a series of cycles which, in and of themselves, also constitute a single large cycle. System development, thus, is a continuous process rather than a linear path between two points. I once heard someone refer to this as *protocycling*.

Second, the model has no starting point. A project can begin at any point along the rings. For example, a project can start from the testing phase. Components, especially off-the-shelf components, can and should be tested as soon as they become available on the market. Once certified they can be incorporated into the design and development phase. In fact, some of the more advanced software shops I work with support a so-called strategic group whose only job is to explore newly marketed third-party tools, test their viability for future products, and certify their quality.

Likewise, a project can start in development, or prototyping, if you will, and move back to the specification and design phase. This is especially useful in migrating legacy systems where an old, mainframe system can be quickly prototyped in VB to construct a benchmark from which changes can be specified.

A third unique feature of the Olympic rings paradigm is backtracking, or the ability to move back and forth along two adjacent rings without disturbing the overall flow of the project. This is no more apparent than in the specification and design phases when the development team and user team continuously reshape the prototype to fit the needs of the user. Of course, some people may notice that this backtracking ability had always existed in earlier models. Debugging, for example, always meant looping back and forth between development and testing. What is new is how extensive the backtracking feature can be—applying to all phases of the project and not just testing—as well as the expanded range of issues that can be handled without any adverse effects.

Notice, however, that despite the versatility of this model, there are certain paths one cannot take. For instance, one cannot move back from implementation directly into development. The path must include design and, possibly, specifications, or, if backward movement is desired, testing. This means that should the users still see a need for improvements after installation, new specification and design phases must be initiated. Conversely, if bugs were to be found during installation, the testing phase should be fired up again to initiate a bug fix. And, likewise, the path from development to implementation should always include testing as there is no feasible way to move between the two phases directly.

The cyclical nature of this model, combined with component-based tools, and the continuous process pattern, permits and in fact encourages parallel development. Specifications, design, development, testing, and to some extent, implementation can all be taking place simultaneously, albeit, not necessarily while working on the same component. And so, while developing a single business system, specification of an Accounts Payable module can be initiated while the design and development of Accounts Receivable is well under way, and all the while, testing of Payroll is going on.

Documentation has been purposely placed in the implementation ring. Unlike traditional development techniques where the documentation phase may start as soon as the specifications are written, in the C-RAD environment, changes in the looks and functionality of the system may occur very late in the project life cycle. Consequently, it is prudent to try to delay documentation until the system is *frozen* and is about to be installed. Naturally, training should also be undertaken at the end of the project but this is not really a change from the traditional way of doing things.

Some commercial application developers such as Microsoft, for example, freeze the look and feel of a system early in the development cycle allowing documentation to commence earlier than usual. Microsoft can afford to do this because its software development efforts are not exposed to the user community. It is, therefore, not subject to user pressure to modify an application that is still in development. Such luxury is hardly afforded the majority of software development teams, most of whom work in very close proximity to the end user and whose funding depends heavily on user sign-offs. Subsequently, change requests and modifications are to be expected right up to the release date. This situation, although not at all desirable, is a reality one must contend with and, thus, documentation should be one of the last phases for any given module. Of course, component technology allows for piecemeal documentation, which makes this problem less severe.

TQM VERSUS TESTING AS A SEPARATE FUNCTION

Those of you who are familiar with the concept of total quality management (TQM) may question the need for a separate testing ring. The principles of TQM as developed by Deming[1] and his disciples suggest that quality should be built into the product and that responsibility for the product's quality should, therefore, lie with the person who is building the product and not with some outside functionary. Over the long run, the theory goes, the process of continuous improvement, or, in other words, the process of self-correctness eliminates the need for testing as a separate activity. After all, testing is not a value-adding function. The testing activity may be necessary but it is hardly value-adding in the sense that it cannot be sold for profit. As such, the idea of total quality management is to gradually diminish the need for testing and thus improve return on expenditures.

The concept of TQM and its implications on software development will be further explored in the chapter on testing and quality control. For the purpose of this discussion, though, suffice it to say that I agree with the ideals of total quality management wholeheartedly, but I do not believe that software testing will become redundant anytime soon. It may very well be that testing and quality control duties will be shifted from being a separate function to becoming part of the developer's duties,[2] but that does not mean that testing will disappear. Even in the component-oriented environment of VB, software development depends heavily on individual decisions and actions. Perhaps even more so than in any other manufacturing activity. And since to err is human, to test is necessary. The testing ring stays!

AM I ADVOCATING CHAOS?

Finally, the ideas expressed in this chapter are somewhat radical and so some readers may not find it possible to fully comprehend their benefits. Instead of

---

[1] Edward W. Deming, 1900–1993, was an American statistician and quality control expert. Deming used statistics to examine industrial production processes for flaws and believed that improving product quality depended on increased management-labor cooperation as well as inproved design and production processes. He greatly influenced Japanese industry as it rebuilt in the postwar years and was often critical of U.S. corporate management.

[2] The fact that some MIS departments practice cost cutting by eliminating the testing function and shifting the quality control responsibilities to the user does not make the effort conform to total quality management. The elimination of quality control functions without proper training and adequate resources only further exacerbates quality problems rather than solves them.

the traditional orderly and organized development process that can be neatly graphed and monitored, the Olympic rings model suggests chaos. Anything can happen at any stage, the project can start at any place, and movement can go forward or backward. What kind of management is that?

Two observations may help put things in perspective. First, the Olympic rings model does not mean poor planning and scheduling. It merely portrays the latitude and flexibility provided by C-RAD tools. As such, it is just a road map. And like a road map that shows a complex and seemingly tangled web of roads leading from everywhere to everywhere, the Olympic rings model is meant to be used to plan a best-path approach to a particular project. Managers who use the Olympic rings model should, therefore, not be overwhelmed by its fluidity but rather be able to exploit the model's flexibility to produce fast results. In other words, the fact that one can move back and forth from development to specification does not mean one *must* to do so. It is up to the manager to decide whether such a feature should be exploited, how many times the loop should be taken, and at what point the project should move on. This is a vast improvement over more traditional models that provide no such flexibility.

Second, C-RAD is inherently a somewhat hectic process. Events happen very fast in this process compared to older methods. Hence, C-RAD management must be disciplined, well organized, and quick to respond. To paraphrase Tom Peters, the famous management guru, management must be able to *thrive on chaos* (or what to the untrained eye appears to be chaos). If you do not possess such an ability and if you lack the traits listed previously, you may not feel comfortable using the Olympic rings model. In such a case, by all means, resort to the cascading waterfall model until you feel more comfortable taking some of the shortcuts afforded by the Olympic rings model.

CHAPTER 16

How Visual Basic's Reduced Scope of Specifications Saves Money

Among the savings one can achieve as a result of using Visual Basic is the vastly reduced scope of any required specifications. That is because VB specifications more closely resemble an assembly document than they do the detailed blueprint of more traditional development. Before the project is even started, major components are already built and need not be specified from scratch. The application's look and feel is also virtually specified through the prototyping stage. All that remains to define is how the different components work together, the data elements involved, and the overall functionality of each element of the application.

Yet the temptation to create a traditional specifications document is immense, mainly because of three reasons. First, we all tend to stick with the tried and proven so we find it difficult when it is no longer necessary. Many of us learned to program in environments that are much different than Visual Basic where extensive and detailed specifications are not only nice but absolutely necessary. Without detailed specifications we have no idea what the user wants or needs. Therefore, we try to draw the wrong analogy to VB even though such detailed specifications may be superfluous.

Second, specifications have always been viewed as the focal point of the project. From a good set of specifications, the adage goes, one produces a great application, commendable in-code documentation, good testing scripts, and an excellent set of manuals. Traditional software techniques even call for coding around the specifications, that is, starting with the specifications and placing bits of code after each line, thereby avoiding the need to independently insert comments in the code.

Finally, and most important, detailed specifications are a great tool for covering one's back side in a highly treacherous bureaucratic environment. If every detail of the user requirements is written down and the user signs off on the specifications, then a black-and-white document exists that can be produced every time the users pretend they asked for something else. And, I must admit, there is a lot to be said for a device that properly covers one's back side in today's corporate setting.

Nonetheless, in most settings, fully detailed specifications are not technically necessary for a successful Visual Basic project. For the most part, specifying every single detail of the design is a waste of time. So no matter how tempted we are to engage in the process of completely specifying every single aspect of the application, we should not do so.

Before you think me unreasonable, let me point out that there is one exception that may present a perfectly valid need for detailed specifications. This exception is a consulting firm or software house that builds *custom* systems for other companies. If you work for or own such an entity, you know that detailed specifications are the only written document you have to prove that what you eventually deliver is what you are being paid for. In essence, the specifications become part of the contract. In such situations detailed specifications are still not technically required but may be essential from a business and legal perspective. This is very unfortunate as it prevents certain efficiencies from being realized.

But aside from this one exception and the previously mentioned need to cover one's back, full-blown specifications are hardly needed. Instead, I recommend a skeleton specification consisting of the following four parts:

1. Function Definitions
2. Prototype
3. Data Dictionary
4. Entity Relationship Diagram (for database applications)

These four entities are designed to fill in the blanks that exist between the already completed or available components. They are derived from the fact that a business application consists of three elements: the user, the database, and the computer program that interfaces between the two. How the user interfaces with the application is defined by the function definitions (step 1). What the application looks like is determined by the prototype (step 2). How the application interfaces with the database is defined by the data dictionary (step 3). And, finally, what is held in the database is modeled by the entity relationship diagram (step 4). The user acts as the anchor from which we start (see Figure 16.1).

Figure 16.1   *We can specify only four out of five system elements*

THE FUNCTION DEFINITION

Naturally, any specification process must start with the user, and as such, users represent a fixed point in space. Therefore, the first question that must be asked is what the users' needs are. This question is usually answered by a one- or two-sentence *big answer* that can be further qualified by a series of subanswers. For example, the users may need a system to keep track of their investment portfolios (big answer). This includes an ability to add, delete, and modify financial instruments, record dividends, buy and sell additional shares, calculate current market value, and so on. The complete set of big and qualifying requirements as well as any equations and process definitions represents the function definition.

To develop a good function definition, painstaking analysis is required. This is the process by which the users lay on the couch and tell the business analyst all their problems and their dreams. Analyzing the requirements also means visiting the end users environment and actively seeking everyone's ideas. This analysis process culminates by listing all user functional requirements. At this stage, analysis should avoid any user interface issues. Finally, the resulting document should be visited again and again as the users discover other needs during the prototyping stage.

Note that if the application is replacing a legacy system, you need only list the current functionality and any incremental changes in the function definition.

PROTOTYPE

Once the functions are nailed down, prototyping is the next logical step. In Visual Basic prototyping means actually designing each screen and putting the screens together to show flow and edit modes. This replaces the screen drawing and interface definition of days gone by and is much more powerful. Whatever design decisions are made can immediately be incorporated, viewed, and tested.

It is imperative that user representatives be present during this process and that they take an active roll in the design. In the absence of detailed specifications, building a prototype is just not practical without the users. What data fields are to be shown? Where should they reside? What terminology should be used? These are all questions that must be answered by a living, breathing user.

I must admit, however, that there are quite a few people who feel very uncomfortable with active user involvement at this stage. These people agree that user input is important but would rather not have the user actually present during design. They believe that if the users are allowed to participate too closely, they are likely to exert pressure on technical issues over which they should have no control. Also, many people are convinced that users should not be exposed to how easily the user interface can be crafted lest they start to question the need for programmer involvement.

Even though I somewhat agree with these views, I do believe that a good project manager can prevent the inclusion of the users from becoming a pitfall. Such a manager can draw stringent enough boundaries around the users to preclude them from overstepping their responsibilities. This means clearly stating such ground rules as adherence to design and programming standards. If such steps are taken, the users can actually be of great help in this stage bringing into the design process insight that is rarely available to the technical staff.

Little bits of information such as "Oh, don't worry about this field, we never use it anyway" or "We need the stock ID at the top of the page because we change that number often," are precious to a successful user interface design. Furthermore, a user that has helped to *sculpt* the application, so to speak, is more likely to have bought in on it and is much more likely, as one of its creators, to help sell it to the rest of the community. Were we to exclude the users from this process, they would view themselves as mere customers who have no say in the design. They would, therefore, feel little pain if the development effort were to be abandoned or the application would not be accepted by the rest of the user community.

As mentioned earlier, it is perfectly acceptable to go back and forth between the prototyping stage and the function definition as new needs are discovered during prototyping. It is hardly unusual, especially for new applications, for the users to discover that they have forgotten some requirements or that there is an inconsistency in the requirement definitions. Without early user involvement, this usually happens when the product is released rather than during specifications. Hence, the ability to prototype the product greatly increases the chance that such revelations will be made earlier in the development rather than later.

DATA DICTIONARY

Once the prototype is completed, you should possess in your hands two elements: a working shell of a program and a written description of its purpose and the purpose of its individual parts. The next step involves collecting the displayed data field from the prototype and each calculated data field you anticipate from the function definitions. Prepare a questionnaire for these data fields so that you can meet with the user representative and fill in the blanks. Create a database of the following information for each data field:

Item	Obtained From	What is it?
Screen Label	Prototype	What label is given to this data field?
Screen(s)	Prototype	What screens does the field appear on?

Item	Obtained From	What is it?
Description	User or Legacy System	A concise description of the displayed field.
Legacy System Label (optional)	Legacy System	What is the equivalent field name on the legacy system, if such exists?
Control Name	Prototype	What is the name given to the screen element (control) that holds the data in VB?
Data Type	User or Legacy System	Is it a string, integer, float, etc.?
Display Size and Format	User or Legacy System	For numbers: digits and decimals. For string: number of characters. For currencies and dates: the exact format.
Control Type	Prototype	Is this a text box, list box, etc.?
Default Value (optional)	User or Legacy System	What default value, if any, should be automatically entered into the field?
Minimum Value (optional)	User or Legacy System	What is the lowest value that can be entered for this field?
Maximum Value (optional)	User of Legacy System	What is the highest value that can be entered for this field?
Allowable Values (optional)	User or Legacy System	For list boxes and others, what are the allowable values for this field?
Required/ Optional	User or Legacy System	Is the field required or optional?
Calculated or Memorized?	User	Is the field calculated or memorized, or both?
Database Name (If memorized)	To be filled in later on from the schema	What is the name given the data field in the database?
Data Table (If memorized)	To be filled in later on from the schema	What table does it reside in?
Calculation Formula (If calculated)	User	How are the data calculated?
Cross Validation	User or Legacy System	Does the validity of the entered value depend on other elements on the screen? How?
Status Line Message	User or Legacy System	What should be displayed on the status line when this field is entered?
Edit and Validation Rules (other than data types, max., min., and allowable values)	User or Legacy System	Are there any specific edit and validation rules other than data type enforcement, range check, and allowable value check that should be performed?
Validate on Exit or Save?	User or Legacy System subject to good software design standards	Should the validation rules be checked when the user exits the field or upon attempting to save to the database?

A few examples of how this works are shown at the end of this chapter.

ENTITY RELATIONSHIP DIAGRAM

The last part of the specifications is the entity relationship diagram. Having collected all the required data fields during the earlier steps, you now hold most of the information you need to design the basic entities and their relationship in the database. This is not really a final database schema. You cannot produce a final schema since you are yet to decide what database to use. You have not decided on a database because you have not finalized the specifications and requirements of the system. Subsequently, you are yet to uncover specific nuances of the database that may affect a schema. But creating a first draft of the schema—an entity relationship diagram—at this point is very important. It serves three specific purposes:

1. Constructing a data model defines the relations between database elements. For example, the fact that an investment portfolio is really a collection of other financial instruments may not be easily discernible to a programmer who is not familiar with the industry. An entity relationship diagram defines such a dependency. In essence, the entity relationship diagram serves as the road map between the different data elements and, thus, becomes an essential specification tool.

2. Defining the data model also uncovers any relational inconsistencies that are not immediately obvious in the previous three phases. In a sales database application, for instance, a customer contact may be first thought of as an integral part of the customer record. But what if the contact changes companies? Would it not be better if the contact information was independent of the customer, linked to it in a one-to-one relationship? This relational *bug* would not and could not have been uncovered from the prototype, user requirement, or data dictionary. Only an entity relationship diagram can reveal such inconsistencies.

3. Finally, drawing a schema, even a preliminary one, is a great technique to expose any need for additional data fields or attributes—fields that help in audit trailing or securing access to the database, for example. These may include timestamps, userstamps, access codes, and so on. This is also a good time to finalize indexes and keys, making the most out of user input.

Remember, though, that this schema is a fluid working document and is not a final design. It is perfectly acceptable to move back and forth between it and the data dictionary, or even all the way back to the function definition, when an inconsistency is discovered. That is, if a prototype screen is discovered to hold information that is better placed somewhere else, the prototype should be changed accordingly. It is precisely the purpose of this exercise.

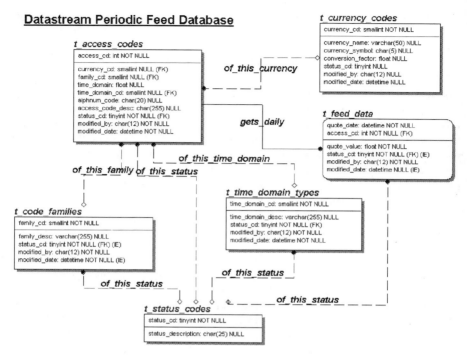

Figure 16.2 *Example of a very simple entity relationship diagram*

At the end of the process you should have a fairly good road map of the data that is consistent with all the other supporting entities—the function definition, prototype, and data dictionary. (See Figure 16.2.) This road map is not the final database schema, as we have already mentioned that such depends on database selection. However, it is a pseudo-schema that is sufficient to complete the picture painted by the other design documents.

SIGN OFF

Having ironed out all the bugs and inconsistencies in all four specification articles, you must now obtain user and management approval for the entire package. This sign-off process is crucial to the success of the project because based on this design you will be setting a schedule, determining a budget and staffing requirements, and making many other managerial decisions. Approved specifications, thus, become a base case from which deviations can be measured. Later on in the process, if a user requests additional features that were not provided for in the original specifications, the effects of implementing such features can be stated in terms relative to the base case: "Yes, we can add the new dialog box you requested but it will take an additional two days and cost $7,500. Is that OK?"

In the absence of formal approval, the user could claim he never would have signed off on a version that did not contain his desired feature. Or, worse yet, the users may question the schedule slip-up and cost overrun since they never understood what they were getting for their money in the first place.

A refusal to sign off is, therefore, a big warning sign. The users may not want to approve the specifications because they disagree with them or they believe that the specifications are not complete. If such is the case, you must work to correct the problem and continue to iron out the details until the specifications satisfy the users.

But if after resolving all their complaints, the users are still reluctant to approve the specifications, you may be walking into a trap. An unwillingness to make a commitment to the application typically signals trouble. It probably means that the project is too risky or that it is not entirely clear what the final product should look like. Either way, it is a no-win situation for you that will most likely result in a career suicide. Proceeding to develop an application that has no champions supporting it should, thus, be avoided at all costs.

VERSION CONTROL

Once approved, all four elements of the specifications must be version-stamped and put safely into storage by your favorite version control application. Both Microsoft's Source Safe and Intersolv's PVCS perform an admirable version control job for files of many different types. You can, therefore, store away in one project and under a single version number the written documentation, the prototype program, the data dictionary database, and the entity relationship diagram.

As modifications are requested and approved, modify the specifications through the version control application. This ensures a commonality of terms for the development team and the user community. Everyone knows what version 1.3 of the specifications entails and everyone works toward that goal. By the same token, earlier versions can be easily retrieved and compared to the current version to show the effect changes have had on the budget and schedule.

Examples of data dictionary items follow.

EXAMPLE OF A STRING DATA FIELD

Screen Label	First Name
Screen(s)	Customer information entry, shipment, order entry
Description	Customer's first name
Legacy System Label (optional)	N/A
Control Name	txtCustFirstName
Data Type	Variable length string

EXAMPLE OF A STRING DATA FIELD (continued)

Screen Label	First Name
Display Size and Format	25 chars
Control Type	Text Box
Default Value (optional)	N/A
Minimum Value (optional)	N/A
Maximum Value (optional)	N/A
Allowable Values (optional)	N/A
Required/Optional	Required
Calculated or Memorized?	Memorized
Database Name (If memorized)	sCustFirstName
Data Table (If memorized)	tblCustomers
Calculation Formula (If calculated)	N/A
Cross Validation	N/A
Status Line Message	Enter customer's first name
Other Edit and Validation rules	Name must contain only letters
Validate on Exit or Save?	Save

EXAMPLE OF A NUMERIC DATA FIELD

Screen Label	Price
Screen(s)	Order entry
Description	Sales item price
Legacy System Label (optional)	Price
Control Name	txtPrice
Data Type	Currency
Display Size and Format	8.2
	$X,XXX.XX
Control Type	Text Box
Default Value (optional)	0
Minimum Value (optional)	0
Maximum Value (optional)	N/A
Allowable Values (optional)	N/A
Required/Optional	Required
Calculated or Memorized?	Memorized
Database Name (If memorized)	cPrice
Data Table (If memorized)	tblInventory
Calculation Formula (If calculated)	N/A
Cross Validation	N/A
Status Line Message	Enter unit price
Other Edit and Validation rules	N/A
Validate on Exit or Save?	Save

EXAMPLE OF A LIST BOX TYPE DATA FIELD

Screen Label	Title
Screen(s)	Customer information entry, shipment, order entry
Description	The customer title
Legacy System Label (optional)	N/A
Control Name	cboTitle
Data Type	String
Display Size and Format	N/A
Control Type	List box
Default Value (optional)	Mr.
Minimum Value (optional)	N/A
Maximum Value (optional)	N/A
Allowable Values (optional)	Mr., Mrs., Miss, Ms. (Take from table tblTitles)
Required/Optional	Optional
Calculated or Memorized?	Memorized
Database Name (If memorized)	sTitle
Data Table (If memorized)	tblCustomers
Calculation Formula (If calculated)	N/A
Cross Validation	N/A
Status Line Message	Enter unit price
Other Edit and Validation rules	
Validate on Exit or Save?	Exit

CHAPTER 17

Database Selection, Design, and Connectivity

At the heart of most business applications is the database. It is an electronic depository where data are stored and with which the application interfaces to add, modify, delete, and report information. While more traditional languages require a considerable effort to fully integrate a database with the application, such integration is much simpler in Visual Basic and other RAD tools—such as PowerPoint, for instance. The database is simply viewed as another component and, thus, treated no differently than a file I/O or screen display.

Of course, the *database* component as referred to in this chapter encompasses not just the data warehousing facility but also a set of tools to extract, view, and manage data. In its most technologically advanced form, such a database component is actually a *data server.* It can be accessed from a local or wide area network and it permits interaction with a wide variety of applications on or off the network. From this perspective, a database component does not only store and manipulate data but also provides gateways for other applications to store, retrieve, and modify data.

The following discussion concentrates on the most advanced of such database servers—those fitting into the client-server paradigm. By definition, therefore, the databases we review here can operate as freestanding applications. These databases run independently of any other application they serve and are not necessarily terminated when the client application is exited. Furthermore, development and some diagnostics can be done directly on the database as well as through clients.

That is not to say that a database server *must* be a separate entity residing on its own network node. Some of the databases discussed here can live quite happily on the same machine as the client application, never knowing that a network even exists. However, since this book concentrates on business applications, non-client-server databases are less relevant. Thus, the focus of this chapter will be database servers. More precisely, we will cover the issues that affect choosing a database application and the decisions that go into the database design and implementation.

MULTITIER ARCHITECTURE

To be able to intelligently discuss client-server database architecture, we must first define some terms. The application that presents the data to the user is the *presentation application*. Editing, addition, and deletion from the database handling as well as calculations are known as *business processing*. A *single-tier* application (as shown in Figure 17.1) is one in which the database, the presentation application, and the business processing application are one and the same.

If the presentation application performs its own business processing and communicates with a database server directly from one or more locations, it is considered to be a *two-tier* arrangement, as in Figure 17.2. In such a setup the server usually resides on a different network node than the applications.

An arrangement that includes one or more processing applications residing between the presentation apps and the database is known as a *three-tier* design. If in a three-tiered design there are several databases and several processing applications on different network nodes, it is considered to be a *three-tiered distributed* design, as shown in Figure 17.3.

All mainframe applications are single tier. Client-server applications can be single or multitiered.

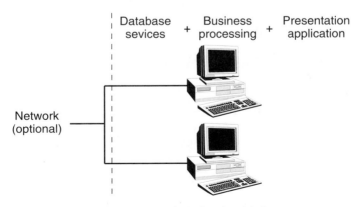

Figure 17.1 *Single-tier host-based design*

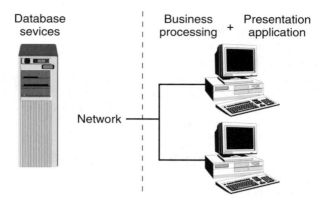

Figure 17.2   *Two-tier client-server design*

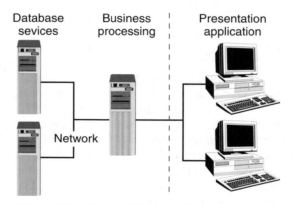

Figure 17.3   *Three-tier distributed client-server design*

DISTRIBUTED COMPUTING:
WHERE TO PROCESS THE INFORMATION?

Back in the days when the mainframe ruled supreme, host-based systems were easily designed because the database, business processing, and the presentation application all resided in the same "box." It did not really matter in the grand scheme of things whether the functionality of such a single-tiered application was accomplished by the database, processing program, or by the presentation program. The three entities shared the same processor so from a performance point of view, very little would have been achieved by shifting the workload from one side of the application to the other.

In the client-server world, where we strive to improve performance and flexibility by distributing processing across many CPUs, things are not so simple. This is because it has never been clear exactly how such distribution should be accomplished. As a result, data processing professionals are perpetually engaged in discussions—actually, heated arguments—as to what is the best way to break up distributed processing.

One group of people, we will call the *server-siders*, advocate that as much processing should be accomplished on the server side of the network, leaving the client PCs free to manipulate graphics and run local applications. This camp seeks to capitalize on the relative inactivity experienced by the server's CPU. Such idle time can be harvested to perform transactions and calculations. Furthermore, increased performance can be easily achieved by upgrading a single machine as opposed to every client. Finally, server-side processing minimizes network traffic since only the results of transactions and operations are sent to the client, rather than the entire data set.

On the other side are the *client-siders* who hold the view that all processing is best done on the client machines and that the server should provide only data services. Their contention is that servers are slow machines that were bought some time ago for their storage rather than computing capacity. These machines are, therefore, not easily upgraded for performance. In fact, since servers continue to serve their purpose long after their performance is surpassed by newer machines, no one bothers to keep them up to date. Compared with the typical servers, client machines are newer and faster and are regularly upgraded as software requirements dictate. Also processing can be achieved much faster if it is distributed and thus done in parallel rather than the serial manner in which the server CPU must work. Thus, the client-siders claim that more efficient processing can be accomplished on the client's box.

Who is right? Who knows? The truth obviously lies somewhere between these two extremes and so the best solution is clearly a combination of the two views. Unfortunately, there is no general-purpose analysis I know of that can reveal exactly where to draw the line between server processing and client processing. So much of this design decision depends on the hardware being used, network performance, the number of nodes, security requirements, and so on. And since all these factors are constantly in flux—software is constantly upgraded, hardware is hauled in and out, nodes are added and removed—there is no guarantee that the design decision made today will be the correct one tomorrow.

So what is a good manager to do? If you choose one approach over the other, you risk having the system made obsolete by new technology. For example, if you place all processing at the client side, you may miss out on advances in database technology and vice versa. Should one fall back and punt? Not necessarily. You may be able to side-step this whole dilemma by taking a conservative strategy. In other words, stick with the same old boring, not-necessarily-optimized, true-and-tested solutions that everybody else is implementing. Deploy the standard client-server design under the assumption that if the industry changes, it will at least make changes that are backward compatible to your solution and so you will not be left hanging high and dry. We will call this the golden rule of client-server design.

This *standard* architecture usually involves performing business processing mostly on the client side but allowing the server to perform all transactions—add, delete, modify. A detailed technical description can be obtained from any one of the number of books written on client-server database technology. It will be further discussed for the remainder of this chapter as well as the chapter on security.

SELECTING A DATABASE

The first decision of the design process is which database to use. In the past, choosing a database for a business system was easy. If you were a conservative MIS manager, you went with the latest and greatest from IBM. Since the proprietary software you were purchasing dictated hardware (and *vice versa*,) you also needed to buy an IBM mainframe. Actually, the only decision you were left to make was how big a machine to buy. So maybe you went with a System 360 as hardware, and DB2 as the database, and then hired a whole lot of CICS programmers to write a whole lot of COBOL-like code. After all, you could never be fired for making the *right decision*—the decision everyone else in the world was making. And, so, life was swell.

If, on the other hand, you were the risk-seeking type and little valued your job security, you might have gone with a solution offered by one of IBM's seven *little dwarfs* competitors. Or maybe you were not the suicidal type but your company was cheap and would not put up with IBM's proprietary merchandising that conscripted clients for life into the IBM family ("glad you have joined our family—now hand over your wallet"). So instead of an IBM, you went with, say, Digital Equipment Company's VAX 780 or 8600 machine on which you installed a Datatrieve database and hired a whole lot of Datatrieve programmers to write a whole lot of COBOL-like programs. And life was groovy.

But now things are different. Not only is the choice of hardware a separate decision from the choice of database but now hardware and software architecture must also be considered. Not to mention the fact that the two applications must typically be developed in two different languages. One application is needed to handle the database and another to manage the presentation (data entry, reporting, searching, etc.). Of course, you must worry about where processing will take place (see earlier discussion). And if life were not already difficult enough, you must also choose from a long list of different database applications all claiming to be the be-all-and-do-alls of the database world.

Luckily, however, we remember the golden rule of client-server design. Therefore, we strive to stick with a proven working solution that will not come back and bite us later on. Such an approach confines the choice to only a few products. Here we will cover three of these: Microsoft Access version 2.0 or later, Sybase System 11 or later, and Microsoft SQL Server version 6.0 or later (SQL is commonly pronounced *sequel*).

All three of these products are *relational databases* or RDBMS—Relational DataBase Management System. Being relational means that data can be defined in relation to other data. For example, suppose you are compiling a national telephone book. A nonrelational, or flat, database design means that each row of data contains name, address, including city name, and zip code. But this is somewhat wasteful since there is an obvious relationship between address and zip code. In fact, similar cities often have the same zip code. And so, do we really need to store what is in fact redundant information? The answer is no, we do not. A relational database allows us to create a relationship between the zip code and the city name and store one of these only once. So if you list names by addresses, the database can then go and fetch the appropriate zip code from the associated zip code lookup table. In fact, even the city name need only be stored once and be pointed to by an index. After all, 1654 takes up much less space (4 bytes) than Indianapolis (12 bytes).

Clearly, RDBMS technology saves an enormous amount of space by reducing the need to store redundant or duplicate information. Unfortunately, there is a performance price to pay for the relational approach. Every time the database *flattens* a relationship tree, some amount of additional processing is required. Flat, or nonrelational, databases do not have such overhead and so they are much faster than their relational cousins.

So what is more important: speed or relational representation? Well, remember the golden rule of client-server design: The primary concern of management should be choosing a database that minimizes business risk. A relational feature in a database is generally the single most important aspect of reducing such risk. The relational feature gives developers the flexibility to bend and twist a database so as to optimize both storage space and access speed. A nonrelational database only allows speed optimization. Hence, as the amount of data grows, the relational database grows linearly while a flat database grows exponentially. In the long run, relational databases reduce costs and, thus, risk.

For the purposes of this discussion a new type of database known as an *object database* is being completely ignored. First, object databases are too new and unproven to be viewed as candidates for the golden rule solution. More important, however, they present the same type of a trap that object-oriented languages do. Namely, the added cost due to the increased complexity involved far exceeds the benefits they may provide.

SMALL-APPLICATION DATABASES

For stand-alone or limited usage data applications, I suggest going with Microsoft Access 2.0 or later. Examples of such an application may be laptop computer databases that salespeople can take to the field and with which they can upload their collected information to the corporate data server. Another example is an information system for branch offices or customers into which a portion of the central database is downloaded. (This non-real-time application may be necessary to prevent customers from tying up central communication lines with frequent access to a somewhat static database.)

Is Microsoft Access the best product for these applications? Afraid not. Is it the fastest? Not really. Is it the most efficient? No. So why go with it? Because of the golden rule, of course. We will never regret developing with a Microsoft product. It may not be the best now but it will always be supported and, with time, will become the standard of the industry.

Besides, MS Access supports many good features that are irreplaceable not only in operations but also in user accessibility to the data. It is a superb data extraction tool and by far the easiest system for end users to employ in manipulating or reporting data. Microsoft wizard technology makes querying, reporting, and screen displays a cinch even for the most computationally challenged among the user community.

MS Access includes an all-purpose database engine (called the Jet Engines for reasons that are far beyond my comprehension). Jet is very nicely integrated into Visual Basic. It is actually billed as an all-purpose ODBC database that can talk to just about any database connected through an ODBC driver. ODBC or Open Database Connectivity is technology developed by Microsoft to allow communication through a translator to any ODBC-compatible database. ODBC proves handy when one must access various databases all with the same presentation app, for example, constructing complicated queries that join Sybase tables with MS Access tables to produce a seamless result. By doing so, one can move common data elements to a centralized database (Sybase) while keeping location-specific data on the desktop (Access).

Unfortunately, at the moment, MS Access itself is not an ODBC database. However, this deficiency is not a problem for Visual Basic since it talks directly to the Jet Engine. Another shortcoming of MS Access is that it rapidly becomes less usable as the number of users increases above, say, one. It is, therefore, extremely limited as a database server even though it is an excellent client tool for other central database servers. Finally, Access's security mechanism is somewhat lacking, a fact that makes the application vulnerable to attacks from, if no one else, the audit department.

Given these limitations, I have found that in the client-server environment Access is best employed solely as a querying or reporting tool or as a local support database for a single-tier system. In other words, it is wise to develop an application using Sybase or MS SQL Server as the backbone database server but then have the application or the users use MS Access to produce ad hoc reports or to query the real database.

LARGE CLIENT-SERVER DATABASES

For true client-server applications, Sybase System 11 or Microsoft's SQL Server 6.0 are the databases of choice. These two products have common ancestry. Earlier versions of both products were developed by Sybase and marketed under a joint marketing agreement with Microsoft. Since then, Microsoft and Sybase had a falling out that caused these two products to diverge. (The two companies have started talking to each other again so who knows what will happen next?)

Even though these two databases are no longer exact replicas of each other, they are similar enough that for the purpose of discussing managerial implications I will treat them interchangeably and will call both products SQL Server. Actually, this is no big sin since both products still have a very similar look and feel with Sybase leading in the performance arena while Microsoft concentrates its efforts on functionality. From a business perspective, however, I do believe that SQL Server is the better of the two products because of—yes, you guessed right—the golden rule. When it comes to database architecture, the object of the game is to survive and not necessarily to have the most technologically advanced system. At the moment, Sybase is experiencing a drop in profit margins that brings into question its long-term viability. Microsoft, on the other hand, is having no financial problems whatsoever. Hence, my preference is for MS SQL Server over Sybase. Then, again, Sybase is far from declaring bankruptcy so I may be just playing Chicken Little.

SQL Server is a full-blown relational database management system that can hold and manage multiple databases simultaneously. Each SQL Server database includes the following elements:

Tables	Collections of columns of data. Each column is referred to as a field.
Stored Procedures	Elements of customized code that manipulate the data and which reside on the server. The code is written in SQL (Structure Query Language), which is a universally standardized database access language. SQL is used by a variety of databases and is nonproprietary. Some basic stored procedures are supplied by the vendor.
Views	Predefined queries written in SQL and stored on the server.
Trigger Procedures	Procedures that are associated with tables and that are executed automatically whenever certain actions are taken. For example, an INSERT statement into table X may trigger a procedure to check if the values being inserted are valid.
Rules	A set of definitions regarding edit and validation rules for each field in the database.
Indexes	Just as the name implies, a way to quickly locate a table entry by first looking into an index table. SQL Server indexes can be composed of a single field, that is, Customer's Last Name, or be clustered together, that is, Last Name and City Name.

SQL Server also has its own security and policing mechanism, administrative tools, and logging and backup techniques. But, by far, the best feature of SQL Server is its ability to act, as its name implies, as a server for client applications. SQL Server can be a node anywhere on the system, residing on a variety of different platforms (PCs running Microsoft Windows NT or SUN Sparc UNIX machines). In fact, SQL Server's strongest feature is its ability to manage simultaneous requests from multiple users. Subsequently, the clerical department in New York can be entering new accounts payable information while the management team in London produces reports all from the same database.

As a large-application RDBMS, SQL Server has three shortcomings. First, a single server can service a lower number of users than traditional mainframe databases. Although this number is growing all the time, it is still somewhere between 30 to 100 users at any one time.

Second, the amount of data any one element in a distributed computing environment can hold is limited under SQL Server. This is not really a function of storage device capacity as much as it is the ability of random access memory (RAM) to swap quickly huge amounts of data in and out of storage. Consequently, SQL Server is yet to be able to handle a very large number of transactions with reasonable speed. It is, therefore, not a good choice for such applications as check transaction processing systems, large stock trading systems, or any other system that handles millions of transactions daily.

Both Sybase and Microsoft are aggressively pursuing the large-transaction throughput market by developing a feature called *replication*. True replication means that multiple machines automatically update each other instantaneously allowing database processing to be distributed in different locations. Replication, thus, facilitates the networking of many SQL Servers, thereby allowing piecemeal processing of a large number of transactions. If replication succeeds, the transaction limitation such as the ones described earlier may be eliminated. Suppose, for example, that your system is to process 3,000 transactions a minute, transaction 1 through 1,000 can be handled by server A, 1,001 through 2,000 by server B, and the rest by server C. When all three servers are done processing their portions, they automatically update each other to reflect all 3,000 transactions.

This brings me to the third deficiency of SQL Server: True replication does not yet exist. Instead, limited functionality allows for read-only replication. In other words, only one server processes all the transactions while the other servers listen and automatically update when the master server is done. This is great for backup purposes but it falls short in large-transaction throughput processing.

Furthermore, unless I am missing something, true read-write replication is logically impossible. Just think of a simple example that clearly demonstrates this paradox: Two customers in two different locations place an order for a certain item at exactly the same time. The inventory database shows one item remaining before the first order is received. If a single database server is used, the orders will arrive serially. Consequently, the slower of the two customer reps taking the order will be told to wait while inventory is updated. She will then be able to see that the item has been sold from under her and inform the customer accordingly. Most likely, when the dust settles, the first order will be confirmed while the second will be put on back order.

But now let's look at what happens in a distributed server environment. The orders are received in parallel by two *different* servers so both customer representatives see one item remaining. Both systems then try to fulfill the order at the same time leaving a total remaining inventory figure of negative one. This is, of course, a physical impossibility as well as a customer relations disaster.

And so, without true replication, large-transaction processing must rely on, gasp, a mainframe database. Luckily, however, there are various products available that provide a gateway between traditional databases and the client-server environment. Sybase, for example, is currently marketing the Sybase Open Database environment that provides for accessing any type of database through a SQL Server-like interface. Such a setup provides an adequate, albeit, not perfect, solution until client-server technology addresses the weaknesses of SQL Server.

MIDDLE LAYER

This is a good point in which to unveil some of the magic behind client-server technology. Client applications do not communicate directly with the database server in a client-server configuration. Rather, they communicate by proxy through the network software. This network proxy program consists of a small application on every client machine that sends out network requests and listens for any arrivals. Among other tasks, it is responsible for *stuffing, addressing,* and *sending* the envelopes containing packets of data and then opening these envelopes and distributing the information.

Likewise, a client-server database also requires a network library program residing between it and the network program. The job of the network library is to make the local client process believe it is talking to a local database. It does so by assuming all the network-related tasks, thereby relieving the client application of such responsibility.

If an application must access several different databases in one session, open database technology is an option, that is, a mechanism that acts as, or at least, appears to be a central depository for several databases. Microsoft's Open DataBase Connectivity (ODBC) protocol is just such a device. It provides the translation mechanism by which the application program can communicate with a variety of different databases through an all-understanding interface. This interface resides between the database and the application and consists of two parts: The first, the ODBC engine containing the interface routines, plugs into the application. The other, the database-specific ODBC library containing the translated commands, plugs into the database via the network. The ODBC library is provided by the database vendor while Microsoft provides the ODBC engine.

Even if you have no need for multiple database access, you can still use ODBC as a communication layer by instructing it not to translate the commands being sent to it. This is known as using ODBC's PassThrough capabilities. Certain aspects of SQL Server absolutely require PassThrough since they involve postrelease add-ons. That is, the translator can never understand new data types the developer defined in the database, or any of the stored procedures that run on it. Obviously, such entities were unknown to the vendor when the ODBC library was being developed. You must therefore use the PassThrough capabilities whenever you call a stored procedure or expect to receive data of a user-defined, data type variety.

Alternatives to ODBC include native database interfaces such as Sybase's DBLib or Microsoft's VBSql that do not have any translating capabilities.

When the application issues a command to the database—say SELECT * FROM TABLE_X—the ODBC engine receives this request first. It then standardizes the request in the ODBC language and, together with the database-specific library, uses the information to convert the request to something the database understands. The network library now takes over and prepares the request to be sent to the right database address on the network. It then hands over the whole package to the network software, which, in turn, divides the requests into appropriate packets and attaches a network destination address to each. It then sends each packet on its merry way. (See Figure 17.4.)

A few microseconds later, the database receives the first packet. The network software on the server side opens the envelope, so to speak, and hands the contents to the database network manager. This guy waits for all the packets to be received to complete the entire request and then sends it to the database. The database carries out the requested query and sends the results back to the client. The entire cycle now starts again, only in reverse.

INTERFACE WITH A VISUAL BASIC APPLICATION

A Visual Basic program can communicate with databases in a variety of ways. Since VB is a component-based development environment, any database vendor can provide its very own database communication component. In this section, however, we will concentrate on the three most prevalent middleware technologies: ODBC, the Jet Engine, and VBSQL (not shown). Using any of one of these three mechanisms, Visual Basic can talk to the database in three ways. The most flexible but complicated method is through calls to APIs (Application Programming Interfaces). This is because ODBC, Jet, and VBSQL are really just dynamic linked libraries, and so VB can call their respective routines through the Windows messaging system. To open a database through ODBC, for example, VB can call a routine named SQLConnect that resides in ODBC.DLL.

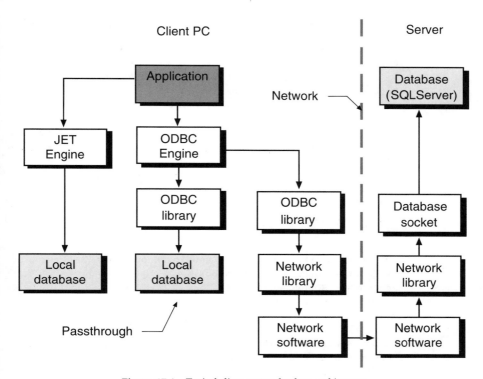

Figure 17.4 *Typical client-server database architecture*

Unfortunately, this is not as easy as it sounds. There is a myriad of memory allocations and error-checking tasks that must take place for this connection to work correctly. The actual code is shown in Figure 17.5 and is a good example of the level of complexity required in using this method.

```
Function fncOpenDatabase(hEnv&, hdbc&, Dsn$, _
                         Uid$, Pwd$, DbName$) As Integer

    Dim RetCode%
    Dim ConnectString$

    ' allocate environment
    RetCode% = SQLAllocEnv(hEnv&)
    If RetCode% = SQL_SUCCESS Then
      ' allocated database
      RetCode% = SQLAllocConnect(hEnv&, hdbc&)
      If RetCode% = SQL_SUCCESS Then

        ' Set login timeout to 5 seconds
        RetCode% = SQLSetConnectOption(hdbc&, _
                        SQL_LOGIN_TIMEOUT, LOGIN_TIMEOUT)
```

Figure 17.5 *Example of an ODBC connect routine using API calls*

```
If RetCode% = SQL_SUCCESS Then

  ' create the connection string
  ConnectString$ = "dsn=" & Dsn$ & _
                   ";uid=" & Uid$ & ";pwd=" & Pwd & ";"
  RetCode% = SQLConnect(hdbc&, _
             Dsn$, SQL_NTS, Uid$, SQL_NTS, Pwd$, SQL_NTS)
  If RetCode% = SQL_SUCCESS _
                   Or RetCode% = SQL_SUCCESS_WITH_INFO Then
    fncOpenDatabase = True
  Else
    subReportSQLError "Could not allocate a database"
    RetCode% = SQLFreeConnect(hdbc&)
    RetCode% = SQLFreeEnv(hEnv&)
    fncOpenDatabase = False
  End If
  Else
    subReportSQLError "Could not set login options"
    RetCode% = SQLFreeConnect(hdbc&)
    RetCode% = SQLFreeEnv(hEnv&)
    fncOpenDatabase = False
  End If
  Else
    subReportSQLError "Could not allocate a database"
    RetCode% = SQLFreeEnv(hEnv&)
    fncOpenDatabase = False
  End If

Else
  subReportSQLError "Could not allocate an environment"
  fncOpenDatabase = False
End If

End Function
```

Figure 17.5 (continued)   *Example of an ODBC connect routine using API calls*

Incidentally, this example may look complex but it is a walk in the park compared to what you would need to do were it not for the ODBC interface
package. Nonetheless, we can still do better. This is because Visual Basic
allows databases to appear like any other component. In version 4.0 of VB,
databases can actually be OLE objects. Subsequently, communication with a
database is just slightly more complicated than communication with a list
box or a combo box. Specifically, a built-in component that is part of the professional addition makes the act of communicating with the database almost
trivial. There are, of course, other off-the-shelf components (custom controls) you can purchase should you find the built-in database object lacking.

For example, the connect routine shown previously in Figure 17.5 looks like the following using the built-in professional edition database object:[1]

```
ConnectString$ = "dsn=" & Dsn$ & _
                 ";uid=" & Uid$ & ";pwd=" & Pwd & ";"
Set MyDatabase = OpenDatabase(ConnectString$)
```

This one line of code does everything the previous example does including error handling. Of course, other database tasks are also easy to accomplish. A program to display the last names of people in the database may look like this:

```
SQLStatement = "SELECT LastName FROM CustomerTable"
Set MySnapShot = MyDatabase.CreateSnapshot(SQLStatement)
MySnapShot.MoveFirst
While Not MySnapShot.EOF
      MsgBox MySnapShot("LastName")
Wend
MySnapshot.close
```

If this is still too complex, Visual Basic provides yet another way to interface with the database. It is known as *bound database controls*. Unlike the database object that is part of only the professional edition, bound controls are part of every Visual Basic installation. Also, unlike the previously described methods, this one requires no code whatsoever. To display a database object you need only place the database control on the form and then *bind* or associate with it the text boxes and list boxes on that form (hence the name *bound controls*). The records in the database are automatically displayed in the bound controls once you run the program and are ready for updating. In a sense, this is like opening up a window in the application directly into the database.

Bound controls are a revolutionary concept that is amazingly simple to implement. Alas, the limitations of currently available databases make this method not yet ready for commercial application. The problem is that it is too simplistic for the complex requirements of real software development. Lack of adequate security mechanisms combined with the inability to validate or manipulate the entered data prior to database updates make bound controls nearly unusable for any commercial application. It is, however, a great prototyping tool.

ODBC VERSUS VBSQL AND DBLIB

As mentioned earlier, if ODBC is used only in PassThrough mode, it provides similar functionality to other available database access tools. Two such

---

[1] These examples are taken from Visual Basic version 3.0. This syntax is still supported in version 4.0, but it is highly recommended to use the newer syntax provided in the new version.

tools include VBSQL and DBLib. VBSQL is sold by Microsoft while DBLib is marketed by Sybase. Both provide API support very similar to the API capabilities of ODBC run in PassThrough mode.

Using these native middleware packages improves performance over ODBC. This is because these alternative methods do not pay the penalty ODBC has to pay due to the translation and multidatabase overhead. Unfortunately, neither VBSQL nor DBLib provides component-like interfaces. This shortfall requires the user to develop the complex type of API calls demonstrated earlier in the chapter.

PESSIMISTIC VERSUS OPTIMISTIC LOCKING

Whenever a situation exists where multiple users access a single database, there is always a possibility that two users will change, or at least attempt to change, the same record simultaneously. To solve this problem, one can choose from various standard solutions. The least flexible, most secure method is to lock any database record that is being so much as browsed by any user. This is called *pessimistic locking* because the application assumes the worst. It assumes that if a record is being accessed, it will most likely change. In other words, if John Smith brings up the inventory record for available widgets, no one but John Smith can change the record. If John now goes to lunch for two hours while the record is displayed on his computer, the record is unavailable to other users for the entire two hours. If John goes on vacation . . . well, you get the idea. Incidentally, this locking occurs even if John never intends to change the record.

Even though pessimistic locking seems on the surface to be an asinine way of doing things, it actually has some very valid uses in the real world. Since it is very simple to implement, pessimistic locking is actually not a bad solution for high-speed, high-volume transaction systems. In other words, your bank's check processing system might access only a single account out of millions of accounts for a few milliseconds at a time. Consequently, the chances that two different processes will hit the same account at the same time are slim. But even if this happens, the time the second process has to wait for the record to be unlocked is very short. It is, therefore, perfectly acceptable to use a pessimistic-locking technique with such a system.

Optimistic locking, on the other hand, does not lock the record until it is actually changed and ready to be written. Contrary to pessimistic locking, this technique assumes that browsed records will not change. Our friend, John Smith, can now freely take a three- to four-hour lunch without hurting his colleagues' ability to change the number of widgets in the database. Alas, this is not a perfect world. When John returns from lunch he sees the same number of widgets on his computer that were there when he left. We know that this is now an erroneous number because *we* did not go to lunch and saw other people change this number. But John knows no such thing. When a customer calls to place an order for three widgets, John enthusiastically sells her an amount that may or may not be in inventory.

One way to solve this problem is to let John's computer know that the displayed record has changed since he first retrieved it. This can be done by periodically comparing the displayed record timestamp to the one in the database. When the two timestamps do not match, the user should be alerted.

DATABASE DESIGN

Keeping the database design simple is probably the single most important aspect of sound database programming. Other rules include:

DESIGN THE DATABASE TO MATCH APPLICATION DESIGN. Determine ahead of time the maximum number of users, total number of records, and performance requirements of the system and select the appropriate database accordingly. The last thing you wish for is that your otherwise beautiful, user-friendly, fully functional, and easy-to-use application is tossed aside because your database ran out of capacity.

NORMALIZE THE DATABASE SCHEME. Normalizing a database means taking full advantage of its relational capabilities. It is a highly technical term that would take the better part of this book to explain. Subsequently, I will forgo explaining it here. (A short explanation resides in the glossery at the end of this book.) Normalizing the database doesn't just save you resources but it also makes it very easy to change and expand. Suffice it to say that no data should ever be redundant or duplicative if the database is fully normalized.

USE DESCRIPTIVE NAMES. In other words, don't abbreviate. Since we no longer have to worry as much about memory, it makes absolutely no sense to abbreviate or encrypt entity names. The emphasis should, therefore, be placed on ease of maintenance even if this means *wasting* memory. An innocent reader looking at the code should not have to decipher such things as CurCnt or LNm. Instead, CurrentCount and LastName will do just fine.

Also make sure the name is descriptive enough and not too generic for people other than the developer to understand. For example, the field name Item is not abbreviated and its meaning is well understood but it indicates very little about what it is supposed to represent. So changing it to Inventory-Item is much better.

USE THE HUNGARIAN NAMING CONVENTION. The Hungarian Naming Convention is a standard by which any entity (variables, tables, indexes) is prefixed by a letter code indicating its type. This convention makes it easy to read, understand, and maintain code since the reader never has to refer to the declaration section in order to know what he is dealing with. Here are some suggestions for database design:

Database Entity Types	Prefix	Example of Entities
Tables	tbl	tblEmployees
Indexes	idx	idxEmployeeNumber
User-Defined Stored Procedures	usp	uspGetEmployee-Number
Triggers	trg	trgValidateSelect
User-Defined Views	uv	uvLondonEmployees
Rules	rul	rulTakeStringOnly

Database Data Types	Prefix	Example of Variables
Integer	int	intEmployeeCount
String	str	strEmployeeName
Double	dbl	dblSalary
Date	dat	datHireDate

INDEX EVERY TABLE. Indexes improve database performance substantially. It is crucial, therefore, to index every table using the fields that are most likely to be used in searches.

NEVER USE NULLABLE FIELDS. Being *nullable* means that a value does not have to be initiated for that field. The data entry clerk might, for example, leave the middle initial of a full name blank when he enters an employee name that has no middle initial. Understandably, in this case, it is tempting to make the middle initial field nullable. The problem is that some databases cannot index on a nullable field. Furthermore, most languages do not do a very good job of reading nulls. Subsequently, the application has to first test every retrieved variable before any attempt to display it.

But if fields are not nullable, these problems never occur. The application can deal with the whole issue of *no-response* or blank entries by replacing them with special characters and numbers instead of leaving them blank. This way, they can be inserted and retrieved from the database without any problems.

USE TRIGGER PROCEDURES. In the absence of a trigger procedure, trying to insert a string into a number field causes SQL Server to return a verbose error in half gibberish, the meaning of which is probably a curse on you and your whole family. But if you write a trigger procedure to check for datatype integrity, upon any attempt to insert or modify, SQL Server will be able to politely inform the application that it is attempting to do something very offensive. Subsequently, it will be easier for the application to trap this occurrence. You will, thus, be avoiding the possibility that the users will hate your guts.

FULLY DOCUMENT STORED PROCEDURES AND TRIGGERS. Just because these elements are being developed in a strange language called SQL does not mean everyone instinctively knows what it is one is trying to accomplish. Fully document, test, and exercise proper version control on every piece of SQL code just as you would for any other types of software development.

Watch Out for Date and Currency Conventions. Since applications are often tightly integrated with the database, it is easy to forget that the two are separate programs. For example, many custom controls in Visual Basic inherit the display properties of the Windows system. Currency and dates are, thus, shown as specified by the user in his Windows setup. Yet this setup has no bearing on the database server that, for all we know, could be residing on the other side of the globe. This dirty, rotten, database may, therefore, not understand the otherwise perfect data the application is trying to send it just because it is formatted differently. As a cautionary step, therefore, always convert date and currency fields before you save them to the database and whenever you retrieve them from the database. Do this even if the conversion accomplishes absolutely nothing so your application can be truly desktop independent.

Use Views. If you find that your application is using complex SQL queries repeatedly, you may want to replace them with simple calls to predefined views. These are nothing more than preprogrammed queries that appear to the outside world to be normal tables. Since views, like stored procedures, are compiled code, you can increase efficiencies by using views as well as avoid problems associated with complex joining operations.

Views can also be used to flatten a normalized database so to the end user, the database appears to be nonnormalized and, thus, much easier to use.

Always Use Status and Timestamp Fields in Every Table. Even if your application has no need for audit control, always include in every table a field for status code and another for a timestamp. The status code gives you the flexibility to keep old and changed records in the database should the user require this feature. By including this capability right up front you save yourself from the need to convert the database later on.

Likewise, timestamp is also needed for the purpose of audit control but it has a much more important function. Timestamp indicates the last time the record was modified. This means that under optimistic-locking techniques the application can test this field to ensure that the record it is currently working on and is about to write back to the database is indeed the record that it retrieved from the database. If the two timestamps do not match, it must obviously follow that some other user had retrieved the record and changed it while the current user was leisurely doing her thing. The record is, thus, stale and should not be written to the database.

Use MS Access as Proxy (Optional). There is a large number of technical papers recommending that all database access should be done through MS Access. MS Access allows for the attachment of database tables in such a way that external tables look and feel exactly like MS Access tables. Access can, therefore, perform the database management function relieving the application from such responsibility.

Certainly, there are advantages to this method. First, all the data *reside* (virtually) in a single MDB file that is easy to create and maintain. Next, all caching activity is performed by an entirely separate application. Finally, users can also interact with a central file to produce ad hoc reports.

There are a few drawbacks, however. From a performance objective, Microsoft claims that the Jet Engine, the MS Access communication interface, matches in speed ODBC 1.1 PassThrough. Unfortunately, that is not good enough. This method also does not support a large number of active users because MS Access opens multiple connections to the database for every user request. Consequently, the number of available real *connections* drops substantially.

CHAPTER 18

The Case Against CASE

Back in the days when only third-generation languages were available, I was a strong advocate of CASE—computer-aided software engineering tools. Conventional wisdom at that time suggested that CASE tools assist programmers wrap their hands around very large and complex systems. Since the computer is much better than humans at handling large and complex data structures such as computer programs, then, obviously, it was believed, computers should be able to aid in coding. The programmer needs only to *tell* the CASE tool what it is she wants to program by feeding it a high-level design of the system. The CASE application then proceeds to do its thing and produces a well-written, well-organized software program. Maintenance is also greatly enhanced since the CASE tool holds the program in a data structure that it can easily modify as design changes are required.

Well, times have changed and, with very few exceptions, I no longer believe in the benefits of CASE tools. Certainly, the theory behind CASE is still sound but what is no longer true is that large computer systems must be complex and hard to program. As it turns out, languages such as Visual Basic that hide much of the underlying complexity of a computer system have become extremely easy to program—much easier, in fact, than the average CASE tool. In other words, the amount of training and the level of skill required to use the typical CASE application far exceed the skill set and training needed to write the average VB program. As such, CASE tools are hardly necessary and often superfluous.

Regretfully, however, this simple truth escapes many software shops. Quite a few companies had invested substantial resources in training their personnel to use CASE tools and so they stick to the practice of using them even when it is not necessary. As a result, they also tie themselves to programming languages that are, indeed, complex and difficult simply because their CASE tools know no better. I suppose the last large C program will be written using the best CASE tool on the market sometime in the next few years. After that, CASE will be mostly forgotten.

There are a few exceptions to this analysis as not all uses of CASE tools are inappropriate. Anytime a computer entity—be it a program, a database, or a document—is better represented graphically as a drawing than as text, it naturally fits the CASE paradigm. The reason to use a CASE application in such a situation is not because it reduces the complexity level of the underlying task but rather because such a CASE tool provides a better user interface for these specific instances.

Relational databases are a good example. The mechanical act of creating a database, no matter how complex, on, say, a Sybase database server is an easy enough task. It usually consists of typing in a whole bunch of SQL statements such as CREATE TABLE, and CREATE INDEX, and other such *exciting* directives. No rocket science here. Nonetheless, human beings having two eyes but only one brain tend to comprehend a relational database design much better as a diagram. In fact, there is a good chance that the database design that is being typed in originated in a diagram. As such, a CASE tool that allows one to draw the database schema and then goes on to produce the CREATE statement on the server is very useful. Such a tool saves time, prevents errors, and ensures that the design as shown on the diagram is really the same as the database on the server. Then again, I imagine that in some future time, all database programming will be done graphically and so the need for CASE tools may also greatly diminish.

Incidentally, a company called Logic Works produces just such a database CASE tool. It is called ERWIN/ERX® for Windows and it's the greatest thing since CD-ROMs.

Another exception to the inadequacy of CASE tools is, actually, not really CASE at all. Although, by definition, they aid in the creation of software, *code generators* have never been considered CASE tools per se. But since code generators do run on the computer and do aid in the creation of software, I include them in this category.

Code generators were known as macro recorders before Visual Basic came along. Typically, they provide a way for the user of a certain application to create an entire segment of code in a given application by initiating a series of manual steps to achieve the desired goal. With Visual Basic becoming the standard *macro* language of the entire Microsoft business line, code generators now produce VB code. For example, a user who needs to create a program segment to change the font of a spreadsheet from Arial to Times Roman can do so by recording the actions that change font. The resulting code is perfectly good Visual Basic and so it can be copied and pasted into any application talking to a spreadsheet.

Code generation is a wonderful time saver and should be used whenever possible. If you want to call it a CASE tool, so be it. Otherwise, stay clear of CASE. It is an acronym whose time has come . . . and gone.

CHAPTER 19

The Pros and Cons of Standards

Standards are a two-edged sword. On the one hand, adhering to well-established user interface and coding standards greatly improves productivity and reduces costs. An application that conforms to a companywide GUI standard, for example, diminishes the scope of necessary training and documentation. If users already know how to accomplish certain tasks in, say, the payroll system, and the new accounts payable application looks and feels the same way, then users are most likely to instinctively know their way around the new system. Subsequently, these users require much less training than their counterparts who use applications that do not conform to standards.

Likewise, adhering to *coding* standards reduces maintenance costs. This is because if the software meets widely used acceptable coding standards, then developers can be shuffled around and easily pick up each other's work.

On the other hand, standards, and specifically strict standards, prevent changes that may very well be beneficial and necessary. In other words, standards fail because as the technology and the environment change, they prevent the application from being modified to take advantage of or handle the transformation. Standards are also terribly stifling to those members of the development team who are creative and innovative. Many technologists have had their ideas squashed in the name of conforming to standards when such ideas could have improved the applications or the development process. Enforcing standards in such a situation, thus, becomes a morale buster.

In fact, the resistance to Visual Basic as a development language in itself is a case in point. Clearly and inarguably, the use of VB, even in a limited capacity, is beneficial to any enterprise. Yet VB is often kept out of certain software shops with no other argument other than it does not meet established standards: "The standards of this company set by good ol' Therston Winchester III and his strategic information committee back in 1984 stated plainly and firmly that this company *will* use only C as a development language. These are the standards and we can do very little about it. Carry on." And so, with standards set at a different time and place, companies go on for years adhering to decisions that are no longer relevant or germane.

But standards, and rules in general, have a much more sinister effect than simply stunting innovation. No matter how well intentioned, standards in a bureaucratic environment soon become a source of power. People who otherwise may have very little authority, therefore, use standards in order to exert their will on other people. This is readily apparent, for instance, in a situation where a user disagrees with the development team about what the user interface should look like. Ideally, it is the user that should ultimately decide such issues, yet the existence of standards tilts the power balance in favor of the developers. "Gee, Mike, we would love to give you an additional list box on this screen but our standards forbid us from putting more than three list boxes on one screen. Sorry. (Chuckle, chuckle, chuckle)." And, of course, this *standard* may later be negotiated away for something the developer wants.

SLOWLY CHANGING STANDARDS

So, should we standardize or operate a free-for-all? Well, given the double-edged sword nature of standards, we must not choose to pursue either one of these choices. Instead I strongly advocate an alternative system that I term *slowly changing standards*. Under this system, a company, a department, or a manager, is encouraged to set coding and interface standards and strongly enforce compliance. The difference is that deviations from the standard are permissible in a well-controlled manner as long as they do not occur too often as to negate the overall benefits of standards. Furthermore, approved changes must be included into subsequent standards. That is, there is no such thing as a one-time-only deviation from the standard. If a change has proven to be inappropriate it should immediately be fixed rather than become a one-time aberration.

To make this system work, establish a standards committee. Unlike other, more traditional standards committees whose mission it is to prevent change, charge this committee with the task of approving change. Set a goal of the specific number of changes to the standards you will be expecting the committee to make each period. For example, the GUI standards committee must approve no less then three but no more than six *significant* new rules to the company's GUI standards over the next year. These changes must be solicited from the members of the development staff and the user community but *not* from committee members. This rule prevents a power imbalance from being created whereby committee members approve only their own ideas. Good ideas will, thus, bubble up from the development team rather than be enforced upon them. And, of course, all changes must be reviewed by the user community and be well tested.

As for enforcing these slowly changing standards, I strongly discourage the use of standards enforcement committees. Often such bodies are composed of people who are short on creative skills but who badly desire to control others. These arrogant, presumptuous, and conceited individuals look and act just like the high inquisitors of the Middle Ages. Such people are hardly qualified to pass judgment in these matters.

Instead of a standards enforcement committee, I recommend that you entrust the task of compliance with the testing and quality control team. They have already been given a mission of finding faults with the development effort and so uncovering variations from the standards falls right in line with their other duties. Furthermore, testers are usually least busy in the early stages of the project when the prototype is being assembled. And since this is a perfect time to enforce many of the GUI standards and at least some of the coding standards, testing personnel can be recruited for the job without sacrificing other priorities.

What should go in the standards? That depends on the industry, the user community, the development language, and so on. I have included two sample sets of standards, one for interface design, and another for coding. You can use these as guides for your own standards or throw them away and design your own.

CHAPTER 20

Visual Basic
Programming Conventions

The following standards document was made public by Microsoft Consulting Services. I have made some minor modifications to conform with my own beliefs:

NAMING CONVENTIONS

Objectives:

- To help programmers (especially in multiprogrammer projects) standardize and decode the structure and logic of an application.
- To be precise, complete, readable, memorable, and unambiguous.
- To be consistent with other language conventions (most importantly the Visual Basic programmers guide and standard Windows Hungarian C).
- To be efficient from a string size and labor standpoint, thus allowing a greater opportunity for longer/fuller object names.
- To define the minimal requirements necessary to accomplish the preceding objectives.

CONVENTIONS

OPTION EXPLICIT. "Option Explicit" must always be used to force proper variable declarations and aid good variable commenting. The time lost trying to track down bugs caused by typos (aUserNameTmp vs. sUserNameTmp vs. sUserNameTemp) far outweighs the time needed to dim variables. (From the Options.Environment menu, set "Require Variable Declaration" to True.)

TEXT. All files must be saved as text to facilitate the use of version control systems and to minimize the damage caused by disk corruption. (From the Options.Environment menu, set "Default Save As Format" to True.)

CONTROL NAMING. The following table defines our standard Control name prefixes.

Prefix	Control Type Description
ani	Animation button
bed	Pen Bedit
cbo	Combobox and dropdown Listbox
chk	Checkbox
clp	Picture Clip
cmd(3d)	Command Button (3D)
com	Communications
ctr	Control (Used within procs when the specific type is unknown)
db	ODBC Database
dir	Dir List Box
dlg	Visual Basic Pro Common Dialog
drv	Drive List Box
ds	ODBC Dynaset
fil	File List Box
frm	Form
fra	Frame
gau	Gauge
gpb	Group Push Button
grd	Grid
hed	Pen Hedit
hsb	Horizontal Scroll Bar
img	Image
ink	Pen Ink
key	Keyboard key status
lbl	Label
lin	Line
lst	Listbox
mdi	MDI Child Form
mpm	MAPI Message
mps	MAPI Session
mci	MCI
mnu	Menu
opt(3d)	Option Button (3d)
ole	Ole Client

Prefix	Control Type Description
out	Outline Control (VB3)
pic	Picture
pnl3d	3d Panel
rpt	Report Control (VB3)
shp	Shape
spn	Spin Control
txt	Text/Edit Box
tmr	Timer
vsb	Vertical Scroll Bar

Control Prefix Notes:

1. Menus:

Because Menu handlers can be so numerous, Menu names require a little more attention. Menu prefixes, therefore, continue beyond the initial Menu label by adding an additional prefix for each level of nesting, with the final menu caption at the end of the name string. Examples:

Menu Caption Sequence	Menu Handler Name
Help.Contents	mnuHelpContents
File.Open	mnuFileOpen
Format.Character	mnuFormatCharacter
File.Send.Fax	mnuFileSendFax
File.Send.Email	mnuFileSendEmail

This results in all the family members of a particular menu group being listed right next to each other. This multitiered format provides a very direct way to find a menu handler, especially when there are a great many of them.

2. Other Controls:

For new controls not listed previously, try to come up with a unique three-character prefix. But it is more important to be clear than to stick to three characters. For derivative controls, such as an enhanced list box, extend the preceding prefixes so that there is no confusion about what control is really being used. A mixed-case abbreviation for the manufacturer would also typically be added to the prefix. For example, a control instance created from the Visual Basic Pro 1.0 3D Frame could use a prefix of fra3d to make sure there is no confusion over which control is really being used and a command button from MicroHelp would use cmdmh to differentiate it from the standard cmd control. Each third-party control used in an application should also be listed in the application overview comment section, providing the prefix used for the control, the full name of the control, and the name of the software vendor. As in:

Prefix	Control Name	Vendor
cmdmh	Command Button	MicroHelp

Note: The vendor reference in the prefix is at the end so that similar controls will be listed together in VB's object lists and it is in noncaps so that it does not run together with the instance name of the control. See Appendix A for more information on third-party control naming.

VARIABLE AND ROUTINE NAMING. Variable and function names have the following structure:

<prefix><body><qualifier><suffix>

The prefix describes the use and the scope of the variable, as in iGet-RecordNext and sGetNameFirst. The qualifier is used to denote standard derivatives of a base variable or function, as in iGetRecord<u>Next</u> and sGetName<u>First.</u> The suffix is the optional Visual Basic type char ($, %, #, etc.).

Prefixes. The following table defines variable/function name prefixes that are based on Windows Hungarian C. These must be used universally, even when Visual Basic suffixes (such as %, &, #, etc.) are also used.

Prefix	Variable Use Description (precedes Control prefix and body)
b	Boolean (vb type = %)
c	Currency - 64 bits (vb type = @)
d	Double - 64 bit signed quantity (vb type = #)
db	Database
ds	Dynaset
dt	Date+Time (vb type = variant)
td	TableDef
f	Float/Single - 32 bit signed floating point (vb type = !)
h	Handle (vb type = %)
i	Index (vb type = %)
l	Long - 32 bit signed quantity (vb type = &)
n	Integer (sizeless, counter) (vb type = %, &, or #)
s	String (vb type = $)
ss	Snapshot
u	Unsigned - 16 bit unsigned quantity (must use &)
ul	Unsigned Long - 32 bit unsigned quantity (must use #)
vnt	Variant (big and ugly to discourage use and make sure it gets the reader's attention)

Prefix	Variable Use Description (precedes Control prefix and body)
w	Word - 16 bit signed quantity (vb type = %)
a	Array
	User defined type
Scope or Use (precedes Use prefix above)	
g	Global
m	Local to module or form
st	Static variable
v	Variable passed by value (local to a routine)
r	Variable passed by reference (local to a routine)

Hungarian[1] is as valuable in Visual Basic as it is in C because the Visual Basic type suffixes alone do not provide standard (and valuable) information about what a variable/function is used for or where it is accessible. For example, iSend (which might be a count of the number of messages sent), bSend (which might be a flag/boolean defining the success of the last Send operation), and hSend (which might be a handle to the Comm interface), all *succinctly* tell a programmer something very different. This information is something that is fundamentally lost when the name is reduced down to Send%. Scope prefixes such as *g* for global and *m* for modular also help reduce the problem of name contention especially in multideveloper projects. Hungarian is also well known to Windows programmers and constantly referenced in Microsoft and industry programming books.

Body. The body of variable and routine names should use mixed case and should be as long as needed to describe their purpose. Function names should also begin with a verb, such as InitNameArray or CloseDialog.

For frequently used or long terms, abbreviations (such as Init, Num, Tbl, Cnt, Grp for Initialization, Number, Table, Count, and Group) are suggested to help keep name lengths reasonable. Names generally greater than 32 characters begin to inhibit readability on VGA displays. When abbreviations are used, they must be used consistently throughout the application. Randomly switching between "Cnt" and "Count" within a project will greatly frustrate developers.

Qualifiers. Often related variables and routines are used to manage and manipulate a common object. In these cases it can be very helpful to use standard qualifiers to label the derivative variables and routines. Although putting the qualifier after the body of the name might seem a little awkward (as in sGetNameFirst, sGetNameLast instead of sGetFirstName, etc.), this practice will help order these names together in the Visual Basic editor routine lists, making the logic and structure of the application easier to understand.

---

[1] Referring to the Hungarian Naming Convention.

The following table defines common qualifiers and their standard meanings:

Qualifier	Description (follows Body)
First	First element of a set.
Last	Last element of a set.
Next	Next element in a set.
Prev	Previous element in a set.
Cur	Current element in a set.
Min	Minimum value in a set.
Max	Maximum value in a set.
Save	Used to preserve another variable which must be reset later.
Tmp	A "scratch" variable whose scope is highly localized within the code. The value of a Tmp variable is usually only valid across a set of contiguous statements.
Src	Source. Frequently used in comparison and transfer routines.
Dst	Destination. Often used in conjunction with Source.

USER-DEFINED TYPES. User-defined types are declared in all caps with _TYPE appended to the end of the symbol name. Example:

```
Type CUSTOMER_TYPE
    sName As String
    sState As String * 2
    lID as Long
End Type
```

When declaring instance variables of user-defined types, a small cap prefix is added to the variable name to reference this new type. Example:

```
Dim custNew as CUSTOMER_TYPE
```

CONSTANT NAMING.

- The body of constant names is described in UPPER_CASE with underscores ("_") between words.
- Although standard Visual Basic constants do not include Hungarian use information, prefixes like *i*, *s*, *g*, and *m* can be very useful in understanding the value and scope of a constant, so constant names follow the same rules as variables. Examples:

mnUSER_LIST_MAX	'Max entry limit for User list (integer value, local to module)
gsNEW_LINE	'New Line character string (global to entire application)

VARIANT DATA TYPES. With the single exception listed later, variants should *not* be used. When a type conversion is needed, variant use would probably provide a slight performance win over the explicit basic type conversion routines, (val(), str$(), etc.), but this gain is not sufficient enough to overcome the ambiguity and general sloppiness they allow in code statements.

Example:

```
vnt1 = "10.01" : vnt2 = 11 : vnt3 = "11" : vnt4 = "x4"
vntResult = vnt1 + vnt2        'Does vntResult = 21.01 or 10.0111?
vntResult = vnt2 + vnt1        'Does vntResult = 21.01 or 1110.01?
vntResult = vnt1 + vnt3        'Does vntResult = 21.01 or 10.0111?
vntResult = vnt3 + vnt1        'Does vntResult = 21.01 or 1110.01?
vntResult = vnt2 + vnt4        'Does vntResult = 11x4 or ERROR?
vntResult = vnt3 + vnt4        'Does vntResult = 11x4 or ERROR?
```

Additionally, the type conversion routines assist in documenting implementation details, which make reading, debugging, and maintaining code more straightforward.

Example:

```
iVar1 = 5 + val(sVar2)        'use this
vntVar1 = 5 + vntVar2         'not this!
```

Exception. While working with databases, messages, DDE, or OLE, a generic service routine can receive data that it does not need to know the type of in order to process or pass on.

Example:

```
Sub ConvertNulls(rvntOrg As Variant, rvntSub As Variant)
'If rvntOrg = Null, replace the Null with rvntSub
    If IsNull(rvntOrg) Then rvntOrg = rvntSub
End Sub
```

COMMENTING

- All procedures and functions must begin with a brief comment describing the *functional* characteristics of the routine (what it does). This description should *not* describe the implementation details (how it does it) because these often change over time, resulting in unnecessary comment maintenance work, or worse, erroneous comments. The code itself and any necessary in-line or local comments will describe the implementation. Parameters passed to a routine should be described if they are not obvious and when specific ranges are assumed by the routine. Function return values and global variables that are changed by the routine (especially through reference parameters) must also be described at the beginning of each routine.

  Routine header comment blocks should look like:

Function:	What the routine does (not how).
Params:	Each nonobvious parameter on a separate line with in-line comments.
Assumes:	List of each nonobvious external variable, control, open file, and so on.
Returns:	Explanation of value returned for functions.
Effects:	List of each affected nonobvious external variable, control, file, and so on and the effect if nonobvious.

- Every nontrivial variable declaration should include an in-line comment describing the use of the variable being declared.
- Variables, controls, and routines should be named clearly enough that in-line commenting is only needed for complex or nonobvious implementation details.
- An overview description of the application enumerating primary data objects, routines, algorithms, user interface dialogs, database and file system dependencies, and so on should be included at the start of the .BAS module that contains the project's Visual Basic generic constant declarations. (Note: The Project window inherently describes the list of files in a project, so this overview section only needs to provide information on the most important files and modules, or files that the Project window doesn't know about, such as .ini or database files.)

CODE FORMATTING

Because many programmers still use VGA displays, screen real estate must be conserved as much as possible while still allowing code formatting to reflect logic structure and nesting.

- For this reason, standard (tab-based) block nesting indentations should be two to four spaces. More than four spaces is unnecessary and causes unnecessary statement hiding through truncation. Less than two is not effective in reflecting logic nesting.
- The functional overview comment of a routine should be indented one space. The highest-level statements that follow the overview comment should be indented one tab, with each nested block indented an additional tab.

     Example:

```
Function iFindUser (rasUserList() as String, rsTargetUser as String) as
Integer
 'Search UserList and if found, return the index of the first occurrence
of TargetUser,
' else return -1
    Dim i as Integer               'loop counter
```

```
    Dim bFound as Integer          'target found flag
    iFindUser = -1
    i = 0
    While i <= Ubound(rasUserList) and Not bFound
        If rasUserList(i) = rsTargetUser Then
            bFound = True
            iFindUser = i
        End If
    Wend
End Function
```

- Variables and nongeneric constants should be grouped by function rather than being split off into isolated areas or special files.

OPERATORS

- Always use "&" when concatenating strings and "+" when working with numerical values. Using "+" only can cause problems when operating on two variants. For example:

```
    vntVar1 = "10.01"
    vntVar2 = 11
    vntResult = vntVar1 + vntVar2      'vntResult = 21.01
    vntResult = vntVar1 & vntVar2      'vntResult = 10.0111
```

SCOPE

- Always define variables with the smallest scope possible. Global variables can create enormously complex state machines and make understanding the logic of an application extremely difficult. They also make the reuse and maintenance of your code much more difficult. If you have to use globals, keep their declarations grouped by functionality and comment them well.
- With the exception of globals that should not be passed, procedures and functions should only operate on objects that are passed to them. Global variables that are used in routines should be identified in the general comment area at the beginning of the routine.
- Likewise, try to put as much logic and as many user interface objects in Dialog Boxes as possible. This will help segment your application complexity and minimize its run-time overhead.

APPENDIX A: THIRD-PARTY CONTROLS

The following table lists standard third-party vendor name prefix characters to be used with control prefixes:

Vendor	Abbv
MicroHelp (VBTools)	m
Pioneer Software Q+E Database	p
Crescent Software	c
Sheridan Software	s
Other (miscellaneous)	o

The following table lists standard third-party control prefixes:

Control Type	Control Name	Abbr	Vendor	Example	VBX File
Alarm	Alarm	almm	Microhelp	almmAlarm	MHTI200.VBX
Animate	Animate	anim	Microhelp	animAnimate	MHTI200.VBX
Callback	Callback	calm	Microhelp	calmCallback	MHAD200.VBX
Combo Box	DB_Combo	cbop	Pioneer	cbopComboBox	QEVBDBF.VBX
Combo Box	SSCombo	cbos	Sheridan	cbosComboBox	SS3D2.VBX
Check Box	DB_Check	chkp	Pioneer	chkpCheckBox	QEVBDBF.VBX
Chart	Chart	chtm	Microhelp	chtmChart	MHGR200.VBX
Clock	Clock	clkm	Microhelp	clkmClock	MHTI200.VBX
Button	Command Button	cmdm	Microhelp	cmdmCommandButton	MHEN200.VBX
Button	DB_Command	cmdp	Pioneer	cmdpCommandButton	QEVBDBF.VBX
Button (Group)	Command Button (multiple)	cmgm	Microhelp	cmgmBtton	MHGR200.VBX
Button	Command Button (icon)	cmim	Microhelp	cmimCommandButton	MHEN200.VBX
CardDeck	CardDeck	crdm	Microhelp	crdmCard	MHGR200.VBX
Dice	Dice	dicm	Microhelp	666mDice	MHGR200.VBX
List Box (Dir)	SSDir	dirs	Sheridan	dirsDirList	SS3D2.VBX
List Box (Drv)	SSDrive	drvs	Sheridan	drvsDriveList	SS3D2.VBX
List Box (File)	File List	film	Microhelp	filmFileList	MHEN200.VBX
List Box (File)	SSFile	fils	Sheridan	filsFileList	SS3D2.VBX
Flip	Flip	flpm	Microhelp	flpmButton	MHEN200.VBX
Scroll Bar	Form Scroll	fsrm	Microhelp	fsrmFormScroll	
Gauge	Gauge	gagm	Microhelp	gagmGauge	MHGR200.VBX
Graph	Graph	gpho	Other	gphoGraph	XYGRAPH.VBX
Grid	Q_Grid	grdp	Pioneer	grdpGrid	QEVBDBF.VBX

Control Type	Control Name	Abbr	Vendor	Example	VBX File
Scroll Bar	Horizontal Scroll Bar	hsbm	Microhelp	hsbmScroll	MHEN200.VBX
Scroll Bar	DB_HScroll	hsbp	Pioneer	hsbpScroll	QEVBDBF.VBX
Graph	Histo	hstm	Microhelp	hstmHistograph	MHGR200.VBX
Invisible	Invisible	invm	Microhelp	invmInvisible	MHGR200.VBX
List Box	Icon Tag	itgm	Microhelp	itgmListBox	MHAD200.VBX
Key State	Key State	kstm	Microhelp	kstmKeyState	MHTI200.VBX
Label	Label (3d)	lblm	Microhelp	lblmLabel	MHEN200.VBX
Line	Line	linm	Microhelp	linmLine	MHGR200.VBX
List Box	DB_List	lstp	Pioneer	lstpListBox	QEVBDBF.VBX
List Box	SSList	lsts	Sheridan	lstsListBox	SS3D2.VBX
MDI Child	MDI Control	mdcm	Microhelp	mdcmMDIChild	
Menu	SSMenu	mnus	Sheridan	mnusMenu	SS3D3.VBX
Marque	Marque	mrqm	Microhelp	mrqmMarque	MHTI200.VBX
Picture	OddPic	odpm	Microhelp	odpmPicture	MHGR200.VBX
Picture	Picture	picm	Microhelp	picmPicture	MHGR200.VBX
Picture	DB_Picture	picp	Pioneer	picpPicture	QEVBDBF.VBX
Property Vwr	Property Viewer	pvrm	Microhelp	pvrmPropertyViewer	MHPR200.VBX
Option (Group)	DB_Radio-Group	radq	Pioneer	radqRadioGroup	QEVBDBF.VBX
Slider	Slider	sldm	Microhelp	sldmSlider	MHGR200.VBX
Button (Spin)	Spinner	spnm	Microhelp	spnmSpinner	MHEN200.VBX
Spread-sheet	Spreadsheet	sprm	Microhelp	sprmSpreadsheet	MHAD200.VBX
Picture	Stretcher	strm	Microhelp	strmStretcher	MHAD200.VBX
Screen Saver	Screen Saver	svrm	Microhelp	svrmSaver	MHTI200.VBX
Switcher	Switcher	swtm	Microhelp	swtmSwitcher	
List Box	Tag	tagm	Microhelp	tagmListBox	MHEN200.VBX
Timer	Timer	tmrm	Microhelp	tmrmTimer	MHTI200.VBX
ToolBar	ToolBar	tolm	Microhelp	tolmToolBar	MHAD200.VBX
List Box	Tree	trem	Microhelp	tremTree	MHEN200.VBX
Input Box	Input (Text)	txtm	Microhelp	inpmText	MHEN200.VBX
Input Box	DB_Text	txtp	Pioneer	txtpText	QEVBDBF.VBX
Scroll Bar	Vertical Scroll Bar	vsbm	Microhelp	vsbmScroll	MHEN200.VBX
Scroll Bar	DB_VScroll	vsbp	Pioneer	vsbpScroll	QEVBDBF.VBX

CHAPTER 21

Graphical User Interface Standards[1]

SCOPE

These standards apply to any Windows-based client-server or stand-alone business application.

INTENT

The intent of this set of standards is to create an environment familiar to the user no matter what application he or she happens to be running.

GENERAL RULES

1. Windows and dialog boxes' look and feel should match the operating system's Windows standards. This is easily done by constructing all Windows and dialog boxes through the standard Windows interface.
2. The Windows look and feel should automatically be updated with the Windows operating system upgrade.
3. Every action should be initiated from either the mouse or the keyboard. Give the users the option of using either.

---

[1] This chapter represents only a sampling of the type of items that must go into a GUI standards document. The M&D GUI Standards Document from which this chapter was taken is over 100 pages long.

4. Design the user interface to minimize common user mistakes (that is, List Boxes as opposed to Text Boxes whenever appropriate).

5. Make the interface very forgiving when handling user errors. Self-correct whenever possible. When self-correction is not feasible, point out errors in a user-friendly way.

6. If an element is not covered in this document, the standard look and feel of that element should be the same as the latest version of the Windows operating system standards.

COLOR[2]

1. Data entry elements that require user input such as text boxes, check boxes, and/or radio boxes should be black text on white background.

2. All noneditable display fields as well as all panels, labels, backgrounds, scroll bars, and push buttons should be displayed as black text on gray background.

3. Data entry errors should be signified by turning the label next to the erroneous entry red.[3]

4. Other colors are permissible in the following:

   a) Icons and small bit maps.[4]

   b) Picture push buttons.

   c) Graphs where color can add clarity.

   d) Red can be used to signify a negative number as in standard accounting format.

   e) In a non-data-entry application, for graphical representation of data.

   f) The representation of a very familiar real object on the screen for data entry purposes, that is, a bank check.

5. Never use color to indicate pertinent information since the application then becomes unusable for persons who are color blind.

PROGRESS INDICATORS

When computing or processing information, the cursor should indicate so by becoming the hourglass indicator as specified by Windows.

---

[2] Extensive research has shown that when it comes to data entry applications, boring is best. In other words, color and size differentiation which are so important to advertising and presentations become distracting to people searching the screen for what they should enter next.

[3] An example of deviation from standard Windows applications.

[4] Because of their size, these are very hard to understand in the absence of color.

Progress indicators must be provided for all computations and processing that require significant time to complete. Such progress indicators can be:

1. Flood bars. Flood color is blue. Percent display in black turning to white when flooded.
2. Icon animation (that is, an hourglass dripping sand).

FONT AND SIZE

1. The font throughout the application shall be Arial.
2. Font size is 9.75.
3. Font is bold unless the item is a label for an optional entry field.
4. Italics and underline shall be turned off.

FORMS[5]

Use forms to collect, view, and update information. Forms are detail windows which can be minimized (iconized).

1. All forms are moveable and include a title bar and a control menu.
2. Forms must be sizable for the purpose of uncovering other windows.

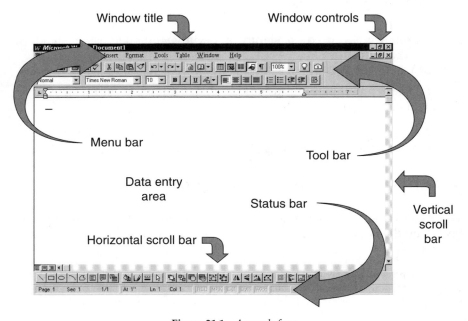

Figure 21.1   *A sample form*

[5] Full screens.

3. Forms must scale with the size of the display terminal.
4. Closing the form window exits the application.
5. Unless data entry or display requires entities which are inherently larger than the entire screen (text document, for example), a form should only contain a single screen worth of information. Forms must, therefore, not be scrollable.
6. Do not crowd data entry forms. Break up a form into two if it contains so many data entry fields that it becomes confusing. Connect the two forms by Next/Previous button combinations.

All forms shall have the following parts, as shown in Figure 21.1.

Title bar:

Conform to Windows standards and appears at the top of the form. The title should indicate clearly the purpose of the screen as in: Claim Entry, New Application, New Hire Information, and so on.

Window Control Buttons:

Conform to Windows standards (clip control, minimize, maximize, arrange, etc.).

Menu bar:

Lists all possible actions. (Further specifications below.)

Status bar:

Displays feedback information including:

1. Display progress flood bar or progress statements.
2. Explain what a particular menu item or toolbar button does.
3. Display status information such as time of day, page number, and so on.

Form can also have, optionally:

Tool bars:

Containing push buttons and other controls.

Horizontal and/or vertical scroll bars:

To move up and down and left and right on the page for the few occasions that require the form to be scaleable.

Frames:

All forms shall have frames except when maximized. Windows in Modal mode should have a double-thickness frame. Non-Modal forms shall have a single-thickness frame.

MENU BAR

The menu bar shall have the following format:

File	Including Open, Close, Save, Save As, recent documents, and Exit.
Edit	Including Insert, Delete, Modify, Find, Replace. *<Application-specific items>*
Window	Including Arrange and a list of open documents.
Help	Including Search, Index, and other entries into context-sensitive help (see Figure 21.2). Also entry into the About screen (see Figure 21.3).

All menu items should have a hot key as well as a shortcut. Likewise, menu items should be grouped together with a separator line between groups.

Pop-up or context-sensitive menus are initiated with a right mouse button click and provide the user with a set of actions appropriate to the current context.

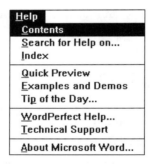

Figure 21.2   *Example of a help menu*

Figure 21.3   *Example of an About screen*

TOOL BAR

All functions represented by a tool bar button must also be accessible with a keystroke. Related groups of buttons should touch one another. The distance between unrelated groups should be a quarter-button wide or high. Dim buttons are not active. The meaning of all icons should be consistent throughout the set of user applications.

DIALOG BOXES

When a complex data structure is to be entered and such information is secondary, as in the names and addresses of beneficiaries, for example, a dialog box can be used. (See Figure 21.4.) Such a dialog box should be launched from the parent form by a button.

Dialog boxes are also useful to gather additional information on the way to accomplishing a user request, as in requesting the number of copies on a print request. As such, a dialog box is initiated by a menu item or a tool button.

Message boxes, specialized dialog boxes to convey a single piece of information as a result of user or program action, should be clarified with one of the following icons in Figure 21.5.

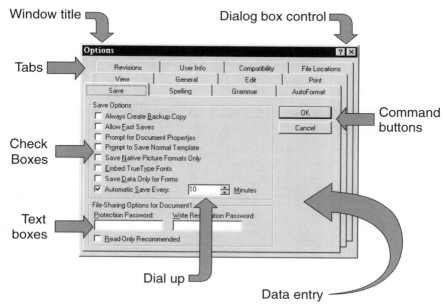

Figure 21.4 *A sample dialog box*

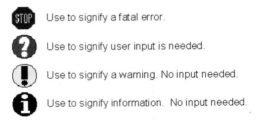

Use to signify a fatal error.

Use to signify user input is needed.

Use to signify a warning. No input needed.

Use to signify information. No input needed.

Figure 21.5 *Message box key*

DATA ENTRY FIELDS

1. Any required data entry field shall be signified with a bold label. Optional fields are signified by a plain label (see Figure 21.6).
2. Currency and Date display format shall inherit the user's setting from the Windows International settings (set from the control panel).
3. For international applications, leave ample room in labels and text boxes for translated text and converted currencies.
4. When users enter a field by positioning the cursor there, give instructions in the status bar. Make the instructions direct, brief, and easy to understand. Use the word Type for text boxes, Click for push buttons, check boxes, and radio buttons, and Select for list boxes and combo boxes.
5. Every field should have a label explaining what information is to be entered.

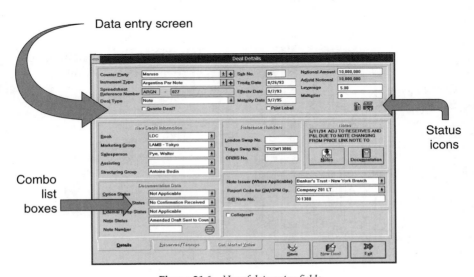

Figure 21.6 *Use of data entry fields*

6. Fields containing similar type of information should be sized similarly.

7. Left justify all labels unless the application is multilingual. Differences in label lengths between, say, Japanese and French, make it necessary to right justify labels.

8. Read-only fields should be so signified by a gray background.

9. Related fields should be grouped together in group boxes or separated from the rest of the form with lines.

10. A logical tab order should be assigned to all entry fields so that the user can tab from one field to the next and on to the command buttons.

COMMAND BUTTONS

1. Every dialog form shall have at least one command button that closes the form.

2. A default button shall always be designated.

3. Whenever possible, provide a Cancel button to take the user back to the state prior to entering the screen or dialog box.

4. Command buttons that are not currently available should be dimmed (disabled).

5. Buttons should be separated by 200 pixels vertically and horizontally.

6. Signify the fact that a button action will open a new window with three dots that is, More . . .

OTHER RULES FOR SCREEN ELEMENTS

1. Use three-dimensional shading to help differentiate between screen elements.

2. Always provide context-sensitive help that the user can invoke by clicking on the F1 function key.

3. Elements that belong to the same group—that is, name, address, telephone number all belonging to a new hire's contact information— shall go on the same panel.

4. Text boxes that display information but are not editable should have a gray background (see Figure 21.7).

5. When using list boxes and combo boxes, the first letter typed should bring up the first item beginning with the letter and as more letters are typed, should continue to narrow down the selection to those items starting with the typed-in letters.

6. Use tabs to move between several pages of the same entity. This is preferable to the NEXT/PREVIOUS button system.

7. Use the following standards for screen elements. These are listed for a 14" screen.

Radio
buttons

List
box

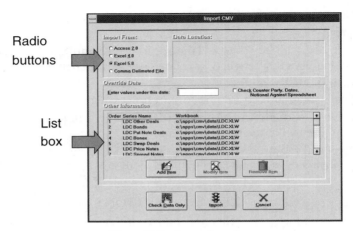

Figure 21.7 *Screen elements*

Element	Width	Height	Three-Dimensional
Push Button	1,500	650	Always
Picture Button	1,500	650	Always
Tool Bar Button	450	450	Always
Text Box	Varies	285	Always
Scroll Bar (H)	Varies	285	N/A
Scroll Bar (V)	285	Varies	N/A

ERROR HANDLING

Always allow the user to recover from mistakes gracefully.

When a user attempts to exit a field, check immediately for type conformance—that is if the user entered text for an integer value field. Also check for violation of *local* acceptance rules. Display a simple error listing the acceptance rule if the data break any of these rules immediately.

Check for errors against a network database only when the user indicates the need to save the entire screen or dialog box. Display a list of all such errors in a message box and return the user to the screen. Labels next to the erroneous entries should be turned red.

MISCELLANEOUS

Use the standard available Windows dialog box (common dialog boxes) for:

File Save As	Print
File Open	Errors

LOGON SCREENS

Figure 21.8 displays a sample logon screen.

Figure 21.8 *The logon screen*

GRAPHS

Figure 21.9 shows the use of a graph in a VB form.

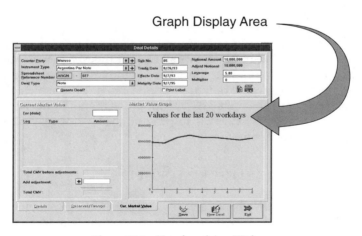

Figure 21.9 *Use of graph in a VB form*

CHAPTER 22

How Is Report Generation Accomplished in Visual Basic?

From a user's perspective, report generation is the second most important feature of any business application taking a back seat only to the data entry features. Between them, these two aspects of the applications cover most of the interaction the user has with the system.

Yet report generation alone usually causes most of the anxiety experienced by users and is the cause of most of the discontent reported to the data processing department. Users often do not understand why they cannot see or print their data according to the format they or their boss currently has in mind. Especially demanding are those users who are accustomed to commercial PC spreadsheet and database applications with which they can arrange their data any which way they want to see them. Thus, the best way to eliminate most user discontent is to provide them with easy data access and flexible reporting capabilities.

LEST WE FORGET!

What would happen if we were to ignore flexible reporting capabilities? Let's review some history: Arguably, the inability to generate flexible, professional-looking reports in a timely manner and within user specification is the biggest single reason for the demise of the mainframe. A close examination of the events leading to the rise of the personal computer reveals that managers and data users hated the mainframe because it prevented them from reading and retrieving data. They were willing to put up with the mainframe's other problems such as slow response time, ugly user interfaces, no pointing devices, and even monochrome displays. But users could not and would not tolerate the long delays they experienced and the countless battles they had to fight in order to obtain reports. And even when, after a long and tiring process, they finally retrieved the report they requested, it was printed on one part computer paper using a fixed-space font that was not very presentable. So they often had to copy the report to some other application like Microsoft Excel, Word, or PowerPoint so it could be presented to management.

Of course, as an old mainframe programmer, I know that this reporting difficulty is not all the mainframe's fault. There are many products on the market that make report generation on the mainframe a halfway decent proposition even for end users. But the CPU of a time-sharing system is a limited resource, as is the time of the data processing department. As more and more applications, users, and report batches are added to the system, the mainframe runs more and more slowly until the entire machine grinds to a halt and becomes useless.

Some corporations got in the habit of solving their capacity-related performance problems by purchasing more and faster mainframes, and, indeed, user satisfaction improved tremendously. Unfortunately, these corporations are no longer with us, having been bankrupted by unwise spending decisions. The ones that are still around—that is, if they have not already moved to client-server technology by now—solved the performance problem by making it very, very difficult for end users to get any time slice, no matter how minute, from the CPU. They did so by removing the CPU-intensive, flexible report generators from their system and by forcing all users to submit report requests through an overworked and underpaid MIS department. MIS personnel, thus, became gatekeepers of the data, and began to fight fierce battles anytime someone tried to obtain the data.

And so, many managers who were subjected to this regime had to wage the equivalent of World War III every time they needed a report. Sometimes they won the war, and sometimes they lost. Either way, dead bodies, ashes, and ruins lay behind each of these efforts. Tired of the constant struggle, users began to take their data, their applications, and their departments off the mainframe and moved, first, to stand-alone personal computers, and eventually to local area networks. Sure, the applications they used in the beginning were primitive and not as robust as the ones on the mainframe, but they could get at the data in any way, shape, and form they wished to view them. This made users very, very happy so they were more than willing to put up with the inadequacies of the early machines. So began the end of the era of the mainframe computer and the dawn of the era of the personal computer.

Of course, there is more to why the mainframe failed as the enterprise's workhorse than just lack of report-generating capabilities, but not much more. The moral of the story is that any system you develop must absolutely, positively have open and free access to the data and allow for flexible, professional reports.

The Golden Rule of Date Reporting: Ignore reporting and data access requirements at your peril.

WHAT ARE SOME BASIC
REPORTING REQUIREMENTS?

Commonly, there are three types of printed output most database applications produce. The first, a line item report, is a textual data dump of some or all the records in the database. It displays some or all the fields associated with each record in one or more tables. This output is often grouped on several levels and contains substantial summary and calculated information. An example of such a report is a sales summary showing sales revenue by product, grouped by region and retail outlet.

A second type of report is the form letter. From a technical perspective it is not much different than the line item report but functionally it is miles apart. The form letter uses name and address data to generate letters to customers, vendors, or employees. The body of the letter may also contain database fields. For instance, a company may use its employee database to send every employee a letter telling him or her how much is vested in the pension plan. In this example, not only are the employee's name and address obtained from the database but also extracted is the amount quoted in the body of the letter.

The third type of widely used report is a graph or other such decision support presentation. A graph displays the summary and calculated data tabulated by the program in a pictorial manner. Returning to the linear report example, the sales by region may be shown as a pie chart.

The line item report is an absolute necessity for any business application such as accounting, inventory, investing, and so on. Form letters are a must for any application whose function it is to communicate with the outside world. Such applications include payroll administration, marketing and sales support, insurance claim systems, and so on. Graphs are required for management decision support and although they may not be viewed as an absolute necessity from a traditional perspective, in today's PC world, no application can survive without being able to produce them.

TO VB OR NOT VB?

Of course, there are many VB components to provide all three reports with minimum effort. The professional edition of VB even comes with a junior version of Crystal Report, which is the leading report generator on the market. This is a robust and flexible report generator with which one can design reports visually via a drag-and-drop method. Database fields are easily bound to the report fields and the result is a very professional report. Moreover, reports can be previewed on the screen before they are printed using the Windows printer definitions and available fonts.

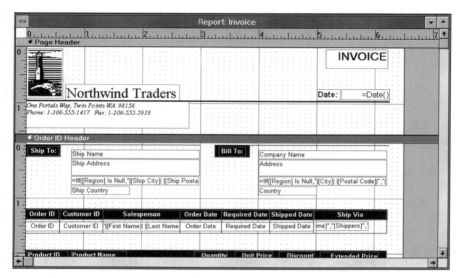

Figure 22.1 *Report design in MS Access: all objects can be dragged and dropped anywhere on the page*

Crystal Report is perfect for line item reports but may not be the best choice for form letters. That is because Crystal Report does not provide enough flexibility to change the body of the letter on the fly. Rather, it is more of a static design tool. A somewhat more sophisticated approach to form letter generation, therefore, is to use an outside database engine such as Microsoft Access to produce such reports. (See Figures 22.1 and 22.2.)

Figure 22.2 *The same report in finished form*

MS Access can be employed to print a form letter by attaching the database data tables to an Access process. Thus, for example, a field named PRINT_ME in the desired table can be set to true by the application in each record for which a form letter is required. The Access process then wakes up periodically—say, once a day—manually or automatically, and scans the record set for those records in which PRINT_ME is set to true. It generates a form letter for each of these records and sets PRINT_ME to false.

The novel aspect of this solution is the fact that the form letter itself, minus, of course, the merged data, resides on the user's PC or on the network. If the letter must be modified, it can easily be done. The drawback is the limited ability to centralize such a database to be modified by several people (it can be done, but not easily).

If more flexibility is desired, a word processor can even be strung up to the Access process. Access can then be used to generate Microsoft Word mail merge documents. Such a mail merge process produces an on-line series of form letters that can be edited individually if needed (see Figure 22.3). Naturally, this last system is limited by available memory and so it is only viable if the system prints a handful of letters at a time.

Access can also produce very professional-looking graphics. As such one may create some canned graphs that are automatically updated by the attached server every time they are printed.

All reports produced with Access can be previewed on-line before printing, thus saving mountains of paper if the produced report is not the one desired.

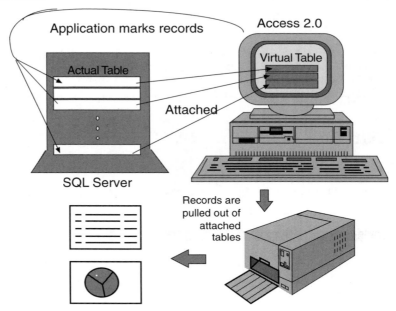

Figure 22.3 *Producing reports with Access 2.0*

So, clearly, no matter which approach you take, report generation is a rather trivial matter compared to the way reporting was done in the not-so-good-old days. But in view of the ease of generating reports with Visual Basic, the question must be raised whether or not you should be in the report-generating business in the first place. Allow me to put forward the proposition that with client-server technology, you no longer have to provide your users with canned reports because they can produce such reports themselves.

If you design your application such that all reports must be generated using the system-provided canned reports, you will, forever, be in the report-generation business. Every time someone will want to see the data in a *new and improved* way, and no doubt, they will, you will have to send your report expert to modify the application so it includes this new canned report. Sure, in the short run this may be a winning proposition. It may only take your expert a couple of hours to generate this report and you may even receive many kudos for your quick response and your ability to produce such nice-looking pieces of paper. That is, until the day you are handed a rush report request from no other than the president of the company and, oh God, you remember that your report expert is on vacation. To make the situation worse, his or her backup called in sick and the only other person who knows anything about the database is in training in Timbuktu. The report is not going to be produced easily, it is going to be late, and as one screw-up wipes out a thousand *at-a-boys*, you will be in hot water.

Let's face it. Report generation is a headache. Your technologists consider it boring, it is time consuming, it sucks up resources like there is no tomorrow, and it gets you nothing but trouble. And as much as we all like to be in charge of big departments with lots of people and responsibility, this is one responsibility you might as well do without.

Luckily, Windows and client-server technology provide an easy and quick way for the users to obtain the data and do whatever their heart pleases with them. Moreover, they can do so safely and without compromising database security. The way this is done is by permitting the users to import the data into a database such as Microsoft Access or into a spreadsheet such as Microsoft Excel. Both applications as well as many others provide very powerful import utilities through ODBC from several database servers. These utilities allow the user to query the data, sort them, filter them, massage them, and format them all in one step, and all with menu-driven or drag-and-drop utilities. Your only responsibilities are to

1. Provide the users with a database map.
2. Name fields and tables in plain English (that is, Employee_Table and First_Name rather than Emp_T0001 and Fname).
3. Send them to commercially available training classes in their front-end application of choice.

Don't worry. There is not going to be any technology shock involved here. By now the end users are accustomed to doing much more complicated tasks on their spreadsheets than the one described here. Chances are that they will take to it like a data junky to a random number generator.

And the users cannot hurt the data because all they are given is Select (or Browse) privileges on the server. They still need to log into the server using an ID and Password but they cannot insert, modify, or delete any data unless you have decided to give them such privileges (not recommended).

The only problem with this scheme occurs if your organization has decided to put a front-end security mechanism between the end user and the server. In this case you may need to supply the client machines with a small (very small) logon utility as an automatically run macro for the front-end application. For example, you can write an Excel macro (in Visual Basic for Applications, of course) to display a logon dialog box, get the user ID and Password, and then do whatever authentication and verification your security system requires. This macro should automatically run every time Excel is launched. Should the user pass the required hurdles, log him or her into the server, and exit the macro. The application is ready to run. Otherwise, display a nice go-jump-in-a-lake message and exit altogether.

The bottom line is: Get out of the report-generating business. Your children have grown up and you are no longer needed. Sob, sob.

_____ CHAPTER 23 _____

Every Application a Component (Object Linking and Embedding)

Object linking and embedding, commonly known as OLE, is a versatile technology that allows users to combine applications in a variety of ways. Through OLE, one can create a dynamic link to a closed application or actually _embed_ an entire application as an object in the client application. Through such links one can send and receive information from the object linked and embedded application (server) as well as initiate and control actions on that server. Thus, for example, not only can the application write a series of data into a word processor document, but it can also print the document it just created by issuing, through OLE, the word processor print command.

Before proceeding, a distinction must be made between _OLE_ and _OLE automation_. OLE encompasses technology that allows applications to be linked together and communicate with each other in several implementation schemes. OLE is, thus, a general term. OLE automation, on the other hand, is one specific way through which OLE is implemented (see Figure 23.1). Namely, it is the method by which one application—the _master_—controls another—the _slave_. The master thus launches the slave application and, in a sense, assumes the role of the user in initiating program actions. This is quite different from other OLE techniques such as embedding where a part or the whole application is embedded in another requiring the user, rather than another program, to initiate actions (see Figure 23.2).

The use of this OLE technology and, specifically, OLE automation, is perhaps best illustrated by an example. Suppose you wish to develop an application that calculates a loan payment schedule given a set of input figures such as principle amount, interest rate, and number of payments. The

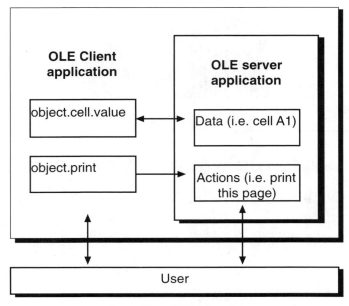

Figure 23.1   *OLE automation*

traditional approach would have required you to develop an algorithm that calculates the loan schedule from scratch. More modern technology, such as an object-oriented approach, may save some of the work by permitting the use of an existing algorithm developed elsewhere and available in some class

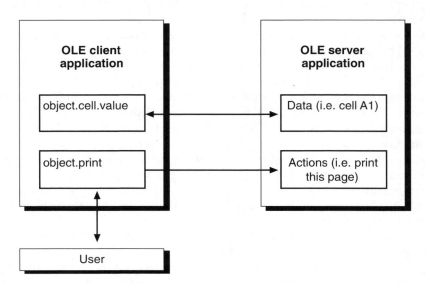

Figure 23.2   *OLE embedded object*

library. Either method, however, requires at least some expertise, and development that is specific to this particular problem. Furthermore, the needed skill set necessary to program the application may not always be the same as that needed to figure out a loan payment schedule.

Using OLE technology, however, allows you to draw on an existing application that already knows how to calculate loan payments. For example, Microsoft Excel, a widely used spreadsheet application, already contains a payment function that returns an array of payments given a principle, interest rate, and number of payments. Subsequently, your application can link up to Excel using OLE technology, call the function, and return the resulting payment schedule to your application.

The mechanics of this call to OLE automation look something like this:

```
Dim xl As Object
Dim payment As Double

xl = CreateObject("Excel.Application")
xl.Visible = False                 'no need to see what
                                   ' is happening
xl.Workbooks.Add                   ' just in case
xl.Range("a1").Value = 0.078  ' interest rate
xl.Range("a2").Value = 3000   ' principle
xl.Range("a3").Value = 30     ' number of payments
xl.Range("a4").Formula = "=pmt(a1,a2,a3)"
xl.Calculate
payment = xl.Range("a4").value ' get the value
xl.Quit                       ' and exit
xl.Close
Set xl = Nothing
```

Alternately, the embedding method could be used instead of OLE automation. That is, Excel can be opened by your application outright as an embedded object. This means that you include an Excel spreadsheet as a *grid*, if you will. The user then enters the input parameters into the appropriate cells and a predefined calculation spits out the result into another range of cells, all within the embedded Excel.

Another example of using OLE automation, this time from a VBA application, involves collecting task names from a Microsoft Project file and putting each task name in a different column heading in Excel.:

```
Dim MyProject As project
Dim MyTask As Task
Dim count As Integer

Set MyProject = GetObject("project.mpp")

For Each MyTask In MyProject.Tasks
    If MyTask.Milestone Then
        count = count + 1
```

```
        Range("Milestones").Offset(count)_
              .Value = MyTask.Name
        End If
    Next
    Set MyProject = Nothing
```

In a way, OLE is the method by which applications become mere components of other applications. After all, there is really no difference, from a
technical perspective, between including a text box object in your form or
including a whole Excel spreadsheet.

Other common uses for OLE include links to electronic mail, word processors, and graphic presentation tools. E-mail is perhaps the most natural
OLE application since just about any business management system produces
some kind of report that then must be distributed around the organization.
Likewise, the information needed by the system is often collected from the
various entities of the organization. An OLE link to e-mail provides for automatic distribution of reports as well as the automatic collection of information
from received messages. Likewise, if, in addition to electronic distribution, a
paper output is required, a word processor can be object linked and embedded into the application to automatically produce such reports.

At this writing, OLE technology is not yet widely used to access databases but this is soon to change. Once databases can be object linked and
embedded, information can be displayed and stored away even more easily
and efficiently than it already is. The Microsoft Jet database engine 3.0 is an
OLE object, for example.

OLE technology is so powerful that Microsoft is currently converting
the technology by which Visual Basic add-ins, known as VBXs, are implemented. Starting with Visual Basic version 4.0, the add-ins can be OLE servers known as OCXs. This means that when one calls on a text box control, one
is really using embedded application technology for communication between the application and the text box.

Alas, OLE is not perfect. Current implementation is somewhat slow
since communication between the applications have to pass several layers of
processing, all of which are subject to the operating system's overhead. Also,
the server applications may, on their own, take a long time to launch. This is
not really an OLE problem *per se*, but it does affect the usefulness of the technology. In the example above, a payment schedule algorithm written from
scratch probably takes the same amount of time to calculate in VB as it does
in Excel through OLE. But if you add on the time it takes to launch Excel, a
process that can last as much as 20 seconds, the OLE approach is much
slower. To remedy this launch time problem, many developers launch the
server application once when the program begins and leave the server open
for the duration of the session.

Perhaps a bigger problem with OLE, specifically, OLE automation, is
that as it is currently implemented it permits little interaction between the
server and client application while the server is performing a lengthy task.

This means that providing progress feedback to the user is difficult if not impossible. Suppose your application instructs Excel to calculate the treasury bond yield rate for the last 20 years and construct a graph for each year. Further assume that because of some user specifications, the task must be performed in the background while Excel is invisible. In such a scenario the whole process can take several minutes to accomplish, all the while the user is oblivious to whether processing is in progress or not. Excel has no easy way of signaling progress back to the calling application and the calling application is in limbo while Excel is executing its request.

It is widely believed that Microsoft and other vendors will shortly solve both the performance issue and the lack of feedback issue with new releases of OLE and OLE-compliant server applications. But for now, OLE's benefits already far outweigh its shortcomings and so I strongly recommend that it be employed extensively. Why write a whole new calculation library when a very good one is already available in most spreadsheets? Why write a distribution program when you can use existing e-mail to send reports around the organization? And why write a reporting utility when you can use a word processor to produce the reports?

MANAGERIAL ISSUES

The number-one managerial concern when it comes to OLE is to ensure that the desktop applications used by the enterprise are OLE compliant. If many of your users' favorite applications can be communicated through OLE technology, it becomes much easier to design custom applications that leverage on the existing data, knowledge base, and user comfort level. That is not to say that wide use of non-OLE-compliant applications is a show stopper. But, in such a case, you may be duplicating systems should you decide to use OLE by installing parallel applications.

This point can be demonstrated with a simple example. If the user community runs an OLE-compliant electronic mail application, it is easy to develop and install an application that calls on such e-mail to distribute reports and other output. But if the e-mail app is not OLE compliant or if it supports only early versions of OLE, you will either have to develop your own report distribution system or install another e-mail program for this purpose only. And since the users are not familiar with the new e-mail application, you will have to train them on the use of yet another new application.

Likewise, applications your own team develops should always be set up as OLE servers if they are to be used by other programs. This enables you to create building blocks from which large systems can be built without having to reinstall much of the software. For example, if a program to enter and maintain inventory transactions is built as an OLE server, it can be called upon by a quality control program to *release* stock into inventory as the product passes inspection. Without such a communication channel, a new system has to be built to consolidate these functions and replace the two applications.

Another neat implementation of an OLE-compliant application is the ability to embed it in a commercially available product. For example, the users may choose to embed your inventory application in their Excel spreadsheet to bring in data directly from the warehouse floor. They may even choose to have a button in their spreadsheet that launches the inventory application. This is a major improvement over the alternative since without an OLE channel, the data need to be exported from the inventory application into an intermediary file and then imported into Excel.

DESIGN ISSUES

Since OLE technology is largely a client-server technology, we must address a traditional client-server issue: Where should the bulk of the processing be performed? This question is very similar to the one we looked into in the databases chapter. On the one side of the argument are those who want to perform all the computation on the client application, using the OLE server for storage of data only. For this group of people, OLE is a useless tool for the simple reason that the technology is designed primarily to be a processing mechanism. Other methods are much better suited for storage and retrieval than OLE.

On the other side of the argument is a group who believes all heavy-duty processing should be done on the OLE server, freeing the client to perform high-speed user interface tasks. Doing this in OLE, however, is not recommended for the reason mentioned earlier. Namely, while the server is computing, the client is suspended.[1]

Obviously, from a user interface point of view, the time the client application spends in limbo must be minimized. Therefore, unless there is a compelling reason to do otherwise, I lean toward the notion that the server should do less rather than more. In other words, use the OLE server for its built-in functionality, but do not add any more functionality by programming macros and subapplications. Instead, let the additional functions be performed by the client application. This way, you have better control over processing, error handling, and exception processing without leaving the user in the dark.

Like all other rules of thumb, however, this one should also be taken with a grain of salt. If you find that certain tasks are more easily performed by the server than the client, by all means, let the server accomplish them. A good example of this exception is text file parsing. Importing an external file and parsing it is a task that should normally be handled by the Visual Basic client. However, Microsoft Excel provides an excellent text parsing function that is both fast and efficient. Using this functionality, huge files can be imported and

---

[1] It is possible to set up a concurrent OLE automation server that goes off to perform its duties while the client application continues to run. However, this implementation is not recommended since it adds a level of complexity to the application that is better left simple.

parsed in a manner of seconds. Subsequently, when it comes to importing text files, it is a good idea to use Excel not only as a calculator but also as a file import component. This is done by programming some Excel macros that read in and parse the text file and then object link and embed the values to the VB application.

REMOTE OLE

With Visual Basic 4.0 Microsoft added the ability of object linking and embedding across the network. This means that the server application need not reside in the same box as the client application. This permits some exciting multi-CPU programming and a substantial acceleration in performance if one were to exploit such capabilities.

Consider, for example, an application that calculates the numerical outcome of a decision tree. Such an application is easily broken into a series of steps. Each step can be run on a different CPU using remote OLE. Thus, if the application takes 15 minutes to calculate a thousand branches, it would only take one minute if broken up into 15 pieces each run by a different CPU.

Remote OLE (Figure 23.3) also has profound implications on distribution of data within the organization. An OLE server can be set up as a data source in a central location while client applications hook to it on an as-needed basis.

VISUAL BASIC AS OLE APPLICATIONS

A Visual Basic application can become an OLE server in two ways. As an *out-of-process* OLE server, the application is a stand-alone executable into which other applications can link. Out-of-process servers can be set up as single-instance or multi-instance applications. Single instance means that only one instance of the application is run no matter how many connections are made to it. A multi-instance application creates a new instance of itself for every caller.

As an *in-process* server, the application becomes an OLE DLL, which looks and acts just like any other DLL. The only difference is that communication between the DLL and the program is accomplished through OLE

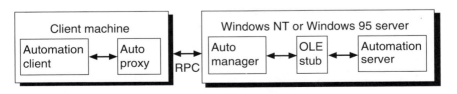

Figure 23.3 *Remote OLE automation*

messaging rather than through the stack. OLE DLLs can be set up as single-instance objects only.

The advantage of an out-of-process executable is that it can be run as an independent application as well as become a component of another application. An in-process OLE DLL can only be called by another application. However, an OLE DLL is much faster than an OLE executable. If performance is important, the DLL is, therefore, the preferred approach.

CHAPTER 24

How to Optimize
Visual Basic Code

This chapter covers some general areas in which Visual Basic code may be optimized. The discussion revolves around managerial, rather than technical, issues due to the scope and nature of this book. However, there is plenty of literature that covers the technical details behind the ideas covered here.

Software can be optimized for speed, functionality, maintainability, size, and ease of use. These goals are not necessarily mutually achievable. Pursuing each can lead to a different set of design decisions. For example, consider an application that calculates current yield on a basket of stocks. If results must be derived within milliseconds of feeding the application new pricing data, calculation speed is of the essence. To gain such speed, the user may be willing to forgo some of the neat display features that are slowing down the program. Maintainability and size may also become less important in view of the desire to gain speed. Clearly, therefore, to begin a process of optimization, it must first be agreed upon what exactly is the optimum and what standards are being sought by optimization.

To determine the optimization goals being sought, pursue a line of questioning similar to the following list:

- Is the program fast enough for the user? If not, what speed is acceptable?
- Is the program producing acceptable precision in its calculations? If not, what is an acceptable accuracy?
- Is the software simple enough so it is easily maintained by the development team? If not, how would performance suffer if you simplify it further?

- Is the application easy to use? If not, would the user be willing to give up some speed to make the screens more user friendly?
- Are people not using the program because it is too large to fit in their computer's memory? If so, can you solve this problem programmatically?

Once you have answered these questions, try to formulate a single optimization goal. This goal statement should strike a balance between the several desired outcomes so that priorities are clear. For example, a goal statement may be: Improve system speed to generate a new calculated yield within half a second per basket of stock, while trying to provide professional-looking screen displays. Such a goal statement sets the priority on speed with a secondary emphasis on appearance.

In the process of arriving at the optimization goal, try to understand more precisely the technical implications of the users' request. Does a desire for higher speed mean faster processing or just faster display? Is the program taking too much RAM or too much disk space? Such pinpointing of the problem beyond simply the ability of the user to express it will save your team from working on the wrong solution.

The next step, of course, is to try to understand why the desired optimization goal is not currently being met. It is imperative that this question be answered before any work is started because the problem may not be caused by the usual suspects. I once worked on a system that, when released, produced reports at excruciatingly slow speed. No matter what we did to optimize the data access code, the reports just would not print quickly enough. Finally, we discovered that there was absolutely nothing wrong with my code but rather another process on the data server was polling the data in such high frequency that the CPU hardly had time to serve our application. We decreased the polling rate and the problem disappeared.

Discovering that the problem is not within your realm of responsibility is hardly a relief. After all, the users are not really interested in who is at fault but they do want their system to work right. The issue, now, becomes a political rather than a technical problem which, depending on the organization, may be easier or harder to solve.

But, if, on the other hand, you find that the problem indeed lies within your system, you must undertake a process that will lead to the desired improvement. It is best to approach this systematically examining the entire application rather than trying to tweak the program here and there. In other words, to reach the desired goal it is often necessary to rewrite some or all the application.

The first step in the process is to review the code in search of the culprit. For example, if you are trying to improve the application's speed, you must determine what statements or functions are taking up most of the execution time. You may want to follow the 80-20 rule, according to which 80% of the execution time will be taken up by 20% of the code. Naturally, you want to concentrate on the problematic 20% of the software to solve the problem and leave the remaining code alone. Incidentally, Visual Basic provides along with the Enterprise Edition a wonderful add-in to help your team determine which lines of code are taking up the most processing time.

Be careful, however, not to optimize too much so as to compromise other requirements. For example, suppose you seek to improve transaction speed to ten items per second, a goal you discover is doable with conventional technology. Your team, however, has devised a complex algorithm that can increase transaction speed to 100 items per second. Contrary to initial reaction and depending on the situation, the second solution may not be best. The complex solution may solve the speed problem but increase code size and reduce maintainability. You will be solving one problem but creating two others. It may, therefore, be better to pursue the conventional solution and save the exotic algorithm for future designs.

Also keep on the lookout for items that are beyond your control. For example, the hardware and operating system puts certain limitations on the application's performance. So, no matter how clever a caching algorithm your team may devise, for instance, in the final analysis, there is a finite limit of how fast you can read from a disk. A faster caching process may bump up against hardware limitations and improve nothing as a result. In such situations you are better off exploring other solutions such as reducing the amount of data read from the disk, or loading it into RAM during startup.

Here are some common optimization hot spots for Visual Basic:

OPTIMIZING SPEED

1. For complex mathematics, it is much faster to use integers and integer math than doing floating-point arithmetic. You can convert floating-point numbers to integers by multiplying by powers of ten and truncating, and then dividing back once the calculation is done.

2. Avoid using variant data types. Aside from the fact that using variants eats up the program stack faster than otherwise, they are handled much more slowly as the program must decide what data type the variant really is and protect itself against illegal values.

3. Whenever reading from or writing to a control, addressing the control is much faster than addressing its default property. That is, *TextBox* returns the same value as *TextBox.Text* but much sooner.

4. Variables are much faster than properties. It is better to do all calculations with variables and only then assign the final result to the property.

5. When using OLE objects, it is best to avoid traversing the OLE tree on every call. Thus, set an object variable to the desired object. That is,

```
SET obj = XLObject.ActiveWorkbook.ActiveSheets.Cells
obj.clear
obj.font = "Courier New"
```

is much better than

```
XLObject.ActiveWorkbook.ActiveSheets.Cells.celar
XLObject.ActiveWorkbook.ActiveSheets.Cells.font = _
    "Courier New"
```

6. VB and Windows use swap files to bring currently executing code in and out of available memory. Swapping is, obviously, a time-consuming effort and it adds little value to the user. To minimize swaps, put all related code in the same module and reduce the number of calls between modules (easier said than done).

7. Whenever possible, try to read files in Binary mode, which is faster than text Input/Random modes.

8. It is better to assign string constants to string variables rather than to assign the literal string. That is, StrVar = EMPTY_STRING is much faster than StrVar = "" when EMPTY_STRING has been declared as a constant.

9. Avoid loading OLE objects repeatedly. Find out if the object is already loaded before creating a new instance.

DISPLAY SPEEDS

1. Don't display forms until they are fully painted. It is faster and it looks much better when you construct and fill in a form in the background prior to display.

2. Hide controls when setting many properties to avoid repaints.

3. Turn the AutoRedraw property to off while writing to the form and then, if necessary, turn it back on when done.

4. Turn off ClipControls.

5. Use Image instead of Picture Box.

6. If memory size allows, keep slow-loading forms in memory by hiding them and then showing them on demand. Discard fast-loading forms by unloading them and reloading as needed.

7. Improve *apparent* speed by using progress indicators such as percent completed or status bar. This at least gives the appearance of faster processing even when no other improvements are made.

OPTIMIZING DATA ACCESS

1. Try not to use the bound data controls available in VB. These controls are clumsy and carry enormous amounts of overhead. Instead, use the database objects provided for in the professional edition.

2. Always use transactions when writing to the database. Use BeginTrans when starting, and then CommitTrans or RollbackTrans when done.

This way, if anything goes wrong during the writing operation, your database is safe and free of partially written records.

3. Try to avoid using the MoveLast method as it is very slow, reading and indexing every record on the way to the last one.

4. Limit the number of records your program returns from the database to the absolute minimum necessary. The bigger the snapshot or dynaset your program manipulates, the more time it will take to process the data.

5. Whenever possible, use snapshots rather than dynasets. Snapshots do not lock the database since the data cannot be changed. Subsequently, other users will not have to wait for dynasets to be closed before they can perform their operations.

6. Optimize the ISAM settings in VB.INI in your Windows directory. See PERFORM.TXT, which comes with VB for further details.

MEMORY OPTIMIZATION

1. Reclaim strings after use by setting them to an empty string.

2. Reclaim objects after use by setting them to NOTHING.

3. Avoid using variants. Each time you declare or pass a variant, 4 bytes of the stack are used up.

4. Use dynamic rather than fixed arrays. Redimention as needed and clear (erase) when done. This will ensure that only necessary memory is used.

5. Remove dead code before making the final EXE. Declared variables that are never used, functions and subs that are never called, and debug statements should be taken out of the code prior to release to reduce the application size.

6. Use 16 color display drivers rather than 256 color drivers (4 bits versus 8).

7. Use Metafile graphics, which are often much smaller than comparable bitmap images.

8. Load pictures only as needed, and share pictures and icons at run time.

If, after trying some of these suggestions, the application's performance is still not acceptable, you may have to resort to converting some time-critical code to a C or even Assembler DLL. Compiled C or Assembler carry less overhead and thus can perform certain tasks faster than Visual Basic. On the other hand, such code is much more difficult to debug, maintain, and modify.

Personally, I have never found the need to develop a DLL to improve speed, opting instead to solve the problem in Visual Basic. Typically, the user community has been very satisfied with such solutions. However, I am not about to completely rule out some instances where other solutions may be necessary.

_____ CHAPTER 25 _____

Application Security

Application security involves defining the users' ability to access, modify, and retrieve data and the mechanism by which this is to be accomplished. Naturally, it is a crucial feature for those applications that require only controlled or limited access. For example, financial institutions that regularly handle multimillion dollar electronic transactions heavily depend on the security features of their systems to prevent theft, unauthorized transactions, and ensure compliance with banking regulations. Likewise, public-sector institutions also require a high level of security for reasons that are somewhat more obscure. In fact our very own federal government is absolutely paranoid about security.

Other industries have somewhat less stringent security requirements but the notion of security is pretty much the same. Basically, most data processing departments are obligated to ensure the integrity of the company's books and records and prevent data corruption. It makes no difference whether the threat to last year's budget projections emanates from a virus created by a malicious college student or from the actions of an incompetent clerk who would delete all files from memory if left to his own volition. In either case, data integrity and corporate assets are at risk. Subsequently, application security is an integral and important function of all computer systems and not just those of banks and the government.

This chapter covers the different security issues involved in application development. Since large volumes can be written on the subject of application security and data encryption—and, indeed, large volumes have been written on the subject—the topics described here are only discussed with a management perspective in mind. Moreover, this chapter does not cover hardware security issues nor does it discuss systemwide security concepts such as virus protection. Both topics are beyond the scope of this book.

THE PHILOSOPHY BEHIND APPLICATION SECURITY

If one examines the various notions of software security, one finds that there are really two extremes. On the one hand are system administrators (SAs) who insist that the user should never be allowed to operate a computer. According to these SAs all aspects of the system must be protected to the nth degree, the keyboard should be disabled and put under lock and key, and the whole computer ought to be placed in a safe in the basement of Fort Knox. If you need to perform any computing, the SAs will be happy to do for you. "Just submit a request. Oh, and by the way, we are so swamped it will take a few days before we get to it."

One can hardly blame system administrators for being so adamant about security. After all, they are the ones who are responsible for the continued operation of the computer systems as well as for the integrity of the data. If something goes wrong, they are the ones who are awakened in the middle of the night and called on the carpet to explain why the firm could not calculate its stock portfolio value when the computer failed. The user who has the power to destroy data or to crash the computer is, thus, the system administrator's worst enemy. And since any user is capable of doing such damage, whether or not he or she realizes it, system administrators strive to build the equivalent of the Great Wall of China around every computer.

But this zeal goes much further than any reasonable explanation would suggest. At times it seems as if every system administrator has been brainwashed to believe that every visitor is an intruder. Paranoia reigns supreme. Consequently, security at the hands of system administrators sometimes gets out of control.

Consider this bit of anecdotal evidence. System administrators tend to ask for and receive from various software vendors a large latitude of control over both the system and any business applications that run on it. Upon system implementation they immediately seize this control and lock out as much functionality from the user as possible. A recent example shows how ridiculous this can become. Microsoft's latest operating systems, Windows NT and Windows 95, allow for exclusion of just about every feature of the operating system from being accessed by the users. This was not the case in earlier versions of these products but Microsoft was strongly urged, by you-know-who to add such capabilities to its systems. In most companies the system administrators use these new access restrictions to take away from the user features the user community previously had no trouble using. In some places users can no longer even change their wallpaper (the screen background) or the screen saver.

Arguably, there may be some good reasons to limit user access to data. But it is absolutely ludicrous to suggest the users' ability to change their desktops' look and feel is a security risk to the firm. Furthermore, by preventing users from using perfectly legitimate functions, the computer Gestapo is setting back the advances PCs made in empowering those users in the first place.

Of course, on the other side of the security spectrum is the user community—the people who actually use the systems on a day-to-day basis. They are the ones who enter data, produce reports, and reconcile statements before 5:00 P.M. today or "your job is on the line!" These people hate security. To them, security is just another bureaucratic obstacle they must circumvent in order to get their work done. They just do not understand why their management can trust them with all kinds of responsible tasks—such as managing a multimillion dollar portfolio—yet not allow them to operate a computer.

Keep in mind that today's user community is increasingly sophisticated. Users do not at all resemble the Mongolian hoards that typically live in the imagination of the system administrators. The stock trader who develops a complex statistical model to predict market movements probably first encountered computers in college or high school. Perhaps he even took one or two computer courses while in school. At home, he owns a powerful machine used not only to balance his checkbook but also to trade his own portfolio, communicate with the rest of the world, and obtain information. Such a user is well aware of what a computer can do. Yet he is often restricted from using the computer at work to its utmost capabilities because of security concerns.

But users hate security for another reason. Client-server systems often require interaction between many systems. As each system's security is being increasingly beefed up, the users find it harder and harder to navigate their cyber universe. Consider the typical setup in many banks. In the morning the user must log into her Windows NT—first password. This process may require logging into a secondary network—password number 2. She then has to log into her e-mail—third password. Each one of her business systems is password protected—some more passwords. Her database is also password protected. Her electronic organizer (PIM) is password protected. Her Bloomberg terminal is also password protected. And her trading floor voice communication system is password protected. When she retrieves her voice-mail messages she has to punch in yet another password. These days, there are some sadistic institutions that even password protect their copying machines.

And all these different systems, of course, have password-protected screen savers that require additional steps every time one takes a coffee break or leaves for a meeting. Each system has a different password expiration cycle, has different rules for which passwords are legal, and does not allow repeated usage of the same password. Given this mish-mash, are we really to condemn the user for being frustrated with security?

As a project manager, it is easy to be caught in the cross fire between the two extremes. So rather than side with one group or another, try to custom fit the application's security with the needs of its constituents—be they users, the company, or government regulators. Begin by developing an independent list of security criteria that the system must meet. For example, you may want to list that the security mechanism of your application should:

- Allow only authorized users to enter new data.
- Allow only authorized users to view data or produce reports.
- Allow only authorized users to modify data.
- Protect data from corruption and/or inadvertent changes.
- Conform to federal, state, and local laws and regulation.
- Meet company security standards and policies.

Next consider the following design issues in view of the foregoing goal statement.

REGULATORY SECURITY REQUIREMENTS. Is the Federal Reserve Bank likely to shut your company down once it reviews your security mechanism during a normal audit? Will the defense department procurement office cancel a contract with your company if it knew what users can freely do on your system? If the answer to such questions is yes, then you are not meeting the most rudimentary regulatory requirements of your industry.

> Take the time to review industry regulatory requirements or hire a knowledgeable consultant to assist with this process. Design your security accordingly.

FIDUCIARY OR CUSTODIAN RESPONSIBILITY. Does your security scheme adequately protect company resources? How about customer resources? Can a user transfer company funds to his own bank account in Switzerland without secondary authorization? Can a user buy herself a car using the brand-new purchasing system you just developed? Can a user delete or modify records that are considered part of the company's books and records? If so, you may have a problem.

> Review company policies regarding action authorization, especially those that have to do with money or material transactions and/or customer transactions. Design the system to meet all such policies.

NETWORK SECURITY. Does your system run on a network or communication lines? If so, will an evil-minded person be able to *sniff* a password just by listening to the line? Can another mischievous person connect into the network past the security gate to do what mischievous persons normally do? If so, is this a problem?

> Review the need to encrypt all or some messages across networks and communication lines.

OTHER LAWS. Does your proposed security scheme require an encryption algorithm that is not allowed to be exported? If so, is your system going to be used by your company's overseas office? That is a no-no. Lose two turns and pay $50 to the bank. Encryption technology is protected by the Defense Department and cannot be installed on your foreign offices.

> See if any laws require or preclude the use of certain technology. Again, hire experts if this is outside your area of expertise.

MULTILEVEL SECURITY. Is PC-level security tight enough to ensure correct access? Do you need application-level security? How about server-level security? How about network-level security? Do you need record-level authorization, table-level authorization, or some other, more complex mechanism?

> Determine the security needs at each and every level of the system and develop appropriate security schemes for each.

USER PRACTICES. Is the user community security conscious or do users regularly trade passwords with each other? Does this level of user compliance fit the overall security needs of the system? Are the users likely to attempt sabotage if they are relieved of their duties?

> Decide if the user community must be assisted in its security compliance using such mechanical devices as daily password generators, eye-retina readers, palm print readers, and so on. Decide on the interval between password changes, the length of a password, and rules for new passwords (all numbers not allowed, no birthdate, no last names, etc.).

AUDIT TRAIL. Does the application require an audit trail so all changes to the data are memorized? If so, do you need to store just the changes or also the data and user who changed the data?

> Determine the need for an audit trail feature in your application.

EXISTING TECHNOLOGY. Based on your previous analysis, can you use an existing scheme that is widely accepted in the industry? Normally, by using industry standard security methods you can meet most of your own company's requirements.

> Read up on what your competitors are doing about security and what your industry's accountants, MIS professionals, and regulators think about such practices. Try to have your design use generally accepted technology.

STANDARDS. Does your company have a standard security mechanism? Do you have standards for password length, rules, and change frequency?

> Keep to existing standards to ensure cross-application uniformity.

AUTHENTICATING VERSUS AUTHORIZING

Prior to any further discussion, a distinction must be made between *authenticating* and *authorizing*. Authenticating a user means ensuring that the person attempting to log into the system is really the same person the computer knows and expects. For instance, requiring the user to enter a password is an authenticating technique since, presumably, only that user knows his password.

Authorizing, on the other hand, means granting the user authority to perform certain actions such as adding, deleting, or modifying the database.

Most systems require both authentication and authorization. But certain applications can be deemed perfectly secure even if they perform only authentication. For example, a managerial decision support system that allows users to only query data—one that permits only certain data to be viewed—need not have an authorization procedure. Basically, everyone who logs in—thus, *authenticated*—is assumed to be authorized to view the data.

On the other hand, an inventory system, for example, usually requires both authentication and authorization to be secure. It is not enough to verify that the person trying to log in is really Joe, the inventory clerk, but the system should also enforce the fact that Joe is only authorized to enter shipments and should not be allowed to make inventory adjustments. Otherwise, Joe will likely grow rich selling the company's product from his garage and then make the appropriate adjustments to the inventory.

THE LOGIN

The login dialog box (Figure 25.1) should be the first thing the users encounter when they attempt to run the application It is the application's first line of defense against unauthorized intruders. At the very minimum the login dialog should prompt the user for a user ID and password. Only a correct response to both of these prompts allows entry into the application.

Typically, the password text box display is scrambled so whatever is typed in is not discernible. This is so someone watching over the user's shoulder would not be able to read the password.

Some security schemes require an additional entry called the secondary password. This is either a day password generated by the system administrators each day or a password generated by a calculator-like device assigned to each user. Such a password generator runs an algorithm that is similar to the

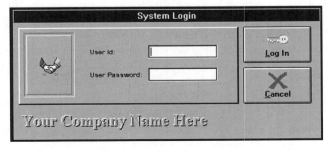

Figure 25.1   *The Login dialog*

one run on the authenticating entity so that at any given situation and time, the password generated is exactly the same for both the client and the authenticating server. This method solves the problem of unauthorized access by people who had left the organization but whose accounts have been left alive for business reasons. It also eliminates the need to encrypt passwords since any given password is only valid for one entry.

More sophisticated techniques require an additional input device such as a fingerprint reader, voice recognition device, retina scanner, or simply just a physical key. This is so a stolen password would not be sufficient to enter the system. A bank ATM machine uses both a password—the user Personal Identification Number (PIN)—and a key—the bank card.

Regardless of what method is used, all login processes perform two functions:

1. Authenticates the user: Ensure the user is really who she says she is by matching the user ID to the password and other information.
2. Collects information for authorization, namely, user ID.

There are certain generally accepted rules associated with password authentication:

- Users should be compelled to change their password periodically. Two months seems to be a good interval.
- The new password should not be a repeat of previous passwords. Have your application remember the last ten used.
- Passwords should be of a minimum length to ensure a large enough number of permutations. Do not permit fewer than eight characters.
- Passwords should differ from the user ID.

PASSWORD ENCRYPTION

From a technical perspective, the login process on a stand-alone computer is very simple: It consists of obtaining the user ID and password and checking them against a list of users in the database. Networks and phone line communication, however, require an additional level of complexity. This is because when one computer authenticates a user on another, the password passes through network or communication lines. Presumably, these lines can be *sniffed* or listened to and the password and user ID can be extracted.

Therefore, it is generally a good idea to encrypt the password before it is sent to the authenticating entity or anytime it must travel across communication lines. The password should then be unscrambled on the other side.

AUTHORIZATION

Unless your company already has an authorization mechanism in place, your application must determine what the user who logged in—authenticated—is *authorized* to do. Many business applications restrict or allow user access by broadly defined functionality. That is, the user is authorized or not authorized to read, add, modify, or delete information on an entire application basis. Other applications further restrict these four functions by database entity. That is, a user can read, add, modify, or delete only in certain databases, tables, or records.

The more granular the restriction scheme, the more complex the security mechanism becomes. A security scheme that is based on record by record privileges—for example, users can only modify records in the customers table and only those records that are in the state of New York—is, perhaps, the most complicated approach. It is much easier to restrict by table or even by database.

Mechanically, such restrictions are accomplished by assigning the user a so-called *ticket* during the login process. This electronic ticket holds information about what entities and what functions the user is authorized to access or execute. The login process creates this ticket by obtaining the information from the security database. Such ticket information may look like this for table-level security:

Table	Read	Add	Modify	Delete
Customers	Yes	Yes	Yes	Yes
Orders	No	No	No	No
Parts	Yes	Yes	Yes	No
Salespeople	Yes	Yes	No	No

Whenever the user attempts to perform an action—say, add a customer—the application checks the ticket and determines if the user has the authority to do so. In this case the authority exists so the program can proceed with the addition. Otherwise an error should be displayed.

AUTHORIZATION GROUPS

It is much easier to administer user privileges if authority is designated by groups rather than by user. Users can then be assigned to groups based on their levels of security and inherit the group's privileges.

Group authorization allows for adding and removing privileges for an entire set of users. Likewise, as new users are added, they can be easily assigned a whole range of privileges simply by associating them with one or more groups. Thus, inventory clerks can belong to the Inventory Clerks Group, which is allowed to add records but never delete or modify them.

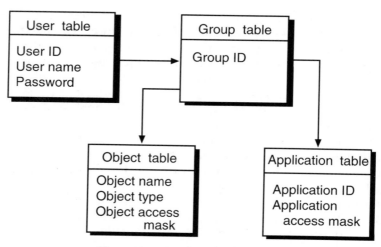

Figure 25.2 *A typical security database*

A global security database should be set up to store all user and access information. It is a multitiered design by which users are assigned to access groups that are, in turn, given permission to applications by object. (See Figure 25.2.) Each object has a bit mask associated with it that the application can use to decipher specific privileges.

For example, Mr. John Smith, user ID SmithJ, is a new user added to the User Table and assigned to the Add Record Group (Group Table). This group can add and modify entries in the inventory database (Application Table).

When Mr. Smith is added to the database, he is also given database access capabilities (in this case Select only) to certain tables. This is done by invoking a stored procedure that grants capabilities based on the application needs. This stored procedure serves an additional function by synchronizing Mr. Smith's user ID and password with the server user ID and password.

If Mr. Smith is to log onto the server using any tool other than the application, he will only be able to view the data but not update or delete data. But when he logs into the application, the application checks the access mask and allows him, through the all-powerful gatekeeper, to enter and modify data.

AUTHENTICATING SERVERS

Some security specialists advocate the installation of authenticating servers on the network. These are servers that reside between the client PCs and the data servers and act as gatekeepers. When the user logs in at the beginning of the day, she is authenticated and assigned a ticket holding *all* of her privileges for every application. During the day she can launch other applications using her tickets, without having to be reauthenticated, because the gatekeeping application ensures compliance.

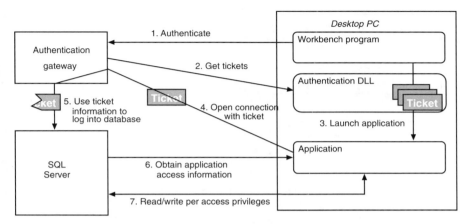

Figure 25.3 *Authenticating server scheme*

This method has a major advantage of increasing systemwide security and centralizing all security functions for a uniform look and feel. It also eliminates the need for users to have to log into every one of their separate applications. Unfortunately, authenticating servers (Figure 25.3) are somewhat limiting when it comes to some of the technology discussed in this book. Because the *gatekeeper* resides in the middle layers of the network, it also interferes with OLE and ODBC object technology. Subsequently, it is rather difficult to implement such a scheme at this point.

DATABASE SERVERS

Database servers present a unique problem for client-server security. That is because database servers are in and of themselves complete applications that can operate on their own as well as through other applications. Subsequently, no matter how well secured one client application is, someone can always circumvent the security mechanism by accessing the database directly or through other applications.

Luckily, most database servers, and certainly Sybase and Microsoft's SQL Server, have their own security mechanism that includes both authentication and authorization. (See Figure 25.4.) So, for example, when a user attempts to access data on SQL Server that were entered and maintained through the application, he can either be prevented from logging in or be given only browse privileges.

Alas, since the user server privileges are very limited or nonexistent, the front-end application cannot use his account to log in. Instead, when he logs into the application—rather than the database—the application, in turn, must log into the database as a superuser. The application then acts as a gatekeeper and decides, based on its own security scheme, what actions the user should be permitted to take in the database.

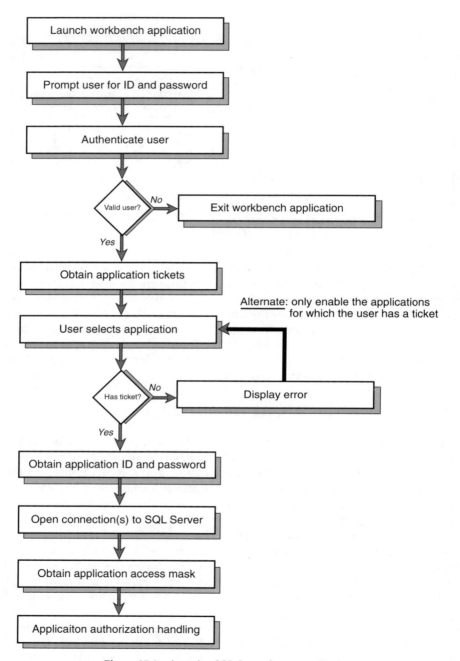

Figure 25.4　*Accessing SQL Server from an application*

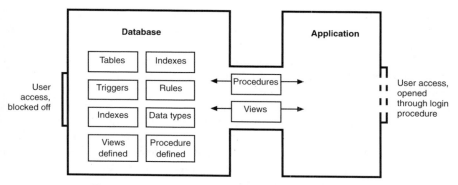

Figure 25.5 *Using stored procedures and views to access data*

Generally, client applications should accomplish processing on the server by proxy rather than by directly issuing server commands. In other words, rather than permitting the application to directly write or modify a table in the database, the application must execute server stored procedures to do so. (See Figure 25.5.) This way, no one, not even the application, is given permission to change the database. Only the database can change itself through the execution of stored procedures. The application should only be granted the right to execute stored procedures. (Am I starting to sound like a psychiatrist?)

There are basically four conventional client-server schemes of ensuring adequate client-server security when it comes to databases:

Adopted Authority:	The most common approach. All updates are done via stored procedures owned by the *application* with update authority to underlying objects. Users are granted authority to stored procedures but do not have update authority to any table. This method has the effect of encapsulating the database.
Login IDs:	Employs different login IDs for updates and queries, logging the user on and off to the server depending on the desired task.
Gatekeeper:	The most sophisticated approach, it controls all logins with a custom-written, front-end gatekeeper. All requests to the server must pass through this program which, in turn, determines the privileges needed by the requester.
Triggers:	This technique places update control logic inside triggers associated with each table. For example, the triggers could check a table to make sure the requesting user is authorized for updates.

The Login ID and Trigger methods are not optimal for most business applications due to their lack of flexibility, increased network traffic, potential degradation in performance, and complexity.

The Adopted Authority method covers most generally accepted audit requirements but fails by allowing access to the same data from multiple applications. Take, for example, a user named John Smith who normally enters new inventory into the database using an internally developed application but then moves on to produce ad hoc reports using Microsoft Access. Alas, a straightforward implementation of the Adopted Authority method would allow Mr. Smith to also update his data from Access by running a stored procedure. He would, therefore, undesirably be bypassing the edit and validation rules of the application.

The gatekeeper approach covers this problem but fails to meet many generally accepted audit requirements of banks and other institutions.

Consequently, I recommend a hybrid approach of the two more acceptable methods. An Adopted Authority Gatekeeper scheme administers all user actions through a GUI front end, checking first for permissions, with all updates accomplished through stored procedures. Yet only the gatekeeper has a right to execute these stored procedures, thus eliminating the ability of anyone to update the data other than through the application. (See Figure 25.6.)

Under this scheme, the user logs into the gatekeeper application using his global user ID and password. The front-end application then logs into the server as a super-user with full access capabilities. Before each requested action, the gatekeeper checks for the user privileges.

When the user logs into some other accessing applications—for example MS Access—she logs into the database as herself and, thus, has limited

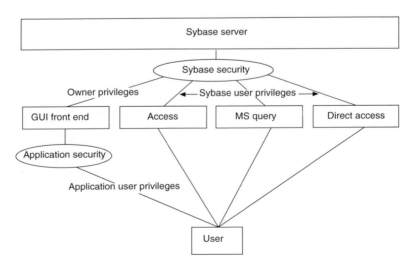

Figure 25.6 *Adopted authority gatekeeper scheme used on a Sybase database*

privileges. For example, she may only be allowed to query *some* tables, but not view others or update any of the tables.

SEPARATION OF DATA FROM CODE

Physically separating database maintenance from code maintenance is an important security practice. It means restricting programmers' access to live data while at the same time restricting database administrators' access to the code. This ensures that crooked programmers—don't know any—are not able to change the company's data by circumventing their own security schemes while at the same time, database administrators are not able to use program code to access the data.

This separation is accomplished by enforcing four policies:

- Developing and testing the application using only a nonproduction copy of the database.
- Adhering to the data server security scheme described in the previous section, and, in particular to the use of data processing by proxy (by executing stored procedures).
- Granting database administrators access only to executable modules, never to the source code.
- Storing the master password by which the application logs into the database in a place accessible only to the database administrators.

AUDIT TRAILS

An audit trail is the information residing within the data that can tell who changed what and when. It is necessary because regardless of how foolproof your authentication and authorization techniques are, no security system can prevent human error. The data are, obviously, not safe just because only authorized users are allowed to enter the system. People who are permitted to use the application sometimes make mistakes. There are some bad apples who even cause intentional harm. In fact, the system itself may be destroying good data because of some obscure bug. In any case, it is essential to keep a record of changes to the data.

As with other aspects of security, there are several ways to maintain a history of changes. One way involves timestamping and userstamping every record. When a record is added, it includes within it who it was who added it and when. If a user changes a record, it is copied with the new timestamp and user ID and the old record remains in the database, flagged as modified. Deleted records also are copies of modified records, flagged as deleted.

By this method, every change made is recorded with the time and user ID never to be modified again. It is a very thorough way of keeping a trail but it is not very efficient. A large number of changes can use up an enormous portion of the storage medium. Also, change reports are difficult to produce since the entire database must be scanned for records that have recently been changed.

On the other hand, this method allows for much easier restoration of data in case of a mistake since the changed data are intact and complete. All one needs to do is change its status from modified or deleted to active.

An alternate way of implementing an audit trail is to remember only the changes, rather than the entire record, in a dedicated changes table. Each field in the database is given an index number. As fields and records change, the changes are remembered along with the time and user ID in the changes table. This allows for a quick report of database changes but not for easy restoration of data. In case of a mistake, actions have to be *played back* in order to be reversed.

CAVEATS

Now that we have thoroughly covered the concepts behind security, we must talk about the potential pitfalls of any good security system. The first issue deals with the notion that any application's security system is only as good as its weakest link. In most schemes, the weakest link is the password. Most of us know that passwords are not very secure yet, except in the most sophisticated and complex systems, a password is all one needs to enter an application. And once the password security is breached, it really matters little how sophisticated the rest of the system is. Everything is open to the user.

Regrettably, users are not very security conscious. In just about every place I have been, users share passwords, write them on their monitors, never change the original login password, or use the same password as their ID. There is really little an application development manager can do to alleviate the problem. Sure, we can try to force compliance by expiring passwords and enforcing password rules. But in reality, a password is a nuisance to the user and so it is not a very reliable key.

Audit trails and physical authentication devices (fingerprint readers, voice recognition, etc.) are a good technique to beef up this downfall, but they are expensive. Even with such devices, no amount of technology will replace user cooperation. It is therefore imperative to instill security conscientiousness as well as accountability into the user community. This can be accomplished by training, hanging posters, and frequent reminders on voice and electronic mail.

A second problem with some security schemes is that the interaction of different MIS policies and security mechanisms can potentially open up a gap in the security fence. For example, I know one major New York investment bank that enforces a strict separation of source code and data. Database administrators cannot modify code and programmers cannot modify the database. At the same time the bank also has a strict policy concerning code maintenance. Once in production, programmers cannot change the code but, instead, must submit macros that change the code. This way, the code is always kept by a third party that ensures auditability and integrity of the source code.

This seems, at first glance, to be a very secure scheme. Yet, on a closer examination, one may notice that taken together, this setup opens up a way for a Trojan horse to be sneaked into the system. In other words, a not so well-intentioned programmer can submit a macro to the code management administrators that, when executed, causes a transaction to be processed on the database. Something like a virus-by-proxy, if you will. The programmer may not have access to the database, but the keepers of the code do. Subsequently, the programmer gains access through a third party.

It is important to ensure that not only your system is safe but that your policies and algorithms do not open gaping holes in other systems.

CHAPTER 26

What Are DLLs and How Do They Affect Implementation?

DLL is an acronym for a dynamically linked library. A DLL is, thus, an executable code library that is loaded and linked into by an application. Once loaded, it can also be shared with any other running applications. A DLL remains loaded in RAM as long as any of the calling applications are running and, therefore, are linked to it. For example, a Visual Basic application may use CTL3D32.DLL, a library of routines that facilitates the 3D display of screen elements. Once loaded, the routines in CTL3D32.DLL can be called upon not only by the VB application that loaded it but also by any other running application, say, Microsoft Excel, for example. CTL3D32.DLL stays loaded in RAM until all the linked applications are terminated.

Mechanically, there is nothing new about shared modules. Programmers could always share libraries by declaring external routines and then compiling and linking their application with existing modules and libraries. The resulting executables then contained copies of the shared object code. The new concept DLLs bring to the table is the ability to link dynamically while the application executable is being launched, and without a formal, manual linking process. As a result, multiple applications can share the same code in memory, thus saving precious RAM resources. As an added benefit, DLLs provide for similar look and feel across many applications since, naturally, sharing libraries means sharing appearance and functionality. (See Figure 26.1.)

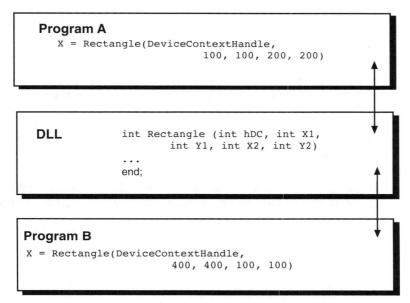

Figure 26.1 *DLL interface in RAM*

Not surprisingly, most Visual Basic components are, themselves, DLLs. That is, the screen controls, whether VBXs or OCXs,[1] are really dynamically linked libraries incorporating code, data, graphics, and event responses. This setup saves tremendous amounts of memory when multiple applications draw on the same resources.

Many Windows modules are also DLLs, which means that while Microsoft Windows is running, any program can call on Windows routines and examine Windows data. Programmatically, the interface with the Windows (or any other application) DLLs is done through what are known as Application Programming Interface (API) calls. These are little more than calls to external procedures.

In VB, the loading and linking into a DLL is initiated by a directive at the head of any module that declares an external procedure. For example, the API declaration to create a window in Windows is:

```
Declare Function Rectangle Lib "GDI" (ByVal hDC As Integer, ByVal
     X1 As Integer, ByVal Y1 As Integer, ByVal X2 As Integer,
     ByVal Y2 As Integer) As Integer
```

This tells the VB program that the Rectangle routine resides in the GDI library. If it is not already loaded—in this case it is because it is part of the Windows operating system—it will be loaded the first time the routine is

---

[1] Technically, OCXs are not really DLLs since linking is accomplished through OLE technology rather than by a more primitive means. Practically, though, they look and act as DLLs.

called by the program. For instance, when a window is to be drawn the program can call this external procedure by:

```
X = Rectangle(DeviceContextHandle, 100, 100, 200, 200)
```

This call opens a 100 by 100 window at location 100, 100 of the device whose handle the variable DeviceContextHandle holds. It returns the handle for the window.

Alas, the DLL's most important feature, the ability to dynamically link into shared libraries, is its most devastating shortcoming. Indeed, if you asked most experienced Windows programmers about their number-one pet peeve you will surely be told: DLLs.

How can something so useful be such a pain in the neck, you ask? The answer is simple: Under current Windows implementation, DLLs with the same name do not have to be unique. This means that two programmers, working separately, can each develop and install a DLL named MY.DLL, each performing an entirely different task. Programmer A uses his MY.DLL in his *super-duper* cash flow analysis program. Programmer B uses her own MY.DLL in her Profitability Analysis module. The unsuspecting user starts the cash flow forecasting application and does whatever bean counters do with cash flow forecast applications. Naturally, MY.DLL of the Programmer A variety is automatically loaded into RAM. After a long morning of very productive number crunching, the user decides that she has enough data to determine the profitability of the company. So she gingerly attempts to start the profitability program only to find Windows spitting a nasty error at her. If she is lucky and uses the latest 32-bit operating system, the error will tell her that a certain function call cannot be located. But if she uses earlier versions of Windows, she is likely to crash the system. What is happening is that MY.DLL of Programmer B is not loaded. Windows fails to load B's DLL because it thinks it is already loaded since the names are similar even though the contents are quite different.

Notice that MY.DLL of Programmer A does not have to physically reside on disk anywhere near MY.DLL of Programmer B. Windows is smart enough to load the version from the working directory of the program that calls it first. If it does not find it there, it will search in the Windows system directory. If it is still not located, Windows will search along the path and load whichever MY.DLL it finds first. In other words, this problem is multi-faceted since under certain conditions a mix-up could have occurred even if the second program were to never have been started. One never knows for sure, without much toil and trouble, which DLL is currently loaded.

"So what?" you probably say to yourself. With 26 letters in the alphabet and ten additional digits to play with, the number of combinations to produce an eight-character (for now) file name is astounding. If file names are unique, you probably reason, the problem just described should go away. Indeed, I would grant you the chances are minimal that a cleverly enough named DLL will be duplicated by another developer. And in an ideal world, you would probably be right and we could all go on to read the next chapter. But since we live on earth rather than in heaven, even uniquely named DLLs can cause a problem by, gasp, stepping on themselves.

How can that be? Well, remember that applications are rarely released only once. Bug fixes and the need to improve and expand functionality means that additional versions of the same program are developed roughly every 12 to 18 months (or, in the case of Lotus, whenever someone kicks their butt with a better product). Unfortunately, this is also true for DLLs. That means that the X3RG56Y.DLL version 1.0 you purchased with your Flux Capacitor application will most likely be competing with the X3RG56Y.DLL version 1.1B purchased with your Trash Resistor application. Sure, the new DLL should be upward compatible but (a) what if it is not, and (b) the newer software may still be missing features if the older DLL is loaded first.

Yach! We can clearly see why a DLL is the natural enemy of an application developer. But how do you solve this problem? Well, first, let me admit that I am not convinced the problem is completely solvable. In fact, I believe that this is the Gordian knot of Windows programming and that whoever finally solves it to the satisfaction of all will be immediately crowned king of all programmers. Nonetheless, let's review the conventional wisdom on this subject with the notion that at least some improvement over nonusability is desirable.

We must begin with the understanding that DLL incompatibility is not a Visual Basic problem—it is a Windows problem. As such, it does not really matter what language is being used to develop applications. In fact, you need not develop any application at all to be hit with this particular issue. As seen earlier, you may simply and innocently purchase two different applications that use two different versions of the same DLL to cause absolute chaos. Visual Basic is only a victim of the situation, and perhaps more so than any other application, because it uses off-the-shelf DLLs as building blocks. Consequently, you are more likely to run into DLL incompatibility problems if your company is engaged in multiple VB project development.

Once this culpability is understood, many managers resort to attempting standardization. This means that the corporation as a whole tests and certifies DLLs by version. An approved version is then used by all applications and development efforts. No un-approved DLL can ever be loaded on the network or desktop and so no DLL incompatibility is encountered. New versions of DLLs can be loaded only after they have been certified to work correctly with all applications.

In theory, this scheme works great. In reality, however, it fails miserably. It is a classic example of correctly identifying the problem only to end up reaching a very wrong solution. First, anybody that has ever breathed corporate air for even a second of their life knows that corporations cannot easily reach a conclusion on anything, let alone on a little thing such as a DLL. If you attempt to implement this solution, you will soon discover that the downtown New York developers do not agree with the requirements of the

Hong Kong developers who, in turn, fight tooth and nail the recommendations of the midtown New York developers. Each development effort has its own DLL requirements and since each development team reports to a different manager, the chances of cooperation are slim. Multiply this situation by hundreds of DLLs and . . . well, you get the picture. Let's just say that I have never seen anyone succeed in standardizing DLLs and I have seen many attempts to do so.

The second problem with standards is that they are very tough to enforce. Even if your company had successfully published a list of all approved DLLs and went through the costly step of removing unapproved DLLs from everyone's desktop, you can only be sure that at that moment in time that standards were met. People routinely and frequently load new applications on their machines with or without the administrator's approval. They test their son's new football game or their wife's new checkbook application, they load new utilities, and upgrade their old personal stuff. (I guess that is why it is called a *personal* computer.) Developers are especially guilty of this unruly behavior as they just love to test new, not always fully completed, software. Unfortunately, each new application comes with its own set of new DLLs, some of which conflict with existing DLLs.

We must also question the concept of setting standards from the perspective of progress. Standards tend to solve problems by halting all change. Yet, arguably, some change is good. Standards cannot distinguish between good and bad changes. To a standards enforcer, all change is bad. In this particular instance, attempting to peg DLL versions prevents the company from benefiting from new and improved applications simply because one of the new application's dependent DLLs is not certified. In my opinion this is clearly a case where the benefits of standardization are far outweighed by the downfalls.

If you are still not convinced that setting standards in this situation is the wrong approach, consider costs. Every time a new application or an upgrade is released, someone must test each of the scores of accompanying DLLs with every application known to exist on the company's machines. Add to that the fact that upgrades and proposed applications are released daily with an ever-increasing number of supporting DLLs. Clearly, any attempt to keep up certification even in the best of companies is a resource hog. Can you justify to upper management the act of dedicating a team of testers whose only job is to ensure DLL compatibility? Doubtful.

A somewhat less effective solution in theory, although much more workable in real life, is application self-enforcement. This is a method by which an application checks loaded DLLs to ensure that it is compatible with them. There are several Windows APIs that provide loaded module information and allow for the extraction of version information from the files. A good application should always check the list of loaded modules against its own internal list of needed DLLs to see if some of these are already loaded. If a match is found, the application should extract version data from the loaded

DLL and see if the data match its own requirements. If so, the application should continue to run as normal. But if a version incompatibility is found, the user should be given a choice of not running the application or at least be told that it may not act as originally designed.

There are several commercially available components and programs that accomplish this task so the functionality need not even be programmed from scratch. VersionStamper™ by Desaware is one such component.

As promised, however, this approach is still not ideal. First, it is not clear what constitutes version information. Many software developers forget to increment the version information in the headers of their programs and so two subsequent versions may show the same version number. This is a terrible sin and any programmer found to be guilty of it should be spanked repeatedly for six straight days, but there is hardly anything we can do about it. Some people try to get around this oversight by also checking the file size and the creation date but these, too, may be misleading. It is also not obvious what is to be done if only one out of the three indicators—version number, date, or file size—is different. Has the file really changed or only copied recently so only the date changed?

Second, this method does not work in reverse. That is, even if your application does all the version checking in the world, other applications may be in conflict with your own DLLs. Unless these other applications do their own version checking, you may, unknowingly and unwillingly, be the one causing the damage.

But perhaps the biggest shortcoming of this method is that it only alleviates the symptoms but solves very few of the underlying causes. Even with version checking, DLLs cannot be magically aligned on the disk or in memory. In essence, version checking simply indicates to the user that she may only think she is driving a Rolls Royce but in reality she may be driving a Chevy. But this method does not provide any way whatsoever of changing what is already in memory.

That is not to say that there are no ways to remove from memory unwanted DLLs. One can certainly do so but the original calling application will surely crash when it is reactivated. In some cases, Windows may crash with it. This undesirable situation comes about because by uprooting an active DLL, a program may attempt to execute a piece of code that is no longer there. The calling stack is no longer valid and so the computer must be rebooted. But I guess we are getting a bit too technical for the purpose of this discussion.

The bottom line is that at this writing, version checking is the best we can do. It is the most cost-effective, realistic solution that a middle manager can hope for. Despite its shortcomings, version checking is not a bad solution to an otherwise very difficult problem.

CHAPTER 27

Is It Soup Yet? Quality Control

Software testing is the least glamorous of all software development chores. Clearly, no statue has ever been erected at Arlington National Cemetery depicting seven brave testers struggling to lift a flagpole over some system. In fact, no statue has ever been erected to commemorate any testing effort, anywhere, at anytime in the history of mankind. As if this lack of recognition is not discouraging enough, testing is also viewed as a self-distracting force within the development team. After all, a successful test cycle typically results in finding fault with the team's handcrafted masterpiece. How *dare* they? Who the hell do they think they are? Let *them* try to manage memory any better . . . and so on.

But if there is no glamour in testing, there is definitely an unspoken notion that testing, or rather, lack of adequate testing, is solely responsible for all software failures. So while it may be acceptable for programmers to produce imperfect code, and for analysts to write incomplete specifications, testers are never permitted a failure, no matter how minor.

"It ain't so," you protest? Just witness how companies and the media treat the discovery of product defects: In 1995, Intel discovered an obscure bug in its flagship Pentium processor chip that under extreme circumstances miscalculated floating-point arithmetic. Intel finally agreed to spend over $200 million to replace the chips after a ton of embarrassing publicity. But did anybody suggest that Intel's defective chip shipped to market with a bug because some engineer screwed up? Noooooo! Rather, everyone agreed that it was the quality control department that failed to detect the problem and that must take the blame. And NASA's Hubbell telescope did not blast off into space wearing the wrong pair of prescription glasses because some drunken fool read the specification upside down. No, it was quality control that fell short and should be fired promptly.

So, obviously, from a management perspective, testing translates into everything to lose and nothing to gain. It takes up resources but produces no tangible product. Yet without testing, the project is lost. In this chapter, therefore, we will touch on not only testing but the whole issue of quality and quality control. As with other subjects, only the managerial implications of testing will be covered. More detail and technical information can be obtained from the numerous books on the subject that are currently in publication.

TOTAL QUALITY MANAGEMENT

There are two truths we must all agree on if we are to hold an intelligent conversation on software quality control:

1. *Testing, as a separate organizational function, does not add value to the product.* Testing may very well be necessary to ensure a bug-free roll-out but, in itself, it adds no tangible value to the customer.

   This is, perhaps, a subtle distinction but a very important one. No one buys or is willing to pay extra for the testing that goes into a certain application. Instead, one buys the application assuming that it is bug free. For example, if both application A and application B are bug free, the purchaser is not likely to pay extra for application A just because more testing went into it. The customer *is* willing to pay, in contrast, for features, ease of use, and functionality. These are all value-adding aspects of the products and thus can collect a price premium. Testing, on the other hand, is not value adding and so the investment in it cannot be recovered.

   Note that I am not at all suggesting that testing is not necessary. It may very well be needed as a stopgap measure in the absence of any other quality control technique. I am merely saying that one cannot charge a premium for the fact that testing was conducted.

   I am also not implying that bug-free software is not preferable to bug-ridden software and thus cannot be more pricy. On the contrary, of the two otherwise similar applications, the one that contains less defects will surely be able to fetch a higher price. Rather I am suggesting that centralized testing as an independent function must be separated from the concept of quality. People may be willing to pay extra for quality but not for testing. In fact testing may not necessarily be the most cost-effective way of achieving a high quality.

2. *Software applications can and must be bug free.* Let's return to the Intel Pentium classic quality control nightmare described earlier. In the wake of this fiasco I read several opinions by respected members of the software industry proclaiming it impossible to produce software that is com-

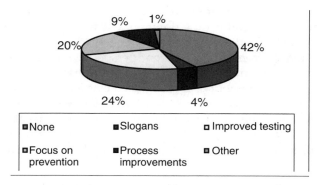

Figure 27.1 *How companies pursue software quality*[1]

pletely bug free. This argument is based on the fact that large applications are intrinsically very complex and that these applications interact with other very complex systems. This combination cannot possibly be duplicated in a development/testing environment. It, therefore, becomes increasingly costly to find and correct the last few bugs of an application—so much more expensive, in fact, that it may not be worth doing.

I am strongly opposed to this point of view. Clearly, it represents a cop-out on the part of the software industry which, in effect, is saying: "We have done the best that we can and we cannot do any better." By saying so, they are denying that producing bug-free software is doable and within their ability and so it must be our goal. Failing to even attempt reaching this goal is against everything we technologists believe.

You need only observe other industries to realize that doctrines such as the one just expressed are not new. There were times when people believed that airplane crashes are inevitable; that it is acceptable for

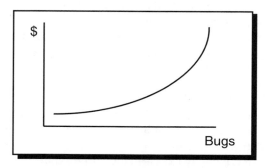

Figure 27.2 *Marginal cost of discovering additional bugs*

[1]Graph taken from Edward Yourdon, *The Decline and Fall of the American Programmer*, (Englewood Cliffs, NJ: Yourdon Press, 1993), pp. 199–201.

one out of several thousand cars to be a lemon; or that telephone and electrical service can be interrupted periodically. Yet, today, none of these opinions is popular because they have all been proven invalid. Airplanes do not have to crash, certainly cars can be made defect free, and it is no longer acceptable to live even one second without a telephone or electricity. Those who operated within these respective industries and did not think likewise are probably not in business anymore.

In his book *Decline and Fall of the American Programmer*, Edward Yourdon talks about this issue:

> One popular characterization of quality today is 6σ [Six Sigma] quality, where σ is the symbol for *standard deviation*. In terms of software, [6σ] translates into a defect rate of approximately three to four defects per *million* lines of code; by contrast, the typical software product produced by the average software organization in the United States has three to four defects per *thousand* lines of code. . . . Does this matter? In other industries, the best-in-class companies are typically at 6σ level of quality and they dominate their markets. And in some industries, customers have come to depend on this level of quality: the airline industry, for example, operates at 6.4σ.[2]

> Similarly, it should be our industry's golden rule that software applications can and must be bug free. That is a technologically achievable goal as it has been in any other human endeavor known to date.

So how does one marry the desire to produce bug-free applications to the notion that testing is neither a desirable nor a feasible path to achieving such a goal? The answer is by following the generally accepted concepts of total quality management (TQM) practiced in other industries, albeit slightly differently. Since total quality management applies well to production and not as well to design and development, we must slightly alter these ideas to better fit the application development cycle.

STATE YOUR GOAL

The goal of any development project should be zero defects, so anything less is a failure.[3] Even one bug discovered by the user after final release is not acceptable. Therefore, your role as a manager is to ensure that zero defects is the only quality control goal your team strives for. Send memos, hold meetings, hang posters, have zero defect *pow-wows*, do whatever works best in your organization, but make sure that everyone is on the same page. If nothing else, your people should be able to instinctively yell "Zero Defects!" in the middle of the night should they happen to suddenly wake up.

---

[2] Ibid.

[3] Note that 6σ quality is only a milestone toward the zero-defect goal.

You will, of course, encounter opposition to this goal. Surely, at least one person on your team will adamantly insist that zero defects is not achievable. But whatever the arguments are, you must never give in on the zero-defect goal. Make it a nonnegotiable issue and discourage any discussion to the contrary. It may even be wise to co-opt the whining person by placing him or her in charge of coordinating quality control. Make sure everyone understands that the position carries with it the responsibility for success as well as accountability for failure. You will be amazed how soon such resistance will dissipate when you have instilled religion into the nonbelievers by virtue of changing their job functions.

On the whole, however, you will probably be pleasantly surprised to find that many of your programmers appreciate this new push toward quality. Many software professionals take pride in their work and prefer not to distribute shoddy products. This can easily be observed every day in any given company where application developers engage in heated discussions with their management arguing that the product is not yet ready for release, only to be overruled by management. By stressing the zero-defect goal, therefore, you will most likely be reinforcing the team's own conviction.

MANAGEMENT COMMITMENT AND
EMPOWERING YOUR TEAM

The number-one impediment to achieving zero defects is lack of management commitment. The number-two obstacle is insufficient authorization by team members to affect the quality control process. The two problems are related, sharing similar symptoms, as illustrated by the following scenario: Management preaches quality control at every opportunity but when a developer reports a bug at some late stage of the development cycle, the manager pats her on the back and sends her back to her cube without taking corrective action. The manager may even say something like, "We will just publish a technical note with a work-around. After all, you don't really expect us to stop the release process, do you, now?"

Such lack of management commitment to the zero-defect standard is exacerbated by the inability of the developer to do something about it. As a result, a programmer who encounters such a situation typically concludes that her management's expressed desire to publish bug-free code is artificial. That is, management is really only paying lip service to the latest fad and should be ignored. She will soon forget about quality control and may even forgo reporting newly found bugs since, apparently, no one really cares.

Management commitment and employee empowerment are important to any corporate effort but these ideas are crucial to quality control. Surely we have all heard, by now, about Japanese factories that install stop switches along their assembly lines. The idea is to enable workers to stop the line should they detect any defect in the product, no matter how minor. No doubt, stopping the line costs these companies dearly but they are willing to incur the expense so that their product leaves the factory defect free. More importantly, they want their employees to know that management is committed to quality and so they empower every worker to be able to do something about it.

As it turns out, the lines in Japanese factories do not stop any more often than in American factories that have no such switches. Evidently, Japanese employees, assured beyond any doubt that management is not faking its desire for quality, put in the effort to make the product defect free right from the start. The need to stop the line, therefore, diminishes significantly.

Software development is not a factory assembly line, but the concepts of management commitment and employee empowerment still apply. As a manager, your commitment to quality must show in your actions as well as in your speech or the team will disregard your directives. Team members should know that the product will not be released unless each and every one agrees that it is bug free. They should know that if they discover a bug, no matter how minor, at any stage of development, no matter how late in the game, they will be allowed to fix it even if it means delaying a long-awaited release. And they should know that each and every team member has the power to participate in the quality control process. From the janitor all the way up to the chairman of the board, everyone can *stop the line* to prevent a defective application from reaching the user.

But management commitment does not stop at your department's boundaries. It also goes far beyond just empowering team members to control and affect the quality of the application. Users, for instance, must also be convinced that their quality problems are addressed promptly. Software development teams are notorious for allowing bugs to live forever in applications as long as these problems are small enough or there is a valid workaround that prevents the problem from happening. Yet, ignoring a problem or developing a work-around is not an acceptable solution to most users. Aside from failing to solve the user's immediate need, such an approach advertises to the user community that the software producer is not as committed to quality as advertised.

Every bug found in the field, no matter how minor, if verified, has to be fixed! You must provide a true fix upgrade to at least the complaining user, no matter how much it costs you.

I can hear the arguments already: "Releasing bug fixes will cost too much"; "it will make version control a nightmare"; "it is not workable," and so on, and so on. Oh, grow up! Most major software companies already engage in such practices with their best customers. At one of my clients we installed versions 5.0a, 5.0b, and 5.0c of Microsoft Excel before the client was satisfied. Yet, Microsoft is hardly on the verge of going out of business as a result. Nor is it struggling with a version control nightmare, is it?

The fact of the matter is that in the long run, quality saves money and increases revenues. Showing a customer that you care enough about quality to go out of your way to fix a problem will most likely cause the customer to be more satisfied than if he were never to have discovered the problem in the first place. As a result, he is more likely to come back and buy your products again.

This point has been proven repeatedly by Motorola, AT&T, Ford, and many Japanese companies. When GM's Saturn car company replaced each and every one of its customers' cars in the first few months of product introduction because it found a problem with the engine, none of the customers complained. In fact these customers flocked back in large percentages to the same Saturn dealers four years later when it came time to buy new vehicles. Did it cost Saturn a small fortune to replace the vehicles in the first place? You bet! But did they end up collecting higher revenues as a result of their actions? Evidently. In the final analysis, they were better off for replacing the vehicles than they would have been were they to tell the customers to go fly a kite, as is the practice in other car companies.

Finally, remember that upper-management commitment to quality is just as important as that of lower management. This means that the need to cut project cost should never mean eliminating the part of the budget that has to do with quality control. This last point is so fundamental to any type of development that it never ceases to amaze me how easily so many companies choose to completely eliminate their quality control budgets in order to cut costs. I know that, often, it is a very tempting proposition to eliminate costs associated with certain functions whose output is not clearly visible to the outside world ("What do those people in quality control do all day, anyway?") . I also know that sometimes, costs do need to be cut ("Jim, our profit margins are not growing as fast as Microsoft. Don't just stand there. Fire someone!"). But cutting quality entirely out of the budget serves no purpose whatsoever. You might as well eliminate the entire programming staff because you will achieve the same results. Aside from the fact that such moves abolish the only thing that separates application from garbage, pulling the plug on quality control also sends a loud and clear message to the entire organization and its customers. This message is: We are not interested in producing bug-free code.

Moreover, companies such as Motorola and Hewlett-Packard have repeatedly proven that high levels of quality control actually save costs, while having no quality control is very expensive. Think about how much it cost Intel to fix the Pentium problem or what Johnson & Johnson paid to recall its tainted Tylenol pills. Now compare that sum to the real quality control budget and you will find that the cost of correcting an error after release dwarfs any cost of ensuring no errors are permitted to exist in the final product.

If you do not believe me, listen to other opinions. Chairman John Young of Hewlett-Packard proclaims: "In today's competitive environment, ignoring the quality issue is tantamount to corporate suicide," and John Akers, CEO of IBM, says: "We believe quality improvements will reduce quality costs 50% over the years. For us that translates into billions of dollars of added potential profits."[4]

---

[4] Edward Yourdon, *The Decline and Fall of the American Programmer*, p. 198.

MAKE PEOPLE ACCOUNTABLE

The other side of management commitment and people empowerment is team member accountability—specifically, accountability by the people who produce the application.

Even if we installed all the *line stop switches* in the world on our proverbial production line, we may still fail to achieve zero defects unless we hold accountable the people whose job it is to stop the line if they detect a problem. And we are certainly never going to eliminate the need for an inspection department if we do not inflict the consequences of making a mistake on those people who repeatedly make the same mistake.

This means that all team members must know that not only are they each individually responsible for the quality of their work but also that they will each be held accountable for turning in shoddy workmanship. That is not to say that mistakes are not allowed. It does, however, mean that mistakes should not be repeated, and that over time, the number of errors should diminish and approach zero.

This can easily be illustrated by the graph shown in Figure 27.3. Developers should never be allowed to repeat previous errors. For example, suppose a programmer always forgets to check for an empty string when prompting the user for a file name, causing as a result a major run-time error. This situation is really unacceptable. By repeating the same mistake, the programmer is violating TQM's central notion of continuous improvement. That is, team members should learn from their mistakes. Subsequently, it is imperative that you initiate some kind of disciplinary actions against the programmer and that you fire him should he continue to forget to validate inputs.

Making dissimilar errors is an entirely different matter. Everyone is allowed to make original mistakes since, after all, we are just human. As a matter of fact, from the quality management point of view, the larger the

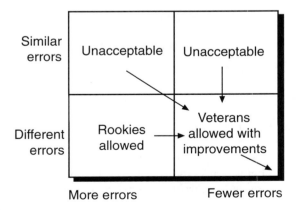

Figure 27.3 *Error types versus continuous improvement*

number of *different* mistakes made the better, since, presumably, if we learn from the mistakes and fix the process that caused them, we are able to engage in the process of continuous improvement.

Subsequently, the key is to enforce the continuous improvement part. In other words, a member of your team who is error prone should be encouraged to learn from his or her mistakes and improve over time. If the number of errors made does not show a decline over time, you may have a careless employee on your hand. Again, it is absolutely essential to initiate disciplinary procedures to discourage this behavior. In a sense, your role in the continuous improvement process is to eliminate those parts of the process—in this case a careless employee—that cause a quality problem.

What does personal accountability mean to individual programmers? First of all, it means testing and fixing their code as soon as they write it. Some programmers hate to test their code and so they simply fail to do it. Others are lazy so they tend to delay fixing bugs they themselves uncover, until someone makes them do it. Yet, there is absolutely no excuse for a programmer to return to the code library an untested piece of software. It is even less excusable for a programmer to have discovered a bug and not to fix that bug immediately. Surprisingly, however, these are normal occurrences in the wonderful world of software development.

No matter how much they kick and scream, developers must be made to produce bug-free code. One way to enforce this is to ask each developer and analyst to submit at the end of each workday a list of the bugs they found and fixed that day (see the chapter on productivity measurement). If the numbers of bugs found by one programmer is well below that of others who do similar work, it may be time to help the programmer recognize her shortcomings. Another way is to fine a programmer for each bug found in his code after he had told you the code is bug free. This can be done by allocating a quality bonus for each programmer at the beginning of the year and then subtracting a predetermined amount for each bug found by the testing department, and double that for each bug found by the end users.

CONTINUOUS IMPROVEMENT

Earlier in the chapter I argued that a centralized testing function does not add value to the software. If you agree with my argument, you would want to minimize this function. The trick to doing so is to progressively reduce the number of defects in the code that programmers turn over to the testing department. Theoretically, at some future time, the number of defects should approach zero, thus substantially diminishing the need for a testing department altogether.

Up to this point, we have touched on some very important methods of reducing the number of errors in pretested code. But by far, the most effective way to reduce bugs is to learn from past mistakes and make appropriate adjustments to the *development process* to prevent mistakes from being made in the first place.

This is no easy undertaking but it is effective. Start by collecting each week all the bugs discovered in the code by either the programmers or the testers during the previous week. Next bring your team together and review each bug with the following questions in mind:

1. How was the bug created?
2. What aspects of the code or the design caused the problem?
3. What steps could have been taken to avoid the *circumstances* that caused the problem?
4. Can these steps be put into a procedure that will prevent the problem in the future?

After each meeting have all members of the team write up the procedures to prevent their particular bugs from being repeated. Keep it short—one or two paragraphs at the most—since, after all, programmers are hired to write software and not books. An example of this process may be:

> The program crashed during run time when an undeclared variable was encountered.
>
> 1. *How was the bug created?* The programmer misspelled a variable name.
> 2. *What aspects of the code or the design caused the problem?* No formal declaration of variables was required allowing the precompiler to skip flagging this error.
> 3. *What steps could have been taken to avoid the circumstances that caused the problem?* The directive "Option Explicit" should have been added at the beginning of every module, causing the precompiler/interpreter to flag the error during development.
> 4. *Can these steps be put into a procedure that will prevent the problem in the future?* Yes. The new procedure is a one-liner:
>
> Always include the directive "Option Explicit" at the start of every module.

Next enter these new procedures into a procedure notebook, and make it available to everyone for review. At the following weekly meeting, go over the procedures developed over the last week before proceeding to review new bugs.

When a new member is hired into the team, have her first study the procedure book before she writes a single line of code or specifications. When a procedure is found to have a bug in it, correct the procedure again and again until it is perfect.

At first this will seem like a big waste of resources. But over time, these procedures will encapsulate the vast knowledge base generated by the very act of studying errors. As more and more procedures are followed, fewer and fewer bugs will be written. In a sense, you will have reduced the possibility of a programmer making a mistake by virtue of standardizing and, thus, reducing the variability and the number of choices a programmer can make at any turn. This is no different than what the best sports team coaches do when they review game films. They look at mistakes made during the game and adjust their player actions accordingly.

REDUCING VARIABILITY

As you might have guessed by now, reducing the variability of the process is one of the pillars on which continuous improvement rests. After all, you can procedurize and debug a process all you want, but this will only help you if the process does not change. The minute the process is altered, new bugs are created and debugging has to start anew. Subsequently, consistent implementation allows the team to reap the benefits of continuous improvements while performing tasks differently each time does not.

Variability in the software development effort can be reduced in three ways. We already talked about one such way, which is writing down development standards and procedures and then adhering to these procedures. A second way to reduce fluctuation is to use Visual Basic and fully utilize the custom control (VBXs and OCXs) capabilities. By testing and certifying a component, one can be reasonably certain that the component is bug free. Theoretically, if the application was built only with bug-free components, it would also be bug free.

Of course, this is not totally true. We all know about interaction bugs that spring out from the confluence of two otherwise perfectly safe systems. A classic example is two Boeing 747 jumbo jets flying behind each other too closely, causing the second plane to lose control in the tailwinds of the first. Both planes are quite safe by themselves but together they can be a problem. But interaction bugs are the exceptions. Most defects sprout within components rather than between them. As a result, the vast majority of bugs could be eliminated simply by using tried and true components. Clearly such an approach reduces system development variability and, therefore, decreases the chance of bugs and the consequent need for testing.

Even if you cannot build the entire applications from tested, previously built components, you should make the effort to reuse code that has already passed muster. VB version 4.0 allows you to make custom objects directly from VB code. To maintain this discipline, purchase and install a good development source library management tool such as Microsoft Source Safe or Intersolv's PVCS. Once approved, code modules should be placed in the library in read-only status. No unapproved changes should be permitted to creep in. If a change is necessary, the module must be put through the test procedure again to recertify it.

Naturally, the fact that a piece of code or a component is certified does not, in and of itself, make for reusability. As a manager, you must religiously enforce the reuse of previously tested and approved code segments in the project.

A third way to reduce variability is in the testing process. Testing conducted by humans is an error-prone process in and of itself. Unless care is taken to reduce bugs in the testing procedures, the entire quality control effort may be fatally flawed. If the instrument by which one measures an application speed cannot be proven to be accurate, for example, one will be unable to intelligently compare performance from one test session to the next. Testing problems must, therefore, be found and fixed much in the same way programming and design bugs are resolved. Likewise, testing standards and procedures must be developed to ensure reduced variability of the testing method.

Perhaps the best way to reduce testing problems is to use automatic testing tools such as SQA Robot. These tools can be programmed directly from the specifications and automatically take a system through the same loop again and again.

SO HOW COME GRAPHS ARE NOT NECESSARY?

Those readers who are familiar with the concepts of total quality management must be struggling with a few nagging questions, by now. You see, I have modified the total quality management *process* a bit to better fit the software development environment. The *theory* of TQM is still intact but the *process*, as preached by the high priests of quality control, is different. One such difference between my method and traditional, more manufacturing-oriented quality management is that I disregard the notion that says processes have to be identified, documented, and then the variability of outcome carefully tabulated and graphed. When the variability approaches zero, the mean outcome around which variability is measured can be improved. Some companies tout themselves as 3σ or 6σ quality control achievers. Technically, this means that their process does not deviate from the acceptable norm by 3 or 6 standard deviations.

Achieving 6σ quality rate is an outstanding result that actually translates to three to four defects in millions parts produced. I do not intend to take away from such achievements but quality management of software development can hardly be approached the way it is for manufacturing purposes. In my opinion—and it is debatable, of course—software development does not allow us the luxury of describable processes. How does one identify the process of writing a parsing routine or designing a transaction screen, for example? Hence, it makes absolutely no sense to measure variability in such an indescribable process to the point where it can be tabulated or graphed.

I do believe, however, that this omission actually makes the methods advocated here much more usable. That is because the manager undertaking the quality programs described in this chapter will likely not encounter the type of frustration associated with attempting to fit a square peg into a round hole. In other words, these methods may not be acceptable to the quality control purists but they are workable in real life. And so, I hope the purists among you will forgive me.

KEEP A BUG DATABASE

Having covered the theory of total quality management, we now must turn to the mechanics of testing. First and foremost among the project quality control tools is the bug database. This is a centralized database that is accessible not only to the entire development team but also to the user community. It lists all the problems encountered to date and their resolution. The database should be easy to use so users can log problems directly into it much in the same way they would send e-mail.

To make this database work correctly, appoint a member of the team to be the database administrator. Among the duties of the administrators should be:

- Distribute bug reports, preferably electronically.
- Produce aging and summary reports for team and management review.
- Mark bugs that are fixed as closed.
- Correct mistakes and reclassify bugs that have been entered incorrectly.
- Eliminate duplicated reports.

There are several off-the-shelf, bug-tracking systems that can be purchased for quick implementation. But whether you develop your own system or buy a commercially available package, the bug database should have the following fields:

Automatically Generated Fields

Reference Number	A serial number for indexing and references. Descriptions can be misleading and, thus, do not make for a good reference.
Report Date	The date the problem was first reported.

User Entered Fields (end user, testers, developers, customer support, etc.)

Reporter Name	Who is reporting the problem? User name.
Telephone Number (optional)	In case the developer needs to ask questions.
Application	What application caused the problem?
Release Number	Which version of the application?
Short Description	A concise one-line descriptor.
Symptoms	What happened?

Circumstances	How did it happen?
Repeatable	Can the problem be duplicated?
Environment	What other applications where running at the time? Which version of the operating system? How much memory was on the desktop, etc.?

Administrator Entry Field

Assigned to Fix	Who should fix this problem?
Status	Is it fixed, pending, canceled, etc.?
Estimate	How long does the developer think it will take her to fix this problem?

Developer Entry Fields

Technical Description	Description of the problem if different from the symptoms.
Cause of Problem	What caused this problem?
Remedying Actions	What did the developer do to fix it?
Prevention Steps	How can the problem be avoided in the future?
Fixed	Is it fixed?
Modules Affected	What code modules, libraries, and/or specifications were changed to fix this problem?
Documentation Change	Does the change require an update to the documentation?
Hours	How much time did it take to fix this problem?
Work-Around	Is there a work-around to this problem? (Remember that work-arounds are not acceptable to the user, but sometimes this information is useful.)

Management Entry Fields

Version Update	Version number incorporating these changes.
Accountable Party	Who is really responsible for the creation of the bug?
Cost to Fix	How much did it cost to fix this problem?
New Release	Is a new release necessary to update the user?
Repeat	Is this a repeated bug? Explain.
Update User	Has the user been contacted and told the outcome of his report?

Reviewed   Has the problem been reviewed with the
                                            development team?
Documented   Has the resolution been documented to
                                            eliminate the possibility of a repeat?

This seemingly complex system is actually quite simple if one realizes that
each player only fills in five to ten fields. This represents ten minutes worth of
work, at most. The bug-tracking system, however, is invaluable to the effectiveness of the testing process and the management of prerelease and postrelease processes.

THE SOFTWARE QUALITY CONTROL PROCESS
AND ITS VARIOUS COMPONENTS

New Component Certifications:

An ongoing process should be the continuous testing and certification of
new custom controls and third-party components. This must be done independently of any particular project, since the components are shareable across
different applications. Once certified as acceptable, components should be
placed in either a source library or a read-only directory structure. Programmers are only to use approved components.

Another aspect of component testing involves certifying each and
every application that uses the component once an upgrade is approved. If
the testing team approves a new version of a certain component to be bug
free, it must also test every application that uses this component to verify
that the new version works correctly with existing applications.

Specification Approval and Prototype Acceptance:

The specifications described in this book including function definition,
prototype, data definition, and entity relation diagram must pass an initial
quality control check. Depending on the system scope and complexity, specification approval can be as simple as sending the specifications to the user
for approval or as elaborate as a formal review session. Either way, the resulting specs should be put into a documentation library and marked with a version number.

Remember that the whole purpose of prototyping is to ensure user
acceptance of the final design before any substantial resources are expended.
It goes without saying, therefore, that prototypes have to undergo vigorous
user scrutiny. What is often forgotten is that this process is no different than
any other testing effort. First, only approved prototypes are to be placed in
the library for further development. Furthermore, prototype bugs, those having to do with misunderstanding the user requirements, have to be studied
carefully to facilitate a process of continuous improvement.

New Code Testing and Modular Testing:

New code should be tested as soon as it is written. This was somewhat more easily done in the 3GL world since each routine was completely specified. A test was, therefore, readily devised by inputting the specified inputs and testing to see what outputs were obtained.

Using RAD tools such as Visual Basic, however, makes this process more complicated. Except for the function definition, there is hardly a written document specifying the details of any given routine. Subsequently, we must rely on the individual developer to conduct such testing before releasing the code. An outside control can be placed on this process by bundling routines into modules that have a clear functional purpose. These modules can be tested more easily since they are specified in greater detail during the analysis stage. The code can then be broken up into routines to be placed into the library. Naturally, only code that passed modular testing is to be placed in the routine library.

Unit Testing:

Once the modules are assembled into a coherent application, the entire assembly has to pass inspection. Of course, by now much of the application is already tested, having gone through components and modules certifications and prototype acceptance. The purpose of this test, therefore, is to uncover any problems that have to do with the interaction of the different, otherwise bug-free, components. Another important goal is to look for any inconsistencies across the entire application. For example, does the application prompt for currency asking for decimal on one screen but no decimal on another? Do field names correspond throughout the whole package? And so on.

Bugs uncovered at this stage that are more basic than just system interaction problems are those that fell through the cracks of earlier quality assurance. As a result, such bugs point to problems not only in the application development effort but also in the testing procedure. Both the development process and the testing process must be corrected accordingly and separately.

Beta Testing and Acceptance Testing:

Beta testing is a sometimes skipped step in which the application is partially released to a select number of end users. The purpose of this test is to put the application through a normal, everyday type of usage similar to what it will be performing once released.

Beta testing is often skipped because it is sometimes very hard to find willing volunteers to undertake such an effort. The user community is busy enough without having to dedicate additional resources solely for testing purposes. Nonetheless, beta testing is a crucial step in the process of bug-free deployment. It is during this stage that we uncover installation problems as well as interaction problems with other applications and the rest of the user desktop.

If you are lucky enough to identify customers or users who are willing to beta test your application, you must be very careful to follow these rules:

- Make sure that the customer knows that the application is not ready yet and may contain some bugs. I cannot begin to enumerate how many development efforts I was part of that by the time the marketing staff finished talking, the customers were convinced our beta release was really a third-generation release of a well-used product.

- Make sure the customer is ready, willing, and able to invest the time required to thoroughly test the application. Often customers volunteer to be a beta test site only because they do not wish to turn you down. Yet, without any real time commitment, the application remains unused and, therefore, untested. And since you are unaware that the system is not being used, you may be left with the wrong impression that the program is functioning perfectly. To defuse such a possibility, ask for feedback on a weekly basis and suspect something is wrong if the only reply received is that everything is working fine.

Another form of beta testing is acceptance testing whereby the application runs in parallel with an existing system for a period of time to ensure correct functionality. Such testing is often conducted on a value-bearing system such as financial transaction processing that requires absolute conformance to existing results. If you are engaged in acceptance testing, you may want to verify bugs before you move to correct them. This is necessary to guarantee that the bug is not produced by the legacy system being replaced rather than by your own application.

Whether you are conducting a beta test or an acceptance test, treat every bug you uncover as a failure of the earlier quality control processes. Consequently, use such problems to debug not only the application but also the testing mechanism.

Documentation Testing:

Documentation is no different than any other component of the system. Imagine a user who expects, based on the provided manual, to enter a string in some prompted field only to be surprised by an error instructing him he is to enter a number. Even though the program may be correct here, the user is left with the impression that the program is defective. It hardly takes an Einstein to realize that all bugs are relative, and that it does not matter to the user who specifically is the culprit.

You must, therefore, put the documentation through the same type of quality control process that the rest of the application must pass. As an added benefit, such a documentation quality process acts as a check and balance to the rest of your quality assurance. If done correctly, documentation testing leads you to uncover problems with the rest of the system simply by comparing the intended functionality to the actual functionality.

Postrelease Quality Control:

Total quality management is not over just because the system is out the door. Training, hot-line support, user group meetings, and newsletters must all conform to a very high standard of quality. Subsequently, test and certify each aspect of these functions before they come in contact with the end user. Hot-line support representatives, for example, should be trained and tested on their knowledge of the system and on how to register problems. Remember, the customer does not really care who or what causes the problems. Any problem carries an equal weight in the decision to reinvest in your product. And so look to debug the entire realm of application development and not just the code development phase.

See Figure 27.4 for a diagram of the testing process.

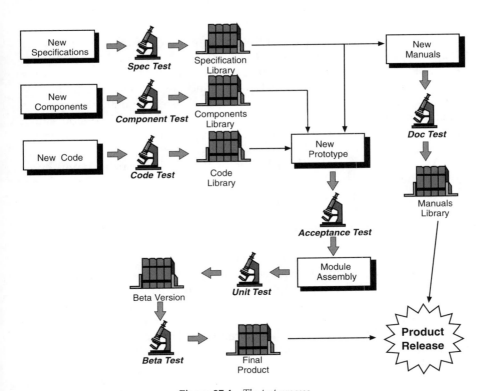

Figure 27.4 *The test process*

CHAPTER 28

What Makes a Successful Deployment?

So the application is complete, all the tests are done, and you are ready for that all-important release. Well, if you work for the typical large company, don't hold your breath. In most settings, there is hardly a natural progression between the defined end of development and actual field installation. At best, a roll-out is a struggle; at worst, it is a disaster. To make it happen, a manager must employ nearly every managerial skill in his possession, call in favors, and bend and twist arms in order to cajole and prod the organization into swallowing the new pill.

What are some of the obstacles that make a roll-out such a painful process? Earlier in this book we talked about one such pitfall: the scope creep. The end of the project means presenting demonstrations of the application to the user community and installing beta test releases on selected desktops. Many users first see the application during this stage. Typically, those users who were not part of the design and prototyping cycle offer a few suggestions, some of which may even be pertinent to an initial release. There is often tremendous organizational temptation to enact these changes.

But changing the application this late in the game is very risky. First, there is the political risk as late changes greatly anger those whose original requirements and design are being altered. Second, taking on change requests usually leads to more change requests. Thus begins a vicious cycle of furniture moving that delays implementation indefinitely. And, of course, every change requires new testing, modification to the documents, and brings about a new set of problems. I have actually seen projects that were completed, tested, and ready for installation eventually get canceled just because they never really ended. Everytime the development team wanted to deploy, the user community had *just one more item* to add or change.

It is, therefore, the job of a good manager to aggressively limit or even try to eliminate scope creep. Customer satisfaction is important, of course, so you should seek to provide a desirable product. Nonetheless, you must realize that you can never succeed in completely satisfying each and every user. Your best bet, therefore, is to stick to the original specifications for the current release. Defuse any potential problems by promising to enact additional requirements and changes in subsequent releases.

If after delaying as many change requests as possible you still discover that there are some show-stopping issues that must be fixed prior to release, I suggest you implement a triage-like process. Put all change requests that must be implemented into the *this version* pile. Describe them in writing and estimate the time it would take to complete them. All other *important* changes and additions should go into the *next version* list. Ridiculous requests go into a *to-be-tossed* list. Have the three lists approved by the powers that be in the user community and restart the development cycle from the beginning to work on the *entire this version list*. Specify, prototype, develop, and test. Avoid at all cost implementing change requests in a piecemeal fashion or the project may never end.

Another obstacle to deployment is a heavy workload—specifically, the heavy workload of the users. Many of today's organizations are operating with such lean resources that they can hardly spare a body to go on vacation, let alone learn a new system. So there you are, sitting on the most beautiful, well-designed, well-built application in the history of humankind but no one will give you the time of day, much less allow you to install it on their computer. You beg and plead to just install it on one machine but all you hear is that it is the end of the quarter and everyone is booked solid through Christmas, three years from now. What will you do?

Unfortunately, I can offer you no magic solution here. The fact that organizational resources are increasingly overstretched is a reality that cannot be easily circumvented. The best you can do is lobby to push your particular project to the head of the priority list. This can be a full-time battle that often requires every ounce of a manager's energy and imagination. If the computers are occupied during business hours, offer to install the system after hours. If you are told no one is available for training, suggest that a temp be hired to free up people one at a time. If you discover a lull in the action, pounce on the opportunity to redirect attention to your application. In short, press on all fronts and do not give up. Sooner or later, the users will start using your application and before you know it, they will not be able to live without it. But if, instead of actively pursuing such a strategy, you sit back and wait for that go-ahead phone call, you will be waiting a very long time.

INSTALLATION

There is really very little complexity to installing a Visual Basic executable on a client-server or stand-alone workstation but, as in any other environment, it involves a tremendous amount of work. Presumably, your testing cycle included testing the application on the network and you have set up all the necessary production databases during development. So by the end of the project, installing the application out in the field should be a no-brainer with one possible exception. This exception involves the complexity presented by DLL files and it is covered in an earlier chapter. Here are the typical steps the development team should take in an ideal release process.

1. Freeze all code modifications and tag the files with a version number. This should be done using a version control software such as Microsoft SourceSafe or Intersolve PVCS. This step is necessary so you will be able to recreate the source code at will.

2. If the application so requires, invite the auditors to review the application and the software and to offer their blessing proclaiming the application ready and secure for enterprise operation.

3. Create a setup utility that installs the necessary files in the right locations, registers the application in the Windows registry, adds or modifies environment variables, and creates the Windows icons and other such niceties. There are various commercially available applications that do this by scripting such as InstallShield or Visual Basic's own setup kit. Whatever method you use, *test the setup program thoroughly.*

4. Cut production disks. Depending on the infrastructure you work with, you may actually be able to install directly from the network. If so, the need to produce floppy disks may be superfluous. Again, there are various applications including DiskLayout by Microsoft that compress and lay out setup disks so that installation can be done automatically.

5. Take receipt of and install any hardware necessary for normal operation. Turn over the responsibility of this hardware to operation personnel. Be nice, they mean well.

6. Install the production server databases and populate as needed. If you are replacing a legacy system, you will likely need to upload the old data to the new database. This can be a very grueling and time-consuming process. Normally, you do not have much time to complete this step because the data may age faster than you can upload them to the new system. If so, load as much as you can and set up a parallel data entry process until the two databases are the exact replica of each other.

   Note that this last step may require your team to write a data conversion program to mold the old data format into the new schema. If such a conversion is required, make sure the program is tested and verified before it is attempted in a production setting.

7. Assign accounts to all the system's users and set their security privileges appropriately.

8. Train the system administrators and other operation personnel on the operation, maintenance, and day-to-day running of the application and the database. Set up backup and replication procedures and define responsibilities for disaster recovery and for routine user requests. Document all such procedures and distribute to all personnel.

9. Hold training sessions for the end users. Give each a set of documentation.

10. Install the application for end user access. In some settings this may be accomplished by installing the software once on the server. Other places require a separate installation on each workstation.

11. Implement a help response procedure for the development team and institute an on-call schedule if such is required. Hand out beepers, cellular phones, balls and chains, or whatever else is necessary to ensure adequate coverage.

    Make sure the users all know who to call and that such calls are promptly answered. Remember that an adequately staffed help line may make all the difference between a successful deployment and a disaster.

12. Install a change request database and a bug database—if you have not done so already. Grant access to these databases to a user representative and to support personnel.

13. Most important, hold a roll-out party. It does not have to be anything wild or fancy but this party does have to convey the message that development is complete and that there is really no excuse for not using the system.

14. Take a long and relaxing vacation.

WHAT TO EXPECT

If ever there was a situation that fits the proverbial Murphy's Law perfectly, a client-server software release is it: If anything can go wrong, it will. As diligent as you may be in following the various steps involved in testing and releasing a new software, you are likely to still encounter problems when it is actually installed in the field. This is mainly due to the fact that the platform on which the application is being installed is not likely to be exactly the same as the one used in development or testing. Slight differences in the user environment as well as system files that are either missing or of the wrong version create havoc for the new application.

Typically, the immediate reaction to such difficulty is to quickly retreat and announce a new release date. Such a reaction is even understandable in view of a tight time schedule, as in having to install the application overnight before the users come back in the morning. However, this off-the-cuff decision to withdraw and return later is often not necessary. Many problems can be solved by an experienced technician within a matter of minutes and even the most complex difficulties are often just paper tigers.

The bottom line is that if the system works on various machines in the development environment, there is no technical reason why it would not work in the field. Keeping this little truism in mind and systematically comparing the development environment to that of the users, any problems can be easily and quickly debugged. Some typical problem areas include:

1. Mismatched or missing DLLs. See discussion earlier in the book.
2. Incorrect environment. Is the path defined correctly? Is the application registered in the Windows system? Are the environment variables defined?
3. Missing license files. Sometimes a third-party product is used in the application that requires a local copy of a license file in order to run. Without this file, the third-party product will not load.
4. Missing hardware. A modem or SCSI card needed by the application may not exist. Worse yet, it may exist but be incorrectly installed.
5. Incorrect or missing network addressing. Check the user's network setting. Is it capable of talking to needed elements through the network? Ping the server to find out.
6. Insufficient memory (RAM) or disk space. Is there enough space for the application to operate efficiently? Enough to swap files?
7. Other applications. Are there other applications running in the background such as an e-mail program or a stock market feed that interferes with the normal messaging pattern of your application? Maybe the background application is clobbering your application's memory space?
8. And, of course, is the computer plugged in?

POSTRELEASE SUPPORT

Naturally, the support your team provides the end users and any intermediate user of your system is crucial to the success of the application. This is especially true in the first few days after release when most users first try to bring up the application. The less painful this startup process appears to the users the more they will like the application and be inclined to overlook some minor shortcomings. In contrast, without such support, the users may decide early on that an otherwise perfect application is problem proned simply because they do not know how to use it properly.

Having said that, I must point out the obvious fact that many applications, both commercial and internal, survive with little or no postrelease support. Even with frustration levels running high, users sooner or later figure out how to use an application they deem important to their work. If upon encountering a problem they fail to make contact with a help line, they hack at it or turn to their coworkers, friends, or Internet bulletin boards (forums) for help. This informal network, in essence, becomes the application virtual support team, allowing the vendor or developer to save much time and resources.

In my opinion, the practice of abandoning the user after release is immoral and abhorrent. I consider it one of the ten worst things one can do to the users, right below inflicting their machine with a virus, and right above forcing them to use DOS. The software industry can get away with this shameful tactic only because computers and software are fairly new to the marketplace. Companies in other industries, by contrast, would not survive a day if they were to follow such practices. But I am happy to report that software companies are waking up to this fact. More and more releases are being backed up by real help lines with real people behind them. Similarly, within corporate walls developers now know that postrelease support is an integral part of their job. They, therefore, no longer mind wearing beepers and answering calls from the Bangladesh office at 2 o'clock in the morning. But we are not quite there yet.

I, therefore, urge you to never skimp on postrelease product support. If the morality of my argument is not sufficient, let's try common sense: Even though a superb application may survive being orphaned, an average application usually does not. Subsequently, it is prudent and wise to minimize the risk and provide support functions after roll-out just in case.

Such support must include a knowledgeable contact who is accessible anytime the system may be in operation. This, of course, means different things to different organizations. A multinational company probably has offices around the globe, which means 24-hour operation. Support is thus required around the clock. For other companies, and for small applications, a cellular phone may be sufficient to keep a person in touch with the users. Sometimes a beeper may do. Still in other situations, a person may need to physically occupy an office, sometimes for no other reason than the manuals take up a couple of shelves' worth of space or the knowledge base is location specific.

The number of people needed to support an application and the caliber of such personnel also vary with the size and scope of the project. Software companies employ dedicated support staffs who have no responsibilities other than to help the user. Most in-house development teams cannot afford such a luxury and so it may be sufficient to partially assign a technician for such duties. The learning curve of the user community must also be considered in determining long-term staffing needs. Clearly, users need more support right after startup than a few months down the line when they have become familiar with the system. This means having to draft several developers to help with hot-line duties early on in implementation but then passing these responsibilities to a single person who may be supporting *several* mature applications.

Whatever the requirements of your situation are, if you can provide accurate and useful information to users whenever they need the information, you are assured that your application will not falter due to misconceptions and misrepresentation.

DOCUMENTATION

In the not so distant past, an application would not be considered ready for release if it lacked a complete set of documentation. A paper manual was the first and only place for the users to find information about the system and its capabilities. Today paper documentation is important, but it is no longer the only place for the users to turn to for help. In fact, many users resist using the documentation and often leave the shrink-wrapped packaging unopened throughout the life of the application.

Instead, on-line tutorials, context-sensitive help, and on-line help files are much more useful to most in the user community than a set of paper documentation. These electronic assistants allow the user of an application to pinpoint the subject of interest without having to go through a mountain of paper. The ability to jump between topics without losing place and the ability to drill down deeper and deeper into a single subject are both important and crucial time savers. Paper manuals cannot compete with such efficiency.

Furthermore, if the look and feel of the application resembles that of other applications the users are already familiar with, then the need for some documentation is questionable to begin with. A manual may still be needed but only to describe the most complex part of the application.

In fact, the entire software industry is struggling with this documentation issue. Many new products are sold without any manuals save one thin booklet on installation. This is a sharp departure from the days when purchasing a new application meant transporting several pounds worth of books back to the office or home. Now, instead of written documentation, vendors offer special deals on their development kits that are shipped on a single CD-ROM disk. Some vendors are even posting documentation on the Internet.

So do you need to worry about documentation? The answer is, of course you do. The more important question, however, is what form should the manuals take? I suggest that an on-line help file and context-sensitive help features are a must. A paper manual, on the other hand, may be a luxury your application can live without. Make the call based on user preference and resource availability.

Whatever media you choose to distribute the documentation, under no circumstances should this manual be written by any of your programmers. Even if a developer does not resent the mere suggestion of having to write the documentation, by definition, he is incapable of doing so. Programmers cannot put together a legible shopping list, much less a comprehensible set of manuals. They tend to write on a level that far exceeds that of the average users, often ignoring entire portions of crucial information that they believe is common knowledge. No user should ever have to be inflicted with manuals written by developers.

Instead, hire a really good technical writer and let her translate the programmer's obscure thought process to something we mere mortals can comprehend. Compile the text into a Windows help file and tie it to the various screen elements and you have got yourself a professional-looking application complete with documentation.

So now, having tried Visual Basic as suggested in this book, you surely agree that happy days are here again.

— I —

Products Discussed in This book

Application	Manufacturer	Notes	Fourth Quarter 1995 Price[1]
Operating Systems			
Windows 95	Microsoft		$ 179
Windows NT v3.51 Workstation	Microsoft		319
Windows NT v3.51 Server	Microsoft		679
Programming Environments			
Visual Basic 4.0 Standard	Microsoft	32 bit only	99
Visual Basic 4.0 Professional Edition	Microsoft	16 and 32 bits	499
Visual Basic 4.0 Enterprise Edition	Microsoft	16 and 32 bits, plus client-server tools	999
Delphi Version 1.0 for Windows	Borland		339
Delphi Client/Server CD-ROM	Borland		1,949
Delphi Version 1.0 Client/ Server Developer Team	Borland		16,875
PowerBuilder Desktop for Windows 4.0	PowerSoft		599
PowerBuilder Enterprise-Windows 4.0	PowerSoft		2,999

Application	Manufacturer	Notes	Fourth Quarter 1995 Price[1]
VB Components (VBXs and OCXs)			
3-D Widgets	Sheridan	3-D Check boxes, list boxes, etc.	89
Aware VBX	FarPoint	Data aware controls	145
Calendar Widgets	Sheridan	Calendar screen controls	100
Code.Print Pro for VB	Pinnacle	Generate reader-friendly code	92
Data Widgets	Sheridan	Data aware controls	95
Designer Widgets 2.0	Sheridan	Tab controls and other screen controls	109
Grapfsman/VBX	Soft-Tek	Fancy graph	138
Schedule/VBX	AddSoft	Scheduling display tools	230
Spread/VBX ++	FarPoint	Very extensive grid	229
ToolThings	Pinnacle	Align controls, remove dead code, and others	99
TrueGrid Pro for Visual Basic	Apex Software	Very extensive grid	95
VB Assist 4.0	Sheridan	Aligning tools, tab order tools, etc.	135
VBTools 4.0	Microhelp	50 powerful custom controls	94
Databases			
Access 2.0	Microsoft	Stand alone Client-server	326
SQL Workstation	Microsoft	Client-server	500
SQL Server Workstation NT	Microsoft	Client-server	949
SQL Server NT Client License	Microsoft	Client-server	156
Watcom SQL 4.0	Watcom	Stand alone	236
Watcom SQL Server 4.0 -6	Watcom	Client-server 6 users	716
Watcom SQL Server 4.0 - unlimited users	Watcom	Client-server	4,529
ODBC Drivers[2]			
Data Direct ODBC Pack V2.10	Intersolv		99
Case Tools			
Erwin Desktop for VB 2.0	Logic Works		199
ERwin/ERX for Visual Basic	Logic Works		3,100
ERwin/ERX for PowerBuilder	Logic Works		3,100

Application	Manufacturer	Notes	Fourth Quarter 1995 Price[1]
Database Administration Tools			
DBArtisan 2.0	Embarcadero Technologies		669
Code Management Tools			
PVCS Version Manager WIN	Intersolv		500
PVCS for Windows NT	Intersolv		500
SourceSafe 3.1	Microsoft		449
Help Authoring Tools			
WinHelp Office	Blue Sky	Complete help authoring kit	699
Doc-To-Help	WexTech	Complete help authoring kit	244
RoboHelp	Blue Sky	Complete help authoring kit	439
Project Management			
Project for Windows	Microsoft		459
TimeLine for Windows 6.1	Symantec		560

[1] Street price.

[2] Most ODBC drivers are free from the database manufacturer. Listed here are only the third-party supplied drivers.

II

Glossary of Technical Terms

3GL *See* Third-Generation Language.

4GL *See* Fourth-Generation Language.

Acceptance Test A test performed by the end user to determine if the system is working according to the specifications in the contract.[1]

API *See* Application Programming Interface.

Application Programming Interface Abbreviated API. A set of routines that an application program uses to request and carry out lower-level services performed by the computer's operating system. An application program carries out two types of tasks: those related to work being performed, such as accepting text or numbers input to the document or spreadsheet, and those related to maintenance chores, such as managing files and displaying information on the screen. These maintenance chores are performed by the computer's operating system, and an API provides the program with a means of communicating with the system, telling it which system-level task to perform and when. On computers running a graphical user interface such as that on the Apple Macintosh, an API also helps application programs manage windows, menus, icons, and so on. On local area networks, an API, such as IBM's Net-BIOS, provides applications with a uniform means of requesting services from the lower levels of network.[2]

---

[1]*Computer Desktop Encyclopedia*, 1996, The Computer Language Co. Inc.

[2]*Microsoft Press Computer Dictionary*, Second Edition, Microsoft Press, 1994, p. 24.

Beta Test A test of hardware or software that is performed by users under normal operating conditions.[3]

Client-Server Architecture in which the client (personal computer or workstation) is the requesting machine and the server is the supplying machine (LAN file server, mini or mainframe). The client provides the user interface and performs some or all of the application processing. The server maintains the databases and processes requests from the client to extract data from or update the database. The server also controls the application's integrity and security. Contrast with centralized processing, in which dumb (nonprocessing) terminals are connected to a mini or mainframe.

Client-server architecture means that the server is used for more than just a remote disk drive to the client. It means that the applications were designed for multiple users on a network. For example, if two users attempt to update the same database record at the same time, the update must be reflected instantly on the other user's screen.

Client-server implies mission critical information systems running on a LAN of personal computers with the same integrity as mainframe systems. Simply downloading files from the server to the client is not true client-server architecture.[4]

Component A component is an object that may not display encapsulation, polymorphism and/or inheritance properties. *See* Object-Oriented Programming.

Control In a graphical user interface, an object on the screen that can be manipulated by the user to perform an action. Perhaps the most common controls are buttons, which allow the user to select options, and scroll bars, which allow the user to move through a document or position text in a window.[5]

Database Management System (DBMS) Software that controls the organization, storage, retrieval, security, and integrity of data in a database. It accepts requests from the application and instructs the operating system to transfer the appropriate data.

DBMSs may work with traditional programming languages (COBOL, C, etc.), or they may include their own programming language for application development.

DBMSs let information systems be changed more easily as the organization's requirements change. New categories of data can be added to the database without disruption to the existing system. Adding

---

[3]*Computer Desktop Encyclopedia.*
[4]Ibid.
[5]*Microsoft Press Computer Dictionary,* Second Edition.

a field to a record does not require changing any of the programs that do not use the data in that new field.[6]

Database Server A computer in a LAN dedicated to database storage and retrieval. The database server is a key component in a client-server environment. It holds the database management system (DBMS) and the databases. Upon requests from the client machines, it searches the database for selected records and passes them back over the network.

A database server and file server may be one in the same because a file server often provides database services. However, the term implies that the system is dedicated for database use only and not a central storage facility for applications and files. *See* Client-Server.[7]

DBMS *See* Database Management System.

DDE *See* Dynamic Data Exchange.

DLL *See* Dynamic Linked Library.

Dynamic Data Exchange (DDE) A form of interprocess communication in Microsoft Windows and OS/2. When two or more programs that support DDE are running simultaneously, they can exchange information and commands. In Windows 3.1 (and later versions), this capability is enhanced with object linking and embedding (OLE).[8]

Dynamic Linked Library (DLL) An executable code module for Microsoft Windows that can be loaded on demand and linked at run time, and then unloaded when the code is no longer needed.[9]

Entity Relationship (ER) Model A database model that describes the attributes of entities and the relationships among them. An entity is a file (table). Today ER models are often created graphically, and software converts the graphical representations of the tables into the SQL code required to create the data structures in the database.[10]

Field A physical unit of data that is one or more bytes in size. A collection of fields makes up a record. A field also defines a unit of data on a source document, screen, or report. Examples of fields are NAME, ADDRESS, QUANTITY, and AMOUNT DUE.

The field is the common denominator between the user and the computer. When you interactively query and update your database, you reference your data by field name.

---

[6]*Computer Desktop Encyclopedia.*

[7]Ibid.

[8]Harry Newton, *Newton's Telecom Dictionary,* 1996. Reprinted with permission from Flatiron Publishing, 12 West 21 St., NY, NY 10010, 1-800-LIBRARY or 212-691-8215, www.flatiron-publishing.com

[9]Ibid.

[10]*Computer Desktop Encyclopedia.*

There are several terms that refer to the same unit of storage as a field. A data element is the logical definition of the field, and a data item is the actual data stored in the field. For each data element, there are many fields in the database that hold the data items.

The terms *field, data element, data item,* and *variable* refer to the same unit of data and are often used interchangeably.[11]

File Server High-speed computer in a LAN that stores the programs and data files shared by users on the network. Also called a network server, it acts like a remote disk drive.[12]

Form A window being designed in Visual Basic. During development controls and code can be placed in the form. In run time, the form becomes an application window.

Fourth-Generation Language Computer language that is more advanced than traditional high-level programming languages. For example, in dBASE, the command LIST displays all the records in a data file. In second- and third-generation languages, instructions would have to be written to read each record, test for end of file, place each item of data on screen and go back and repeat the operation until there are no more records to process.

First-generation languages are machine languages; second-generation languages are machine-dependent assembly languages; third-generation languages are high-level programming languages, such as FORTRAN, COBOL, BASIC, Pascal, and C. Although many languages, such as dBASE, are called fourth-generation languages, they are actually a mix of third and fourth generations. The dBASE LIST command is a fourth-generation command, but applications programmed in dBASE are third generation.

Query language and report writers are also fourth-generation languages. Any computer language with English-like commands that doesn't require traditional input-process-output logic falls into this category.[13]

Gantt Chart Form of floating bar chart usually used in project management to show resources or tasks over time.[14]

Interpret A high-level programming language translator that translates and runs the program at the same time. It translates one program statement into machine language, executes it, then proceeds to the next statement. This differs from regular executable programs that are presented to the computer as binary-coded instructions. Interpreted programs remain in

[11]Ibid.
[12]Ibid.
[13]Ibid.
[14]Ibid.

the same source language format the programmer wrote in: as text files, not machine language files.

Interpreted programs run more slowly than their compiler counterparts. Whereas the compiler translates the entire program before it is run, interpreters translate a line at a time while the program is run. However, it is very convenient to write an interpreted program, since a single line of code can be tested interactively.

Interpreted programs must always be run with the interpreter. For example, in order to run a BASIC or dBASE program, the BASIC or dBASE interpreter must be in the target computer.[15]

ISO 9000 Series   The ISO 9000 series, published in 1987, outlines the requirements for the quality system of an organization. It is a set of generic standards that provides quality assurance requirements and quality management guidance. It is now evolving into a mandatory requirement, especially for manufacturers of regulated products such as medical and telecommunications equipment. ISO 9001, the most comprehensive of three compliance standards—9001, 9002, and 9003—is a model for quality assurance for companies involved with design, test, manufacture, delivery, and service of products. ISO is the International Standards Organization based in Paris.[16]

Join   In relational database management, to match one file against another based on some condition creating a third file with data from the matching files. For example, a customer file can be joined with an order file creating a file of records for all customers who purchased a particular product.[17]

LAN   (Local Area Network) Communications network that serves users within a confined geographical area. It is made up of servers, workstations, a network operating system, and a communications link.

Servers are high-speed machines that hold programs and data shared by all network users. The workstations, or clients, are the users' personal computers, which perform stand-alone processing and access the network servers as required (look up the term *client-server* for more information on this concept).

Diskless and floppy-only workstations are sometimes used, which retrieve all software and data from the server. A printer can be attached to a workstation or to a server and be shared by network users.

Small LANs can allow each workstation to function as a server, allowing all users access to data on all machines. These peer-to-peer networks are often simpler to install and manage, but dedicated servers

[15]Ibid.

[16]Harry Newton, *Newton's Telecom Dictionary.*

[17]*Computer Desktop Encyclopedia.*

provide better performance and can handle higher transaction volume. Multiple servers are used in large networks.

The controlling software in a LAN is the network operating system, such as NetWare, LANtastic, and Appletalk, which reside in the server. A component part of the software resides in each workstation and allows the application to read and write data from the server as if it were on the local machine.

The physical transfer of data is performed by the access method (Ethernet, Token Ring, etc.), which is implemented in the network adapters that plug into the workstations and servers. The actual communications path is the cable (twisted pair, coax, optical fiber) that interconnects each network adapter.[18]

Local Area Network   *See* LAN.

Microsoft Access   A database program for Windows from Microsoft that reads Paradox, dBASE, and Btrieve files. Using ODBC, it reads Microsoft SQL Server, SYBASE SQL Server, and Oracle data. Access BASIC is its programming language, and "Wizards" ask you questions to create forms, reports, and graphs.[19]

Microsoft SQL Server   A Microsoft retail product that provides distributed database management. Multiple workstations manipulate data stored on a server, where the server coordinates operations and performs resource-intensive calculations.[20]

Normalization   In relational database management, a process which breaks down data into record groups for efficient processing. There are six stages. By the third stage (third normal form), data are identified only by the key field in the record. For example, ordering information is identified by order number, customer information by customer number.[21]

OCX   Dynamic link library file that contains user or third-party developed controls for Visual Basic applications and that communicates with the application using OLE technology.

Object Linking and Embedding   *See* OLE.

Object-Oriented DBMS   DBMS that manages an object-oriented database. It is capable of handling complex queries about objects that would be difficult in relational database programs.[22]

---

[18] Ibid.

[19] Ibid.

[20] Harry Newton, *Newton's Telecom Dictionary.*

[21] *Computer Desktop Encyclopedia.*

[22] Ibid.

Object-Oriented Programming (OOP) Programming that supports object technology. It is an evolutionary form of modular programming with more formal rules that allow pieces of software to be reused and interchanged between programs. Major concepts are (1) encapsulation, (2) inheritance, and (3) polymorphism.

Encapsulation is the creation of self-sufficient modules that contain the data and the processing (data structure and functions that manipulate these data). These user-defined, or abstract, data types are called classes. One instance of a class is called an object. For example, in a payroll system, a class could be defined as Manager, and Pat and Jan, the actual objects, are instances of that class.

Classes are created in hierarchies, and *inheritance* allows the knowledge in one class to be passed down the hierarchy. New objects can be created by inheriting characteristics from existing classes. For example, the object MACINTOSH could be one instance of the class PERSONAL COMPUTER, which could inherit properties from the class COMPUTER SYSTEMS. Adding a new computer requires entering only what makes it different from other computers, while the general characteristics of personal computers can be inherited.

Object-oriented programming allows procedures about objects to be created whose exact type is not known until run time. For example, a screen cursor may change its shape from an arrow to a line depending on the program mode. The routine to move the cursor on screen in response to mouse movement would be written for "cursor," and *polymorphism* would allow that cursor to be whatever shape is required at run time. It would also allow a new shape to be easily integrated into the program.

The SIMULA simulation language was the original object-oriented language. It was used to model the behavior of complex systems. Xerox's Smalltalk was the first object-oriented programming language and was used to create the graphical user interface whose derivations are so popular today. C++ has become the major commercial OOP language because it combines traditional C programming with object-oriented capabilities. ACTOR and Eiffel are also meaningful OOP languages.

The following list compares some fundamental object-oriented programming terms with traditional programming terms and concepts.[23]

Object-oriented	Traditional
programming	programming
class	data type + characteristics
instance	variable
instantiate	declare a variable

[23]Ibid.

Object-oriented	Traditional
method	processing code
message	call
object	data type + processing

ODBC Open DataBase Connectivity (ODBC) is Microsoft's strategic interface for accessing data in a heterogeneous environment of relational and nonrelational database management systems. Based on work-in-progress on the Call Level Interface (CLI) specification from the SQL Access Group, ODBC provides a vendor-neutral way of accessing data in a variety of personal computer, minicomputer, and mainframe databases. ODBC alleviates, according to Microsoft, the need for independent software vendors.[24]

OLE Pronounce "oh-lay"; acronym for object linking and embedding, a way to transfer and share information among applications. When an object (such as an image file created with a paint program) is *linked* to a compound document (such as a spreadsheet or a document created with a word processing program), the document contains only a reference to the object; any changes made to the contents of the linked object will be seen in the compound document. When an object is *embedded* in the compound document, the document contains a copy of the object; any changes made to the contents of the original object will not be seen in the compound document unless the embedded object is updated.[25]

Open DataBase Connectivity *See* ODBC.

OOP *See* Object-Oriented Programming.

Path The route to a file on a disk. In DOS and OS/2, the path for file MYLIFE located in subdirectory STORIES within directory JOE on drive C: looks like:

```
c:\joe\stories\mylife
```

The equivalent UNIX path follows. UNIX knows which drive is used:

```
/joe/stories/mylife
```

The Macintosh also uses a path in certain command sequences.[26]

PERT Project Evaluation and Review Technique. A variation on the critical path method of organizing the completion of projects. Projects are examined for the their worst, best, and average completion times. A

---

[24]Harry Newton, *Newton's Telecom Dictionary.*

[25]*Microsoft Press Computer Dictionary,* Second Edition, p. 278.

[26]*Computer Desktop Encyclopedia.*

critical path is determined and overall standards for completion times are created. The PERT technique was created by the military. It is used for organizing complex tasks.[27]

PowerBuilder Application generator for developing Windows client-server applications from Powersoft Corporation, Burlington, MA. It uses a programming language called PowerScript that is similar to BASIC. PowerBuilder supports SQL and several databases, including DB2 and Oracle.

PowerMaker is a subset of PowerBuilder with a simplified interface for power users and departmental use. It accesses popular databases as well as its own relational database. PowerViewer is the query, reporting, and business graphics generator for both products.[28]

RAD Rapid Application Development. The result of using such tools as Visual Basic or PowerBuilder.

Record In a database, a record is a group of related data items treated as one unit of information—for example, your name, address, and phone number. Each record is made up of several fields. A field is simply your last name.[29]

RDBMS Relational Database Management System. *See* Relational Database.

Relational Database A database that is organized and accessed according to relationships between data items. A relational database consists of tables, rows, and columns. In its simplest conception, a relational database is actually a collection of data files that "relate" to each other through at least one common field. For example, one's employee number can be the common thread through several data files—payroll, telephone directory, and so on. One's employee number might thus be a good way of relating all the files together in one gigantic database management system (DBMS). A relational database consists of tables, rows, and columns. Most minicomputers and mainframes today have relational database systems available for business use. Typical examples are DB2 from IBM and RDB from Digital Equipment Corp. Relational databases differ from nonrelational databases in that there are no system dependencies stored within the data; for example, hierarchical databases are not relational because they contain pointers to other data.[30]

---

[27] Harry Newton, *Newton's Telecom Dictionary.*

[28] *Computer Desktop Encyclopedia.*

[29] Harry Newton, *Newton's Telecom Dictionary.*

[30] Ibid.

Schema Pronounced "skeema." The definition of an entire database. Schemas are often designed with visual modeling tools, which automatically create the SQL code necessary to define the table structures.[31]

Spreadsheet Software that simulates a paper spreadsheet, or worksheet, in which columns of numbers are summed for budgets and plans. It appears on screen as a matrix of rows and columns, the intersections of which are identified as cells. Spreadsheets can have thousands of cells and can be scrolled horizontally and vertically in order to view them.

The cells are filled with:

1. labels
2. numeric values
3. formulas

The labels can be any descriptive text, for example, RENT, PHONE, or GROSS SALES.

The values are the actual numeric data used in the budget or plan, and the formulas command the spreadsheet to do the calculations; for example, SUM CELLS A5 TO A10.[32]

Stored Procedures Compiled code on a database server that reduces the processing burden on clients.[33]

Structured Query Language A language used to interrogate and process data in a relational database. Originally developed by IBM for its mainframes, there have been many implementations created for mini and micro database applications. SQL commands can be used to interactively work with a database or can be embedded within a programming language to interface to a database.

The following SQL query selects customers with credit limits of at least $5,000 and puts them into sequence from highest credit limit to lowest.[34]

```
SELECT NAME, CITY, STATE, ZIPCODE
    FROM CUSTOMER
    WHERE CREDITLIMIT > 4999
    ORDER BY CREDITLIMIT DESC
```

SQL Pronounced "sequel" or "see qwill." *See* Structured Query Language.

Table In a relational database, the same as a file; a collection of records.[35]

---

[31]*Computer Desktop Encyclopedia.*

[32]Ibid.

[33]Harry Newton, *Newton's Telecom Dictionary.*

[34]*Computer Desktop Encyclopedia.*

[35]Ibid.

Third-Generation Language Traditional high-level programming language such as FORTRAN, COBOL, BASIC, Pascal, and C.[36]

Unit Test Running one component of a system for testing purposes.[37]

VBA *See* Visual Basic for Applications.

VBX Dynamic link library file that contains third-party or user-developed controls for Visual Basic applications.[38]

Version Control Management of source code in a large software project. Version control software provides a database that keeps track of the revisions made to a program by all the programmers involved in it.[39]

View In relational database management, a special display of data, created as needed. A view temporarily ties two or more files together so that the combined files can be displayed, printed, or queried; for example, customers and orders or vendors and purchases. Fields to be included are specified by the user. The original files are not permanently linked or altered; however, if the system allows editing, the data in the original files will be changed.[40]

Visual Basic for Applications Subset of Visual Basic that provides a common macro language for Microsoft applications. VBA lets power users and programmers extend the functionality of programs such as Word, Excel, and Access.[41]

WAN (Wide Area Network) Communications network that covers wide geographic areas, such as states and countries.[42]

Wide Area Network *See* WAN.

[36] Ibid.
[37] Ibid.
[38] Ibid.
[39] Ibid.
[40] Ibid.
[41] Ibid.
[42] Ibid.

Index